States of Grace

Also by Edie Clark

The Place He Made

Monadnock Tales

The View from Mary's Farm

Saturday Beans & Sunday Suppers

States of Grace

Encounters with Real Yankees

EDIE CLARK

BENJAMIN MASON BOOKS
Dublin, New Hampshire 03444

With the exception of "Wilderness Beekeeper," and "The Man Who Wrote the Book," all of the articles in this collection originally appeared in a slightly different form in *Yankee* magazine. The author is grateful for the opportunity to republish them.

Book design by
Jill Shaffer / Powersbridge Press
P.O.Box 332
Peterborough, NH 03458

First printing July 2010
Printed in the United States of America
10 9 8 7 6 5 4 3 2 1 paperback

Publisher's Cataloging in Publication Data
Clark, Edie, 1948–
States of Grace / Edie Clark
p. cm.
ISBN 978-0-9719934-7-1
1. New England — nonfiction — social life customs — Profiles
I. Title.

Library of Congress Control Number: 2010931355

Benjamin Mason Books
PO Box 112
Dublin, NH 03444

Ordering information: www.edieclark.com

To all those who find their passions and follow them,
regardless of the consequences,
this book is for you.

Contents

Acknowledgments

To all the editors I have worked with over the years, Jud Hale, the late (great) John Pierce, Tim Clark, and Mel Allen, I give my deepest thanks.

To Jamie Trowbridge, Steve Lewers, Katrina Kenison, Maude Odgers, George Odell, Nancy Cayford, Lynn Elder, Annie Card, Sharon Smith, Dean Lunt, for all the gracious favors, large and small, thank you, so much.

Introduction

When I was a young writer in the late 1970s, a friend told me about the writer, Joseph Mitchell, whose stories had been published in the *The New Yorker,* mostly before I was born. Some of his stories had been put into collections but all of them were out of print. I searched far and wide for his most famous, *McSorley's Wonderful Saloon,* which had been published in 1943. Internet searches for rare books have transformed this kind of inquiry into a couple of clicks but back then, I had to be content to poke through old book stores and attend library sales, not exactly hard labor for someone like me but time-consuming nonetheless. At last, at one library sale, I was thrilled to come upon a copy of one of his books, *The Bottom of the Harbor,* the dust jacket protected by Mylar, the Dewey decimals inked at the base of the spine, and due dates stamped in red on the flyleaf. I took the volume home and savored each piece, about a dragger captain, about the caretaker of a cemetery, about a bar keeper, about the things one might find at the bottom of New York harbor. I especially admired the way he included dialogue — not the sanitized quotes usually found in newspaper stories, but conversation so authentic, it felt like you were speaking to that person directly, conversation that told you more about the person than any kind of description a writer could conjure. In addition, Mitchell's descriptions were majestic, his words like poetry, love songs to the common man. And yet an elegiac tone pervaded, as if he were in attendance at the funeral of a great personage.

Eventually, I was able to find all of Mitchell's books, one by one, their dust jackets tattered or missing, pages slightly yellowed, emitting that distinct smell of old paper and aging glue. These volumes will always occupy an honored, separate space on my bookshelf. Aside from everything else, Joseph Mitchell's work provides a wondrous record of old New York, the New York of my grandfather's time. Mitchell wrote about the unsung, the disenfranched, the eccentric, those who were more or less hidden from view but whose stories captured a culture that was fast disappearing.

I grew up outside of New York City, where my grandfather ran a leather belting manufacturer on a side street off Wall Street, near Vesey Street, about which my grandfather always said: you can get anything on Vesey Street. (As nearly as I can tell from reading current maps, his building was right where Ground Zero is today.) As a little girl, I often went with him to work on Saturdays, when things were quieter. This was not the Wall Street we think of today — at that time, the financial district was just a very small part of the neighborhood that surrounded his workplace. The streets were long canyons of endless buildings, each building containing workers creating something different. My grandfather and I rode the train in together from New Jersey and then walked from the station, a fairly long walk made much longer by my grandfather's frequent stops along the way to chat with friends on the street. What I remember most are the people. He seemed to know everyone and there was an easy geniality that permeated the air, always fragrant with roasting chestnuts, engine exhaust, dead fish, and hot pretzels. His friends were colorful, interesting, different, and, to me, fascinating. Their language was distinct and expressive, weighted with words and accents of many foreign lands. When I got older, I realized that this culture, the one into which my grandfather had been deeply embedded, had completely vanished. This passage left a sadness in my heart. Joseph Mitchell's stories always put me in that mood, of the street, of the characters my grandfather seemed to know and admire.

By then, I was living in New Hampshire, where a completely different yet strangely similar culture still existed — the agrarian culture of sturdy people who loved the land and knew it like flesh and blood. I wanted to know these people, to absorb them and the strong values that permeated their lives.

Perhaps having experienced the loss of that old world of New York City, I wanted to somehow retain the New England culture, fast being erased by the arrival of the faceless Walmarts and Dunkin' Donuts. My first attempt to hold onto that culture — though I did not see it that way at the time — was to live back to the land. My first husband and I were disciples of Helen and Scott Nearing, using cash to buy land and then more cash to build our self-sufficient house. We raised chickens and cultivated big gardens and, using our cellar and home canning techniques learned from others, we lived off what we grew throughout the year. In so doing, we met our share of characters. Interestingly, while our choice of lifestyle was somewhat scorned by many of the more traditional residents, it was the old-timers who showed an interest in what we were doing. They not only embraced our endeavor, they helped, offering advice and information we could not have found in a book. They also knew and loved the old culture and wanted to see it carried on. This was almost forty years ago and almost all those who guided us then are gone — a fact I realize only now, in the perspective of time.

I see now that my other attempt to hold back the tide that was rising on New England culture was to work for *Yankee* magazine, where I started in 1978. Of course, at the time, I thought I would work there for a brief period, just long enough to get my bills paid, and then move on. I had no idea where it would lead. Then-managing editor, John Pierce, who hired me initially to do proofreading, encouraged me to write.

Mitchell's work filled me with nostalgia as well as a powerful desire to emulate. But where could I find the New England equivalent of these Bowery preachers, these oystermen, these fortune-tellers?

One of the things I have loved about Yankee is that the magazine has always made space in its pages for the unsung, for the eccentric. Because that is a lot of what we think of when we use the word, "Yankee" to describe a person — Yankees are independent, distinct, not cast from any mold. Reading Joseph Mitchell had already changed my assumption that magazine stories must be about the accomplished, the business tycoons, the movie stars. Aside from the great pleasure I found in the way Mitchell put words together, what he gave me, more than anything, was permission to write about these unconventional people myself.

The first story I wrote for *Yankee* in a Joseph Mitchell state of mind was "The Mushroom King," published in 1982 but prepared and written long before that. (Among other lessons I was learning was the frustration of working for a monthly general interest magazine with a six-month lead time for each story. Then sometimes the story would be held much longer before the right time and the proper space opened up.) I read newspapers to find ideas for stories and one day, in one of the many papers I read, I saw a photograph of an older man holding an enormous tree mushroom in his lap. He was smiling a kind of mischievous grin, as if he knew a secret. The caption on the photo was simply, "The Mushroom King, Tony Anzerino." Curious, I called the paper to find out more and the person I spoke with told me that "everyone knows Tony" and that he always called the paper when he found an especially large mushroom. "What does he do with them?" I asked. The man did not know the answer to that question but he gave me Tony's phone number. I called him up and discovered a voluble man, anxious to tell me all about his mushrooms, which, he said, he usually took down to the local bar to cook up for his friends. This resonated for me, as many of Joseph Mitchell's stories took place in a bar or were somehow linked to New York watering holes. Of course, I didn't put it together that that was because Joseph

Mitchell was, himself, a frequent patron of these places. At the time, I only made the connection that these neighborhood bars could be rich breeding grounds for great stories, for meeting colorful characters.

When I asked if I could come visit him at his home, Tony suggested that we meet at Allen's, instead. "I practically live there anyway," he said. I felt excited, as if my Joseph Mitchell career was about to be launched. So I followed his directions and found the bar, on Rt. 2 on the approach to Greenfield, Massachusetts. It was a low-roofed building, pickup trucks parked outside the door at two o'clock in the afternoon, neon beer signs blinking from the windows into broad daylight. I was a young woman at that time and had rarely been inside an establishment like that, certainly not by myself. I immediately understood my lack, the profound difference between myself and Joseph Mitchell. When I saw what my destination was, I drove right past the bar and kept driving, my mind racing in confusion. Eventually, I convinced myself to turn around and go back but once again my nerve failed and I continued on down the road. A third try and I cautiously pulled into the sandy parking lot and got out. Coming out of the strong sunlight, I stepped into the pitch black environment of the bar. For a full minute, I could not see anything. In that moment, every man at the bar had turned toward me and the din of their conversation quieted. When my eyes adjusted, I saw that, as I'd feared, I was the center of attention.

I only knew Tony from that one photo in the newspaper. After a long minute, a voice called to me from the deeper darkness. "You must be Edie!" I felt welcomed as if into a tight fraternity. As soon as everyone understood I was Tony's friend, the one from *Yankee* magazine, they welcomed me, too. "Ya goin' ta make Tony a star?!" one of them said. And we all laughed.

Tony made it easy for me to feel at home in a place completely foreign and a little scary to me. We sat at a booth in the back and talked there for a very long time as I attempted to take notes in the darkness. (Later, I learned that a tape recorder is a reporter's best friend.)

He was, as was often the case, preparing food for his friends and so, periodically, he got up and went through the swinging doors into the kitchen. That first time, he was making spaghetti sauce, spiced with the mushrooms he had collected the day before. Once, he brought out a little dish for me to taste as he went along in his culinary process. Again, I felt a slight wave of panic — what if these wild mushrooms are poisonous? What if I die, right here in this somewhat ignominious roadside bar? I was learning that when you are in the field, in order to get the story you want, you have to take a few risks. I tasted the sauce. And the next time I saw him, he made a big skillet full of fried mushrooms which he gave me to take home. I had never eaten anything so adventurous in my life. And I had never met anyone like Tony before.

(In rereading "The Mushroom King," I realize that I wrote around that episode with Tony in the bar, only mentioning it in passing, as if the event were in the normal course of my day. In fact, that initial encounter with Tony in the bar became one of the most memorable of my working life.)

After that, I began to look for characters like Tony to write about. It's like looking for a heart-shaped shell on the beach: once you focus on that shape, your eyes can pick them out from among the others. I found Ruby Hemenway who, at the age of almost 100, was writing a column in her local newspaper. I found Floyd Smith, a retired chicken salesman who had taken up beekeeping and who had taken to driving his hives up to his hunting camp in the wilderness of Maine where he left his bees for the summer in order to create his delicate and light-hued "wilderness honey." I found Ruth Farris and Jenny Cirone and Bernie McLaughlin and Barna Norton and Thelma Hanson, all ostensibly ordinary people who seemed to me extraordinary. Eventually, I realized that they were, each of them, living in a state of grace: there was one deep and abiding passion at the center of their lives which endowed them with an elegance and guided them with generosity and good will.

These men and women were not really like Joseph Mitchell's characters at all and few of them were anything like Tony. First and foremost, they were individuals. They were Yankees, after all, dyed in the wool, shrewd, rugged, taciturn, determined, stubborn, and bestowed with the kind of charm Hollywood has never quite understood or, thank God, successfully imitated. More than half of the people included in this book have passed away but many are still alive. Some, such as Dennis Littky, who hails from Cincinnati, and the inveterate Jean Burden who grew up in Illinois and spent most of her life in California, are not "real Yankees." Dennis was not a Yankee but he was drawn into the culture, has wrestled with the bear and, to a great degree, has won, on his terms. Many a Yankee has been very glad he intersected with their lives. And Jean was anything but a Yankee and yet she was Yankee to so many far-flung poets. What all these colorful, spicy folks have in common is that they live inside this state of grace, a condition of their own device, a clemency, if you will, against the increasingly swift currents of mediocrity.

In putting together this collection, I've added updates at the end of each piece. In only a very few cases has the trail gone cold. Mostly, I found them alive and thriving or else I found their legacy alive and thriving. It has been interesting to me, rediscovering these people and in so many cases, discovering that their accomplishments have been recognized and expanded upon. I couldn't help but notice that so many lived into their nineties and beyond, which suggests that leading a busy, passionate life may actually extend it.

Tony was the first of many who demonstrated to me that to prepare these stories is to cultivate a relationship. At first, the journalist is simply doing the job, trying to find out the necessary information in order to write the story. But this kind of writing is not research into genomes. It's all about people and their endless variations in personality and pursuit. No one ever told me that these relationships would be such an abiding, inseparable part of my writing life. So many people I have written about have become, for better or worse, part of my life. For me, this has been a surprise and a delight. If I had managed to notice it, Joseph Mitchell fired a warning salvo in one of his most interesting books, *Joe Gould's Secret,* which was the last article Mitchell wrote for *The New Yorker,* the last article he ever published. A two-part series about Joe Gould, a derelict of the Bowery, self-described genius and fast talker who claimed to have written the history of the world, in nine million words, or so, carrying around his apparently voluminous notebooks in bags. Joseph Mitchell became fascinated by Gould, who he met in a bar and with whom Mitchell apparently identified. He wrote him up and championed his case in the pages of *The New Yorker.* When Joe Gould died, years after the articles had been published, it was revealed that Gould had never written any words at all — all those bags he carted around with him were filled with other bags. No one can say for sure, but the link between this disappointing fact and the fact that Joseph Mitchell never published again — despite showing up in the offices of *The New Yorker* every day for the rest of his working life, some thirty years, all told — might indicate the depth of Mitchell's disappointment, the deep sense of betrayal he must have felt. Throughout those years, however, rumors were constant that Mitchell was working on a magnum opus, rumors he did little to discourage. Yet, like an echo from the past, when he died, none of the rumored, hoped-for writing was found.

A wonderful film, also called *Joe Gould's Secret,* was made of this story in which the sometimes intense, sometimes intrusive relationship that develops between writer and subject is revealed, warts and all. Of course, this does not always happen but in my case, it has happened, time and again, albeit in a much more gentle way. None of my subjects have ever bamboozled or disappointed me. Quite the contrary. They have, each one, expanded my life and inspired me. From them, I have learned a library of information, about beekeeping and about honey, about photography, about slavery, about gardening and plant science, about turtles, about lobsters, about the simple subject of grass, about how one person can make a difference, about magic and relationships, about animals and animal handling, about the natural world, about how to live a long life. The list is very long. When all this began, I had no idea that my desire to be a writer meant that I was signing up to become a student, forever. I've been enriched by all that I have learned from each of these diverse people and immensely grateful to each of them for so freely sharing not only their knowledge but also the details of their lives with me. (Quite a few of these stories were researched and written around the extended period of my husband's illness and death. To say that this work and these encounters kept me going through an especially difficult time would be an understatement.)

As have many of these people, Tony stayed in touch with me for the rest of his life. If I dig down into the files in my attic, I will find remembrances of Tony and his colorful and unique life. The article I wrote about him in Yankee was his greatest moment, he told me. And many of the people I've written about have told me something similar. I regard that as one of the great things about *Yankee* magazine, that the editorial persuasion of the magazine allows such people into their pages so that these homely lives, these Yankee lives, can be celebrated and given quite a bit more than just fifteen minutes of fame.

In the first issue of *Yankee*, published in September of 1935, the magazine's founder, Robb Sagendorph stated his mission for this fledgling publication: "the expression of and perhaps indirectly, the preservation of that great culture into which every Yank is born and by which every real Yank must live." We are all part of this, our culture — who we are and what we do comprise it and define it, most especially these amazing people.

I was not always working on stories like these, but these were the ones that often gave me the most pleasure. It is a supreme privilege to be invited into someone's home, to be invited into a stranger's life. I will be forever grateful to *Yankee* for giving me the platform on which to place these deserving people.

Tony Anzerino turned out to be the only subject I ever met in a bar. I found that, at least in New England, the great eccentrics are often found in their gardens and fields or out in a boat or at their desks, penning words that can always be kept, even if the hands that wrote them pass away. And so, I raise my glass to these many wonderful people, living or dead, with my extreme gratitude for living their lives with such perfect pitch, for allowing grace into their lives through their good works and for allowing me to record their stories. I can't imagine what in my life could have given me greater pleasure than to come to know them, to come to love them. These people make me happy. I hope they will make you happy too.

Edie Clark
Harrisville, New Hampshire
May 2010

Nash Island Millionaire

THE DAY IS ENDING for Jenny Cirone, the eighty-eight-year-old shepherdess, lobsterwoman, and queen of the islands that surround South Addison, Maine's, Eastern Harbor, the surface of which is sparkling up at her now, as she sits in her living room. The late summer sun is angling down, highlighting the upright ears of the sheep that graze so close to her window that she can hear them tear the green grass from its stems. A warm salty breeze comes up off the water and Jenny smiles, sitting back in her big chair. The nearest sheep turns her face up to Jenny and bleats at her.

"Yer waitin' fa me, aren'cha, baby? Ooo, I know it, ya haven't got ya suppah yet. Ooo, you're beautiful, you're beautiful, yes you ah!" she says in the clipped enunciated downeast accent that is so thick, someone from away might need an interpreter.

Four more come close to the window, bleating and stamping. "I'm coming, I'm coming," Jenny says to Easter Lily, Wren, Beauty and her twin, Beast. These are just pets, these ten that graze on the land that stretches from her farmhouse down to the water. Two hundred more of her sheep graze out on Nash Island and its sister, Big Nash. "This is my whole family," Jenny says. "My whole family is completely gone. Counting my mother and father, there were eleven of us and now I'm the only one left."

Jenny grew up on Nash Island, where her father was the lighthouse keeper from 1916 until he retired in 1935. On the island, they had a farmyard with pigs and horses, chickens and sheep. "My father was a great provider. He'd go out birding and come back with forty or fifty. In winter, we'd let them freeze out in the shed and whenever we wanted a duck, we'd just go out there and chop one out for supper." The winter winds on the island were sometimes fierce enough to lift the rugs off the floors. "When the books came off the shelves, then we'd take the mattress downstairs and sleep on it together."

The sheep gave them meat to eat and wool to knit into something warm. "I don't remember a time when I didn't have a sheep," she says. "We used to ride them like horses and harness them up. We'd have them haul coal or hay."

When she was twenty, Jenny came ashore to marry Stanley Cirone and together she and Stan built the house where she still lives, a gray-shingled Cape with barns just steps from the back door. Pretty soon, they bought the islands, for less than what she pays in taxes on them now. She knew it was good grazing land. She's kept her sheep out there ever since.

The kitchen door bangs shut and a handsome redheaded man of 40 or so strides into her living room.

"Hey, Cappy," he says. Alfie Wakeman, Jenny is very proud to tell you, is a doctor now, but he's been going out with her on her lobster boat since, as he says, "before I could see over the side of the boat." He calls Jenny "Cappy," short for Captain, his captain. Alfie grew up in Connecticut and came here to this fishing village for summers. South Addison was the home of his great-grandfather and his grandfather, both friends and fishing companions of Jenny and Stan's. In 1989, Alfie moved to South Addison with his family for good and they now live in the house next door to Jenny. He has three daughters, the oldest is named Lily, after Jenny's sheep Easter Lily, the middle girl is named Wren after another of Jenny's sheep, and the third, the youngest, is name Genevieve, after Jenny, for that is her real name. Although he works as a physician's assistant at the health center in nearby Harrington, for the past twelve years, he and Jenny have been in business together, hauling traps. On his days off, they go out lobstering in Jenny's boat. Tomorrow, Alfie has a day off.

"Did they set out the bait for us?" Alfie asks Jenny.

"Said he'd put it on the dock and put a crate over it so's the gulls won't get it, how about that?"

"Oh, man," says Alfie.

"We'll go at six o'clock?"

"Yup, should be enough light by then. How many do you need?"

"I need five," Jenny says.

"Well, I need three," Alfie says.

"You've got to have three, Alfie? Oh, Godfrey. Well, we'll see now."

"We'll get eight out of that second trap by the high head!"

Alfie grins widely at Jenny, his blue eyes looking straight into hers, which are almost as blue, set in the brown, crinkly skin of a woman who has spent her life outdoors. Her eyes sparkle back at him. "We'll get eight, yes, that's right Alfie!"

"OK, Cappy, six o'clock!" he says as he heads back out through the kitchen.

"Six o'clock!" she calls after him.

Once Alfie is back outside, the sheep bolt over toward the barn. From the window Jenny watches as he unlatches the barn door and lets them inside. With effort, Jenny gets to her feet. They are slow now. Over the past ten or fifteen years, she's had both knees and her hip replaced and a broken shoulder that never healed properly. Using both canes, she works her way out to the barn, carrying the feed that Alfie set out for her.

Inside the barn, her sheep bleat and shove at the sight of Jenny. "Stop it! Stop it!" she cries. "Godfrey, you're not dying, you're just hungry."

She lowers the dishes into the pen on a fish line, so that she can easily retrieve them herself. The sheep nuzzle into the feed and the barn resounds with the solid crunch of their blunt teeth coming down on the hard corn. "There, there, you beauties," she says. "There, there."

AT FIRST LIGHT, Jenny stands at the edge of the harbor, the rising tide lapping at her canes and her high-top rubber boots. This evening there will be a concert in town and songs written in honor of Jenny Cirone will be sung. A video, recording her life growing up on Nash Island is being sold to raise money to restore her father's old lighthouse, which has not guided ships for sixty years. Jenny has become a local celebrity. She thinks little of it and files it in the "I'm not sure about this" section of her sharp mind. Right now, her mind is on lobsters.

Alfie is pulling the tender in from its mooring and when he's got it, he deftly bales the rainwater from its bottom.

"You're spoiling me, Alfie," Jenny says. Jenny's had this rowboat since 1947, the year she had *The Convincer* built for herself. Using that big lobster boat, Jenny and Stan tended two hundred and fifty traps, every day. In her off hours, Jenny liked to race *The Convincer*, which had a reputation for being the fastest boat in the harbor. "I've been a kid all my life," she says now. "I don't know why I don't grow up out of it but I don't."

The Convincer has gone to boat heaven. The "new" boat is *Tubby*, a twenty-foot Eastporter with a forty-horse outboard and a green tarp rigged onto the bow to protect their gear.

Jenny steadies herself on Alfie's hand as he gently lifts her feet over the side of the tender.

"You want me to row this morning?" he says as she settles into the boat. "I'm letting you off a year and a half early!" For some time now, Alfie has said that when Jenny turns ninety, he'll start doing the rowing for her.

She grins again as Alfie sets the oars and pulls out toward *Tubby*. When they reach *Tubby*, Alfie once again helps Jenny aboard, saying, "There you go, just like a spring chicken, you are!"

"More like a dead rooster, I'd say," Jenny comes back, laughing. From where it's been stowed, Alfie gets Jenny's oilskin apron. She raises her arms so he can get it over her head. With the crippled shoulder, it's hard for her to get things over her head. Then he pulls the big rubber gloves onto her hands, carefully pulling each finger tight. She settles onto the plank that's rigged high so it's easier for her to sit. She sets the bait bucket in front of her and a bucket full of empty bait bags beside her.

The engine is new, hanging black and shiny from *Tubby*'s stern. Alfie presses the starter by the wheel and the big engine shivers to life, then murmurs in neutral. "This motor's so quiet," Jenny says. "I can't get over it!"

Alfie maneuvers out of the harbor, a deep pocket of blue water, famous for its sheltering reach. In silence, Jenny stuffs the bait bags with the fresh cut herring while Alfie cuts bait with his free hand and drops it into the bucket for Jenny. It's a fair day with only a gentle breeze. "Not every day is like this one!" she says. Jenny and Alfie go out regardless of the weather. "We go when Alfie has the time," she says.

They keep forty-eight traps just outside the harbor and around Nash Island. They've had a good summer. They take the lobsters that they want and sell the rest at the wharf for the going rate. Today it's three dollars a pound, which isn't bad. They were hauling at a great rate in July, sometimes bringing in forty a day. Usually, the hauling is best in the fall but it's been a strange summer and their luck has not been so good in the past couple of weeks.

As he comes up on one of Jenny's buoys, Alfie snags it with a boat hook and pulls it on board. The traps are down about sixteen fathoms so he hauls the line, hand over hand, for quite a while before the trap appears. He pulls it aboard, streaming seawater and seaweed into the cockpit.

As Alfie hauls up each trap, he unfastens the empty bait bag and hands it to Jenny as she hands him a full one, stuffed with herring. The ripe smell of the rotted fish fills the air. He winds the bait onto the bar in the middle of the trap, closes the trap and balances it on the side of the boat as he brings the engine up to speed again. When it's right, he lets go of the trap and it drops back down into the deep. He holds onto the line, cleaning the seaweed off the line as it slithers through his gloved hand and back into the clear green water. He pulls up a half a dozen like this. Cool sea air riffles the water.

"All zeroes, Alfie?"

"Poverty baskets, Cappy!" he says.

"Well, if this one don't have four in it, Alfie, I'm going to have to fire you!"

Alfie smiles and hauls up the trap which has two sea urchins and a big crab inside.

"Oh, Alfie, what are we going to do!" she says, her voice like song.

He lets out a low hoot as he pulls in the next trap. Inside, three lobsters flap against the sides of the wire basket. Alfie takes hold of one and measures its back with his calipers. Legal-size lobsters have a narrow target size: no bigger than five inches and no smaller than three. Lobsters that fall outside those figures have to be thrown back.

"Well, I've got my three, Cappy," he says. "We can head in now." Jenny gives a bighearted laugh. He sets them in the basket next to Jenny, whose job it is to capture their claws with big rubber bands.

In the next trap are two good-size, hefty lobsters. "I'm glad you took those three smallest ones, Alfie," she says and they laugh hard together.

Four hours pass this way. By the time the sun is up high enough to warm them, they've checked most of the traps. Before they head in, Alfie ducks under the tarp and comes out with a clean water jug. He leans overboard and fills it with seawater. Jenny will cook her lobsters in this, what she calls Nash Island water.

On the way back to the wharf, they pull off their rubber gloves, wash the bait from the deck and Alfie breaks out the Ziploc full of Jenny's sugar cookies and Hermits, the breakfast they have not yet had. They've got twelve lobsters in the bucket, eight to keep and four to sell, which will give them just enough to cover the cost of the gas and the bait. Dolphins wheel up by the green can.

"We've hauled for one, maybe even zero," Jenny says. "I think there's been a time or two when we've come up with nothing. But it's been an awfully good summer, a good three years, hasn't it, Alfie?"

THE FAINT FRAGRANCE of steamed lobster lingers in Jenny's kitchen. The lobster pot is clean and resting in the dish drainer. In the quiet of her kitchen, Jenny waits for her neighbors to pick her up to go to the concert. Since coming in from the sea that morning, she has recorded their catch into her record book, dug a few potatoes, cleaned house a little, and cooked a lobster dinner for friends.

Jenny's days go by swiftly but the nights are harder. Stan has been gone now for eleven years. "I never thought I'd be alone," she says, apparently still surprised. "I was always used to a crowd." But there's no self-pity in her words. What Jenny says more often than anything is how lucky she is, especially to have Alfie. "I never knew anyone so patient as he is. I don't know what I'd do without him. I don't. And that's the truth."

In the evenings, she sometimes falls asleep in her chair watching "Who Wants to Be a Millionaire." The show amuses her.

"I don't want to be a millionaire. If I were, I mean, I would be just the same, nothing would change. I don't envy anyone who has more than I do. I don't know how my life could be any better. I'm so lucky I have so many friends. When it came time to buy that new engine for *Tubby*, one friend of mine said to me, 'You don't need that engine! Put your boat ashore and you can get your friends to take you out.' I told her I don't use my friends like that. So long as I can do this myself, I'm better off. Then she says to me, 'Do you realize how old you are?' And I said, 'I know how old I am! If I drop dead tomorrow, then I'm dead and that's all.'

"So I got the engine anyways. And I've got that motor paid for. I'm lucky about that. I'm just lucky to be here. Yes, I am."

April 2001 Yankee magazine

JENNY AND ALFIE *continued to fish together until November 2003. That winter, Jenny fell ill. Alfie and his family kept close watch on her. She died on February 3, 2004, at her home in South Addison. "We all had a good dinner together and then I sat with her through the night. In the middle of the night, she took a couple of deep breaths and then she was gone," Alfie says. She was just shy of ninety-two. "She had a little note tucked into her mirror that said, 'Someone please take care of my sheep when I'm gone,'" Alfie says.*

Soon after, Alfie bought Jenny's house and he takes care of her sheep, taking them to Nash Island in the summer, just as she did. "We try to keep everything the way she had it," he says. "We've fixed up the fences and we have a few cows over there now along with the sheep." He's got seven sheep, some of Jenny's plus some new ones. Wren, Beauty and Beast have passed away but Easter Lily is still alive. Alfie still fishes on board Tubby, *with his three daughters, Lily, Wren, and Genevieve, and that good, new motor.*

A Company of One

THE BIG GREEN Twin Lights bottles jostle and clatter and clink, a distant music that's been heard on Broadway in Rockport, Massachusetts, for the past ninety years.

"Ninety-one," Pierce Sears says, over the din of the bottle washer. He is standing at his post, at the end of the conveyor, where the bottles, now filled with pale dry ginger ale, teeter out from under the capper and inch down toward his waiting hand. He takes hold of each one by the neck, upends it and raises it aloft. Using the light that spills in from the big window beside the machine, he squints through the clear green prism of the glass and ale. Satisfied that all is as pale as it ought to be, Pierce brings the bottle down into the big wooden delivery box with a swift, sure motion. He does this, bottle after bottle. When the box is full, he hefts it over to a stack of crates near his pickup truck. As he works, the bottles keep coming, ganging up at the end of the line like so many little men, waiting.

Pierce Sears, sixty-five and counting, works with the sleeves of his plaid flannel shirt rolled above his elbows, his strong arms exposed. He is a bantamweight, a trim fighter for Twin Lights, a company of one. Pierce ("I *hate* to be called Mr. Sears!") is the sole survivor of this long legacy of cold sweet drinks that has quenched the summer thirst of the North Shore since just after the turn of the century, when Pierce's grandfather stepped into the frenetic arena of making soda pop. At the time, Twin Lights was as big a name as Coca-Cola. Perhaps, in Rockport or Gloucester or Beverly, Twin Lights was a bigger name. Every bar, every tavern, every store, every restaurant carried the big bottles with the jazzy emblem of the two historic lighthouses that blink from Thacher's Island. "Business was booming," Pierce recalls. He has worked at the plant, which is just a stroll across the asphalt driveway from the Sears' home, since he was old enough to stand on his own. Back then, there were nine workers busy every day, washing, bottling, and loading. A fleet of big Chevy trucks, painted sky blue with white piping and the Twin Lights logo big as day on the rack overhead, plied the roads along the neck, delivering soda to eager customers. One of the trucks remains, a caged lion in Pierce's garage. The paint is still bright, the Twin Lights logo prominent, the scrolling perfect. Pierce uses his relatively new pickup truck for deliveries now. The antique truck has only 65,000 miles on it. "I've had offers," Pierce acknowledges. He would no sooner part with this truck than he would with the very logo itself.

Times have changed. Pierce's pickup has no sign on it. In fact, there is no sign on the Twin Lights building. In 1960, Pierce's father, George Sears, had the building painted and the signs, which were big as the side of the building, were taken down. Somehow they never got put back up. Those who know what goes on behind that plain white door at 71 Broadway have no trouble finding Twin Lights. Summer visitors often stop to say hello and show their children how the soda is made. It is what their own parents did.

A friend has come to help Pierce this morning, and he stands at the end of the big old bottle washer, feeding dirty soda bottles into its open end. Trembling from the quake of the old machine, the bottles disappear into its deep innards, a great, long white sarcophagus that fills the length of this narrow, cement-floored room. Water spurts from the network of pipes that surround the old machine. The whoosh and clank of the machinery has a pleasant, soothing effect that seems to say: *the world is at work, mak-*

ing wonderful things for us. This particular machine, known in the trade as "The Dixie," is sixty years old and could not be replaced for all the money in the world.

The Twin Lights bottling process is fairly simple. The dirty empties go in and wend their way through the washer, a bath that takes a full fifty minutes. The bottles emerge, sparkling and upright, on a short conveyor belt. They nudge each other along. Caps trickle down a chute, rattling like coins. Gushing and gurgling, the bottler grips the bottle and squirts syrup into the bottom. A spray of carbonated water fills the bottle, which is rotated and then bestowed with its crimped crown, a royal moment.

"They don't make these bottle washing machines anymore," Pierce explains. "The bottlers now just rinse the new bottles before they fill them, because those bottles will never come back to them again. We exist on second-hand bottles."

Secondhand is an epic understatement. Some of the bottles being fed into this machine are forty years old and have been through the wash and back countless times, thanks to the beauty of the bottle deposit.

The sound of shattering glass is followed by a geyser of ginger ale. Pierce jumps and hits the kill switch. The machine stops, and there is a moment, like a sigh, while the room comes into silence. Only the drip of the pipes and the soft whir of the idling engine can be heard. The sharp odor of ginger fills the air.

"Ah, working perfectly, as usual," Pierce's friend says, winking at the visitor.

"That bottle has just been through too many times. It was time to go," Pierce says, as he clears the belt of broken glass and mops up the floor.

The bottles are one part of a three-part formula vital to the lifeblood of Twin Lights. The other two are the Dixie and Pierce Sears himself. If any of them go, it will spell the end of Twin Lights. "It's a dying business," Pierce states plainly, as he switches the machine back on and the *clinkety-clank* begins anew. "But as long as I stay in bottles and can keep the machinery going, I'm going to keep going. It's something I like to do. And folks still seem to like our soda."

Twin Lights exists on these old bottles and the prayer that this machine will continue to come to life when the switch is thrown on the mornings that Pierce decides to bottle. Pierce confides that his friend is more mechanically inclined than he is, a truth that is borne out when he occasionally tweaks the machine with the help of a crowbar or, even, the heel of an old, rusty, open-end bottle opener.

A white Ford El Camino rolls into the driveway, and an old man gets out. He comes in to Pierce and they converse briefly, as the newly crowned bottles congregate at the end of the line. The man drives his truck around to the loading bay, and Pierce returns and tries to catch up. He is smiling. The man's aunt died and he was cleaning out her house when he found two cases of empty Twin Lights bottles in her attic. He has brought them home to Pierce. He might as well have brought gold bullion.

The bottle problem is not new. "We have always lost bottles," Pierce says. "This being a summer resort, people would look upon these bottles, with the picture of the Twin Lights, as a cheap souvenir."

What's different now is that they don't make these bottles anymore. Only the old bottles, which were thicker and more rugged, will fit into the Dixie.

It's ginger ale this morning. It could be birch beer or sarsaparilla or grape soda. Twin Lights has eleven different flavors, nothing you haven't heard before in the soda line. While once the Dixie chugged along five days a week, turning out three hundred to four hundred bottles a day, Pierce only bottles one day a week now, filling the four hundred bottles he has, and no more.

Twin Lights soda can be found in only one store in Rockport. The Richdale, just a few blocks down from Pierce's house, stocks Twin Lights on the bottom shelf of the soda cooler. Down there, beneath their snappy, punky, fluorescently labeled, peachy, mangoed, kiwied peers, the dowdy Twin Lights bottles look like a mistake, a soda caught in a time warp.

"We don't sell through stores much anymore," Pierce says. "I sell mostly to private customers, homes and clubs. My regular customers understand how important it is for me to have these bottles back."

To lure back his waning supply of bottles, Pierce has tried to increase the deposit. "We were getting twenty cents a bottle and I raised it to forty. Double! But, I don't think it had any affect at all." Twin Lights bottles can be found in antique stores sometimes for as much as $20. The arithmetic is not difficult.

Only a small percentage of the bottles he sends through the Dixie are actually Twin Lights, the beautiful old green glass with the white and red painted logo seared onto the glass, forever distinct. Pierce gleans any old returnable bottle that he can get and sends them through. At the end, he pastes a paper label over the logo of White Rock or Highland Club. These are the bottles he takes over to Richdale. Fewer to be lost that way.

Pierce knows that every time he sends a bottle out into the world, it may never come back to him, which puts him one step closer to the end of a long run.

"I'm alone here," Pierce says, stating the obvious. "My friend helps me when I bottle but otherwise I'm alone, since my dad died four years ago." Pierce's father worked the Dixie just about to his dying day, which came when he was eighty-seven years old. Pierce hopes for the same for himself. "It pays the taxes, keeps the buildings up. I'm semiretired. This is what I do."

The Coca-Cola clock above the machine reads five until noon. The Dixie suddenly blasts air and Pierce lurches to hit the switch. That's it. The ginger ale he mixed this morning is all gone. There are only five bottles left in the machine, ready to be filled. "That came out just about right," Pierce says to his friend. In the afternoon, they will be bottling creme soda. "Take a good long lunch," he tells his friend.

"I might take a nap," the man says.

"Good, that's fine," Pierce says. "Take your time."

Steam rises and warm water drips from the Dixie. It is quiet inside the Twin Lights plant. The wooden crates filled with fresh ginger ale sit stacked on the loading bay. After lunch, Pierce will mix the syrup for the next batch. Tomorrow, he'll do his route. Pierce dries his hands on a towel that hangs from a pipe and he walks across the driveway to his house. There will be lunch and then, perhaps, a nap.

August 1998 Yankee magazine

Twin Lights Beverages *turned one hundred in 2007. Pierce Sears is still mixing the ginger ale and the orange soda and the other classic flavors before sending it through The Dixie (which he reports is cranky but still chugging along) and capturing it in the inimitable Twin Lights bottles. "The bottle supply is at a low ebb," Pierce reports. "But I've got enough to last." The company remains devoted to and dependent upon recycling.*

Wilderness Beekeeper

At dusk on a day early in June, seventy-five-year-old Floyd Smith waits outside his home in Walpole, New Hampshire, for the last of his young honeybees to return. They have spent the day feeding on the early spring blossoms of the basswood and locust trees that cast shadows across his lawn. Smith is a round, clean-shaven man with the stern presence of a parson and watchful eyes the color of mink fur. Now, as the daylight squeezes out and the lines of bees decrease, he begins to seal the first of the fifteen wooden hives that are housed in a peculiar bee yard: an open-air trailer, 8 feet by 22, roofed over like a gypsy wagon, surrounded by chain-link fencing, and hitched to the back of his Ford F-350 pickup truck. Floyd is hurrying, stuffing cotton into the hive entrances and stapling them over with screening.

These million or so bees will be on the road with him all night on a non-stop journey to North East Carry, Maine, three hundred and sixty-nine miles and about nine hours from Walpole, a town nearly dead-center in the span of New England, a fact that might surprise until you look at the map. Floyd is heading northeast, to his hunting camp up at the tip of Moosehead Lake. It's a long way to carry bees. By sunrise, if all goes as he has planned, the bees will be at home for the summer, deep in the chilly spruce forests of northern Maine, where they produce what Smith calls wilderness honey — a honey very delicate in flavor and so clear you could read the newspaper through it. He believes there is no honey like it, anywhere.

As he works, strapping each hive tightly to the trailer, Floyd Smith explains that this overnight trip is the only way he can transport his bees. They'll stay in the hives when it's dark — processing honey, not sleeping — but at the first sign of daylight, they will begin to stir, anxious to be out again gathering nectar. So the timing of this trip leaves no room for meal stops, side trips, or engine troubles.

Satisfied that the hives are on the trailer to stay, Floyd loads the back of his pickup with a duffel bag, the variety of tools he uses to work with the bees, and a Styrofoam cooler packed with enough food to last several days. Behind the seat he tucks a jug of black coffee and a brown bag of sandwiches. He gives a whistle for his bird dog, Lady, who hops in, trembling with excitement. Right on schedule, he pulls onto I-91 north.

THE FRAGRANCE of lilacs is everywhere and the peach trees are in bloom — signs of spring that broke a month ago in more southern parts of the region. If spring comes late to Walpole, it comes even later to the north woods of Maine. Floyd has to schedule his trip after the end of mud season, making sure that the dirt roads leading to his camp are passable and that the intensive spraying for spruce budworm by the paper companies is over. Two days ago, he got word from the forester that all was clear. Floyd plans to stay at his camp several days, long enough to get the bees settled. He will return twice during the summer to check on them and to collect honey. At the end of September, he'll bring the summer-weary bees back home to Walpole, along with, he hopes, a harvest of a thousand pounds of honey — which he has no trouble selling to friends and neighbors.

Floyd drives cautiously through the early evening, keeping an eye on the trailer in his side-view mirror. The trailer is heavy — the hives alone weigh almost two thousand pounds — and he takes most hills in second gear. Smith, a man of fierce likes and dislikes, ordinarily spends the first three hours of each day, which he begins unfailingly at 4 a.m., reading from a stack of newspapers and magazines. When he finds his conservative values challenged, he'll fire off a letter to the editor. But tonight, no matter how fired up he is about the welfare fraud he read about this morning, his talk keeps coming back to the bees.

"You might have noticed that we've got an extra hive on board," he says to me. "Just yesterday I got a call from a friend over in Saxtons River. She said there was a swarm of bees over in the churchyard behind her house. So I took over an empty hive and sure enough, there was a nice ball of bees, big as a peach basket, hanging from a crotch in the pear tree. I set the hive down right under where they were a-buzzin'. I had on a glove, which I didn't really need because when they are swarming, they are not in the mood to sting. I was after the queen, who's generally right in the center so I reached right up into the middle of that ball of bees and I pulled it down, fast, toward the hive. I must have hit it right because they went down — the queen deep down into the box where it's dark the way she likes it and the rest of them following right behind like good little children."

We follow the Connecticut River up the interstate that slices between Vermont and New Hampshire, then we twist along the brow of the White Mountains and cross into Maine onto a kind of road you don't find very often in New England. Floyd, who spent most of his life as a traveling salesman, calls these "long straights," flat stretches of highway that run through sparsely populated farmlands and towns with names like Norridgewock, Mexico, and Harmony.

FLOYD HAS MADE this trip hundreds of times. He first leased his camp in 1940 from the Great Northern Paper Company and over the years it's been a special haven for him for hunting, fishing, and solitude. Lillian, his wife of fifty-six years, with whom he remembers having had just three arguments, ever, has never been there. Only in the last five years has he shared it with his bees. Originally, he was curious to know if the bees, born and bred in Georgia, would produce any honey at all in the northern words, where the season is brief and the flowers tiny.

"The first swarm we took up to Maine — I was in on this with a friend at first — the challenge was to keep the bears away," he says. "So we carefully fixed a platform on top of the boat house where the bears couldn't get at the hive. The first morning we let them out, the DC-3s went over, spraying Sevin for spruce budworm. Sevin kills bees faster than you can shovel them and we did lose a lot, but we still made forty pounds of honey that year. It was clear to us then that there was plenty for them to feed on up there.

"I've gotten a lot of honey from these bees," Floyd continues, "sometimes as much as a hundred pounds from a single hive. Since then, I've tracked the bees to find out where all this honey is coming from. Across the river from camp is an enormous bog, probably a peat bog. There are no trees there that are bigger than two or three inches around and the forester up there told me that most of those trees are a hundred and fifty years old. When it's a good flying day, you can see the bees streaming across to that bog. In summer, there's foliage and grass and weeds and all kinds of flowers. If you walk around very slow, you'll discover flowers under your feet, everywhere."

Lady stirs on the seat beside us. The road is long and solitary. We rarely encounter another car. Long into the dark night, Floyd eases the truck onto the narrow shoulder of the road and, like some kind of nomadic night watchman, he gets out and paces, listening to each hive. Most of them give off a sleepy buzz, but one, the one he captured yesterday in the churchyard, is furious, its angry scream carried off on the wind. "They'll just have to hold onto their britches till we get there," he says, chuckling.

Floyd's homemade trailer has a threefold function: It transports the bees, houses them and, wrapped as it is in the chain-link fence, protects them from the marauding bears of the North Woods. Once it reaches its destination, Floyd electrifies the fence, the juice provided by a battery big enough to power a large tractor like a John Deere, 750 diesel. The first couple of years, he accommodated the bees in a small house next to his camp. This house now wears long streaks of deep scratches in the wood, the scars of bee-hungry bears. Floyd says the bears didn't succeed in getting any honey but their persistence set him to work on the idea of this trailer. "So far, they haven't touched it," he says.

WHILE WE'RE STOPPED, Floyd pours black coffee into the cap of his Thermos and shares one of his peanut butter sandwiches with Lady. "Most people think that the bears have a fondness for honey but I don't think that bears like honey so much as they like the grubs, the little baby bees," he says. "I've often been walking in the woods in the summer months and I'll come on an old log that's been thrown about left and right. There's an anthill inside that log, and the bears have torn it up, looking for grubs. And I've been told that that's what they're after when they break up a beehive.

"The other thing is that a bear doesn't want to just eat something," Floyd continues. "He wants to raise hell. Sometimes when I go up in the middle of the summer, I can see where the bears have been. The grass around the trailer's all matted down and you can see where they've rolled around in the grass, just like a bunch of teenagers on a picnic."

Ten minutes later we're on the road again. It's only midnight and there are still a good two hundred miles left. Cool, rainy weather is good for controlling bees and this night is cooperative. We have passed through rain squalls and, as if crossing invisible lines, into patches where the stars are bright, then back into another driving rainstorm. Spring has definitely been left behind: In the light of the headlights, I can see that some of the trees by the roadside are bare.

Floyd is used to the cold, and to animals, and to traveling. He grew up on a farm where one end of the barn was in Vermont and the other end was in Canada. He left the farm at the age of sixteen and eventually got a job with Hubbard Farms, headquartered in Walpole and one of the largest chicken-breeding farms in the world, where he spent forty years as a salesman. During that time, he sold Frank Perdue some of his first chickens and wore out sixteen Chrysler Newports, traveling around, selling chickens.

Over the years, he has come to see his bees as no different from chickens or hogs or sheep or any other domestic animal. He believes that they like to be handled gently and with respect. In working with bees, he classifies himself as a novice. "In the five years I've been taking these bees to Maine," he says, "all I've learned about bees is that I don't know anything about them. As quick as I think I know something, they teach me something different. There are beekeepers and keepers of bees and I try to be a keeper of bees."

"THE BEES ARE secretive about talking to me," he says now after a long silence in the cab of the truck, lit only by the lights of the dashboard. Lady is fast asleep between us. "But it's been found that they have ways of talking to each other. In each hive there are what are known as scout bees. When we get there tomorrow morning, as soon as I pull the cork out of these hives, these scout bees will be out, looking for the honey flow, the flowers that they'll draw nectar from over the summer. When they've found it, they'll come back to the hives and they'll do a dance that will tell the other bees that the honey is, say, one mile away. Then they'll do a second dance that'll tell them what direction the honey's in — northeast or southwest or whatever. And finally they'll do a third dance that tells them of any obstructions or dangers. Ordinarily I can't tell to look at a bee if he's looking at me or at the tree or at the door. But last week I opened up one of the hives and I'll be damned if one of those bees wasn't doing a little dance and the whole swarm was gathered around him."

Floyd rarely wears protective clothing when working with his bees. "If you haven't got a protective suit on," he says, "you're more likely to be careful and respectful of the bees. I know that a guy with five hundred hives has got to go in there with a suit on and go about his business — he's got a lot of work to do in a little bit of time. But he's likely to forget all about the intimate parts of being with the bees.

"When I go up to check the bees in July, I always hope it's going to be a nice, sunny, warm morning so the bees will be flying," he goes on. "I hope that I can work seven of my fifteen hives with nothing but a t-shirt and trousers on — no gloves, nothing. But by then, they begin to be disturbed so I usually put on a veil and gloves. What disturbs them is the thumping around — just knocking the ashes out of my pipe — they don't like that. With the bees, if you tend to your business, they'll tend to theirs."

Headlights flare up fast behind us and the car swerves past, its taillights disappearing into the night. I ask Floyd what would happen if someone came along and hit the trailer from behind. "Well," he says, "we'd probably have a lot of loose bees. And probably some sour neighbors." He laughs. "Last year, a load of pollinator bees — which are the only other kind of bees that get hauled around in a trailer, and for a completely different reason — tipped over somewhere downcountry, and they had very little trouble. The bees stayed right there. No matter how broken up the hives are, they won't leave; it's their home."

It's a good thing the bees feel that way. These bees are thirteen hundred miles from their original home in Jessup, Georgia. In late April, they were sent to Smith, a comparatively modest order of seven swarms. It is an early spring ritual that he shares with more of the other beekeepers in the area: receiving bees, through the mail or by carrier, settling them into hives, and feeding them an initial source of sugar.

The day Floyd's bees arrived, shipped to him by truck, felt much like this raw, cold night we are now riding through. That day, I traveled to Walpole to watch as he worked bare-faced and bare-handed, ministering to his fourteen hives. Seven of his swarms wintered over from last year. They were at home in their hives, drowsy from the cold, the hives so silent they seemed empty. This year, Floyd was increasing his bee yard two-fold. Each box, he explained, contained three pounds of bees that would burgeon to nine pounds by midsummer. They are shipped in pine boxes, each one containing something like twenty-one thousand bees, huddled into a clump no bigger than a head of cabbage.

To start, Smith pried off the wooden cover of the first box with a hive tool, like a small pry bar. The bees stayed solid, like packed raisins, inside the box. He removed the queen — only one to a box. She was housed in her own miniature cage, a clot of nurse bees surrounding her like a fist, keeping her warm. He seated her deep in the center of the hive. Then he upended the box into the hive. The bees poured out in a viscous stream. To coax the last reluctant few, he banged the box vigorously against the side of the hive. With the next box, Floyd urged me: "Put your hand flat against that screen." The other side was crawling with hungry bees. "Go ahead, it's safe. I want you to see how much warmth they generate." Reluctantly, I put my hand against the screen. On that chilly day it was like warming to a heater.

It took Floyd only a couple of hours to introduce the new bees into their hives and supply them with bottles of sugar water to tide them over until spring really arrived. I asked him if this is a money-making operation. "Each of these boxes cost me twenty-five dollars," he said. "Then, to raise all those bees up to where they can go to work, I have to feed them ninety pounds of sugar — I can't keep track of the price of sugar but probably something like fifty dollars. I also feed them a stimulant that costs me about fifty dollars.

"The other thing is it takes about a hundred dollars' worth of gasoline to take them up and bring them back," Floyd continued. "And I don't figure my time, because that's worth about as much as a setting hen. If I can do this and not lose money, that's fine." As Floyd put the cover on each hive, the bees roared, the protest of a single voice. But in time they calmed and the sound coming from each hive was a contented hum.

It's nearly four a.m. when Floyd pulls his rig up at the gate to what is known as the Golden Road, an immense, privately owned network of dirt roads built and maintained by paper companies for hauling logs. A sleepy-eyed woman comes out of the gatehouse in slippered feet. She asks where we're headed, then scribbles' Floyd's license plate number on her clipboard. He asks her what the temperature is. "Thirty degrees," she says and points to a small garden planted in the gravelly soil beside the gatehouse. It is June 10 and her garden is cloaked in tarpaulins against the frost as if it were October.

We jounce onto the last stretch of the trip, a wide dirt logging road, barren of road signs or telephone poles or mailboxes. "On this road," says Floyd, "you have to know where you're going because there isn't anyone here to tell you. At my camp, it's thirty-five miles to the nearest village. And there are no communications to the outside. The loggers all have CB radios but we have no phone and no electricity. If I were to stay with my bees for the whole summer, I might be two or three weeks without seeing anyone."

We are almost there. Lady and I have dozed off and on for the last few hours, but Floyd, well over twice my age, has kept up a running conversation and has barely yawned.

We have counted our sixth moose. In the gray light of morning, we trundle over the washboard of a corduroy road, made nearly impassable by deep ruts and mud washes, and pull up to Floyd's camp, a tin-roofed, two-room cabin made of peeled tamarack logs, which sits tight on the bank of the West Branch of the Penobscot. It is 6 a.m. and we're right on schedule. As we emerge from the truck, we are welcomed by a snow flurry.

Lady anxiously follows Smith inside and noses about while he lights both woodstoves, the Shaker-style box stove in the living room, big enough to heat a logging camp, and the black cast iron cookstove in the kitchen, taking from a good supply of dry firewood that lines the living room wall. Fifty-six pairs of deer antlers festoon the walls, a recipe for baked beans is penciled onto the kitchen wall next to the cupboard, and the West Branch, a river made famous by log drivers, canoeists, and Henry David Thoreau, runs close enough to make you think you could reach out the kitchen window and dip your cup into the deep, black water.

"The bees won't bother to fly until it heats up outdoors, so what do you say we have ourselves a little breakfast while we wait?" Floyd says, rubbing his hands together. From the cooler, he unpacks eggs and slab bacon and coffee. The fire in the big black cookstove, which looks almost as good as the day it was made, has quickly warmed the space. He takes the big black cast iron skillet from the nail on the wall. The pan shines like black enamel. As he works, the fragrance of butter melting in the skillet and coffee percolating fills the cold camp. Warmth spreads. Bacon sizzles. He drops eggs in next to the spattering, thick slices of bacon. I sense that Floyd is as hungry as I am. He slides the eggs and bacon onto thick camp plates and sets them on the rough pine table. While he toasts bread on the top of the hot stove, he directs me to pull a jar of honey from the shelf. It has wintered over in the camp and, though it is crystallized solid, I spread it on the hot buttered toast. "Best thing I ever ate," I say, and mean it. Floyd chuckles like a proud Papa.

"Big name brands are a blend of many kinds of honey," he says. "You get a hundred bottles in a hundred different months and every one of them will be alike, always the same color. They're experts: To make the honey keep well in stores, they heat it up so it won't crystallize and push it through the fancy filter. But I don't process my honey like that. I take it down home and spin it out of the combs and strain it through a wire screen to take out any little pieces of wax or anything like that, and then pass it through a piece of damp nylon into bottles.

"I call my honey wilderness honey rather than wild flower honey," he continues, "because, if you think about it, most all honey comes from wild flowers. It changes its color and flavor along with the blossoms of that time of year. Down home, we have dandelions first, then we have the basswood and locust — each flower will produce a different kind of honey, of a different color. But up here, it doesn't change. Everything grows very rapidly once the spring opens, everything just busts loose.

"The distinctive quality of my honey is that it always has the same light color and the same delicate flavor," he says. "It would seem that the bees would make less honey in conditions like these, but the natural bent of wildlife is to support itself against whatever nature gives it. Like the moose and the deer and the bear — they all feed and grow fat in the summer because they know the winter is going to be very hard. Same thing with the bees: They store tremendous amounts of honey — seventy to ninety pounds to each hive — to last them through the winter. These flowers are all in bloom at once. You wake up in the morning and stuff has grown, just during the night."

Floyd pauses to point out a pair of purple finches that are resting on a branch outside the window. He has just sopped up the last of the egg yolks with the corner of his toast. "To me," he says, "just to be here and see those two little birds, it's a big event. I think that there aren't many deeper thoughts than just going hunting or fishing — in other words, just being here in these woods." He gets up and stretches and says, "Well, I think my bees are going to have to wait just a bit longer. I'm going to have myself a nap."

While Floyd snoozes, I go outside into the still cool morning. There is not a sound until I get close to the hives, where I can hear the bees arguing and muttering inside their prison. It's obvious they won't starve: An abundance of wild cherry blossoms rim the camp's clearing, dandelions speckle the grass around the trailer, and tiny violets lurk in the weeds on the riverbank. I sit with Lady on the camp steps. The sun breaks through the thick clouds and the sky clears off, postcard blue.

Later, Floyd will take me in his canoe up the West Branch of the Penobscot, a river he knows like the road home. We will find our way to Lobster Cove — so-named because it is shaped on the map like a lobster claw — and see, one after another, a dozen moose, grazing in the shallows. Later in the day, we will walk up to the old village of North East Carry, which, at this early time of the season, looks like an abandoned village at the edge of a rough sea. The wind coming up off Moosehead Lake can create cresting waves. North East Carry was once a thriving logging town, where logs were collected and pushed downriver to the mills. When we stood at the edge of those vast, roiling waters, it seemed we were the only two people on the earth.

In time, Floyd comes out into the warming sun. He takes off one of the several layers of plaid flannel shirts he has worn on the journey and hangs it on a post. "Warming up," he says. He climbs up into the trailer and moves gingerly down the narrow aisle to the first hive. I stand close by, eager to watch the bees' release but a bit wary. With a pair of needle-nose pliers, Floyd pops the screening from the hive entrance and pulls the cotton out of the holes. The bees boil out in straight lines, startling me, bouncing off my face and arms like a barrage of buckshot. They don't sting. They soar and angle back and forth, making messages with their lines, elated to see the sun. Their wilderness summer has begun.

June 1982 Boston Globe Sunday Magazine

FLOYD SMITH *died on October 21, 1993 at the age of eighty-eight. Up until three or four years before he died, Floyd continued to take his bees to North East Carry and make the honey they produced while in the wild. This was a unique enterprise and no one, that we know of, has continued this practice. Many of his loyal customers still miss the subtle taste of Floyd's wilderness honey, most especially his children and grandchildren.*

Barna's Rock

It is seven o'clock on a foggy June morning. A small group is gathered at the dock in Jonesport, Maine, a little village at the outer edge of the United States of America. Jonesport is home to fishermen and gillnetters, but, most notably, home to Barna Norton, guide to birders, pilot of *The Chief*, and, until his son, John, joined him, an army of one against the Canadian government. Now Barna and John are an army of two.

The group, which numbers thirteen in all, is hoping the fog will lift enough so that Barna can get them out to Machias Seal Island, which, for all they know, is simply a rock where puffins and razorbills and arctic terns come to light, an island delight to bird-watchers. But along with the terns and the puffins, there is history, history that reaches back into the very beginnings of this country.

John is on board *The Chief*, washing down the decks and readying the forty-foot diesel-powered vessel for the journey to the island. The fog is lifting. The engine burbles.

Barna remembers that he has forgotten paper towels. Some distance into the trip, at least one of these visitors will *need* paper towels as they fall ill to the relentless sway of the wide ocean that separates Barna from his island, the island of his forefathers and, he intends, the island of his descendants. Barna makes a mad dash for his house, which sits up above the docks. Barna is eighty-two, and so his "mad dash" is a little slower than it once was. He is wearing galoshes, a plaid raincoat and a visorless hat that sits plunk on top of his head.

One by one the tourists board *The Chief*, welcomed cordially by John, who speaks sweetly but who has pirate eyes and a mean-looking scar across his nose.

Barna appears again, his arms filled with rolls of paper towels. Light-footed, he walks down the ramp, ready once again to make his claim.

Barna steps aboard and hops up onto the tall stool at the helm, throws open the throttle and guides *The Chief* out into the open ocean. The group talks excitedly among itself about the puffins, the auks. They don't seem aware that they are about to take part in an invasion.

The trip to Machias Seal Island takes about an hour and twenty minutes, if it is fine weather. Today is iffy. Barna has been up since five, making his decision. His guests are often landlubbers. He decided it was safe to make the trip but warns the passengers that they may not be able to make a landing on the island. There are signs on the boat that read: *Warning! Landing on Machias Seal Island can be extremely hazardous. Passengers go ashore on the island at their own risk.*

The passengers keep their binoculars trained on eiders and dolphins. From one side to the other, there is nothing but water and sky. The ocean is big, heaving hills of sea water carrying *The Chief* on a merry roll.

At last a speck appears on the horizon. This is the island of Barna's eye, the only island in his vision now and for all times. With the timing of a master, Barna navigates *The Chief* around the rough and rocky perimeter of Machias Seal Island. He swings her around in the churning sea and cuts the engine. In their intimate choreography, John goes forward and releases the anchor while Barna works the tide.

In the shelter of the island, the sea is no less calm and there is some heated discussion between John and Barna as to whether a landing is safe. The tourists listen politely. They have paid fifty dollars apiece and dearly wish to go ashore. However, it does not look like any easy task.

Good-sized waves crash up onto the rocks, splash powerfully, and pull backwards, exposing seaweed that glistens like oil. John jumps down into the little motorboat that he's towed out behind *The Chief* and the tourists follow suit. They are going to see the puffins.

Up by the lighthouse, the Canadian flag whips and waves on its pole. Barna is the last one off *The Chief.* John pilots the little craft as close as he can to the rocks. Barna watches the waves come and retreat. He waits and then, at the exact right moment, he steps lightly onto the slick cushion of kelp. In his right hand he grips an umbrella. Taped to the top of the umbrella is a small American flag. He never goes ashore on his island without our flag. Years back, he carried a larger one and planted it in the soil, sometimes with the help of his seven-member Territorial Council, who stood at attention as Barna unfurled the lovely colors of his loyal soul. But the big flag is hard for him to handle now that he is older, and the members of his council are getting too old to come out to the island. No matter. The umbrella method works just as well, providing the additional service of protecting him from the sun and from the droppings of marauding terns.

Barna raises the umbrella and makes his march up the slick, rocky approach, to the lighthouse. For about the fifteen thousandth time in his life, Barna Beal Norton has laid claim to Machias Seal Island, for the United States — and for his family's honor.

THIS IS THE WAY Barna tells the story of the ownership of the island, which has been in dispute for decades. If the Canadian flag that waves up at the crest of the island means anything at all, is no longer in dispute, but Canada's claim to Machias Seal Island will never be valid, not in Barna's mind.

"According to the terms of the Treaty of Paris, in 1783, all the islands in the Gulf of Maine to the east and north of Grand Manan went to England. Those to the south and west belong to the United States. Now that treaty said *uninhabited* islands, which is what Machias Seal is. Machias Seal is inhabited only by light keepers and they don't count. According to international law, a lighthouse has no homesteading value. It is considered an aid to navigation or a buoy on dry land.

"In 1865, when we had the Civil War going on, my great-grandfather Barna Beal came out here to this island and laid claim. He was known as Tall Barney. He stood six foot seven inches and he weighed two hundred ninety pounds. He was known for being a rowdy up and down the seacoast. He wanted to lay claim to the fishing grounds to the south and west of Grand Manan. And he wanted to stay way clear of the war they were fighting. So he took up residence on Machias Seal Island. One day Tall Barney was out fishing and the Canadians set after him. They jumped aboard his vessel and tried to arrest him! Well, he smashed their guns against the main mast, broke some of their arms, their heads, tossed them back and forth across the vessel and threw them overboard. Then he made his claim."

The legend of Tall Barney is much broader and more involved than this one anecdote. But for the purposes of this story, this one tale is enough. Barna continues with the story he has told a thousand times, maybe more, not only to interested visitors but to our senators and to the Congress of the United States.

"Well, everything went along just fine until 1915, which is the year that I was born. In his will my great-grandfather said that the first male child named after him would inherit Machias Seal Island. I was named Barna Beal Norton, after Tall Barney, and my father came over and declared that Machias Seal Island would belong to me."

Barna Beal Norton may share his great-grandfather's name, but he doesn't share his brawn. Barna is only five feet and a few inches. But he can muster up a battle just like Tall Barney. When the Machias Seal Island gauntlet was flung, Barna took up the challenge.

It wasn't until 1940, when he was twenty-five years old, that Barna first laid eyes on his land. "I knew about the island since I was a small boy, but we didn't have any money. We didn't even have a boat!"

So Barna set about to build a boat. On his desk Barna has a picture of that old boat, which he called *If.* It was thirty-three feet long and it cost him a precious three hundred and fifty dollars to put together, using an automobile engine he rescued from a wreck. "I cut it down and converted it and in the spring of 1940, I went out with a group of people to show them the puffins and to declare the island mine. I've been doing that ever since."

The Canadians, he says, didn't pay any attention to him at the time. "And I didn't pay any attention to them," he adds.

The plot thickened in 1970 when, for reasons unknown to Barna, the Canadians began to take their ownership of the island seriously. "They showed up one day when I was out there and it got to the point where I was chasing the fellow with an oar and I hit him! Well, they had the law after me and they wanted me arrested! Senator Cohen gave a speech in the Senate defending my ownership of the island."

The battle escalated during the 1970s, culminating in the arrival of what Barna calls "high potentates" in helicopters onto the island. "I was playing pool with the light keeper and they come down and tell me that these High Ups want to talk with me and I says, 'What are you talking about! I'm playing pool!' Well, tremble and shake, they tell me I'd best get myself out there. And I says, they haven't made an appointment to see me and under no circumstances would I go out to them. They were trying to make me kowtow and I wasn't about to! So they said that from then on, there would be Mounties on the island. Well, I guess some Mounties showed up a few times but it got foggy and stormy and pretty soon they stopped showing up at all. And I still kept coming!"

That scrimmage was followed by another battle when Barna's friend Ken Wood was told by Canadian officials to get his lobster traps out of the waters around the island. This was also in the early 1970s. Ken went to Barna for help and Barna told him to stand his ground. "I rallied the troops. We put the traps back out there, and the next time I come out, there's a couple of US Coast Guard cutters out there, and I look to the west and I see these airplanes coming. Oh, it was a mighty day but it went by, and Ken still puts his traps out there. To my mind, that proved right there who owns that area. The United States."

And Barna Beal Norton.

But Canada continues to keep light keepers on the island. Machias Seal Island has the only manned lighthouse in all of the Maritimes. And at great expense. Because of the treacherous landing on Machias Seal Island, the men and their supplies are brought on and off the island by helicopter. This is no mere coincidence. According to Canadian officials, the lighthouse keepers are there for "reasons of sovereignty."

Barna explains: "They don't *dare* take people off from it because they know that if they did, I'd be sitting up in that lighthouse myself. They know that's the truth."

PAUL CRANFORD has been a Canadian light keeper for more than twenty years and he has served on Machias Seal Island since 1991. He knows Barna well and is glad to see him when he comes ashore. Barna sometimes brings him treats from the mainland, strawberries and broccoli, such things that, when you are living on a rock in the Atlantic Ocean, are more valuable than gold. While the tourists hoist binoculars to their eyes and ogle puffins and eiders, Paul welcomes me into his lighthouse and offers a cup of hot tea. He speaks diplomatically when I raise the issue of the island's ownership.

"Yah, Barna shows me old papers and this and that and he tells me old legends of people who fought with different people a hundred years ago or whatever and I guess that's why it's disputed, because there is truth to both sides."

On the other hand, Cranford recognizes the benefit he enjoys as a result of Barna's persistence: "I suppose it is good for me because it provides me with job security!"

Cranford believes that the reason this particular island and its boundaries are of interest is not because of an old pirate's claim to

Machias Seal Island, but because of the potential importance of offshore drilling rights. But the reason is perhaps irrelevant. The reality is Barna's persistence.

"Of course, Barna is not interested in oil!" Cranford says, laughing good-heartedly. "He is interested in the island and the birds. And the *pride*!"

Paul Cranford, a native of Prince Edward Island, is a writer and a fiddler who uses his time on Machias Seal Island to write and to compose. Due largely to his long months on the island, he has issued a CD aptly named *The Lighthouse*. The tunes are shot through with references to this desolate place: "The Puffins' Return," "After the Storm," "Gale Force," and one called "*The Chief*," after Barna's boat.

Outside, Barna makes his way up the stony hill to the lighthouse. He is carrying his umbrella and before he enters, he pokes the flag in the doorway and waves it tenuously. "OK?" he calls in.

"Come on in, Barna!" Paul calls warmly and Barna enters.

"I thought you might be scratching the bow," Barna says.

Paul welcomes any opportunity to work his fiddle, so he picks it up and begins to play a reel. This one is called "Barna Norton," and Barna taps his rubber sole to the rhythm.

"We've got to go, you know," Barna says when Paul puts down the fiddle. "The tide is right." There are only a few moments when it's right to get on or off the island, a little window through which Barna has stepped with precision for more than fifty years. He saunters back outside and raises his umbrella. The little flag flutters in the northwest wind. Holding the umbrella high, like the flag of victory he knows it to be, Barna marches back down the hill where John is waiting to load everyone safely back onboard *The Chief*.

John takes the helm on the way home. He and his father have sometimes come to blows and he has lived in other parts of the country at times, including six years in San Francisco during the sixties. But he is fifty now and home is where he wants to be. John, the only child of Barna and the great-great grandson of Tall Barney, plans to carry on Barna's fight when Barna is no longer able to make the journey to plant his flag. John has only one child, a four-year-old daughter named Whitney. When she was seventeen days old, John took Whitney, daughter of John, granddaughter of Barna Beal Norton, and great-great-great granddaughter of Tall Barney Beal, out to the island. "I planted her little tiny feet on the island and I said, 'It's all yours, darlin'. It's all yours.'"

June 1998 Yankee magazine

BARNA NORTON *passed away in January 2005 at the age of eighty-nine. At that time, his son, John, continued running the puffin tours to Machias Seal Island, simultaneously keeping the Norton family claim to the island alive. On June 8, 2008, John Norton died of cancer. His partner, Holly Davis, and John's daughter, Whitney Norton, continue to guide birdwatchers out to Machias Seal Island aboard Barna's boat,* The Chief, *which still defiantly proclaims its port of registry on the stern: Machias Seal Island, U.S.A. Whitney will turn nineteen next year and plans to get her pilot's license at that time. She visits the island at least fifteen times a year to maintain the Norton family's claim and America's stake in Machias Seal Island.*

In Paradise

In the distance the red tractor moves soundlessly across the hayfield. It is eleven o'clock on a Tuesday morning in July in Shirley Center, Massachusetts. The thermometer by the kitchen window of the Longleys' farmhouse reads eighty-six. The sun is hot and round, rising high in the sky. The tractor comes close enough across the grassland to hear, until the engine's noise takes over the landscape and Melvin Longley brings it to rest between the red brick house and the barn. He presses his forefinger on the kill switch and silences the *chum-chum-chum-chum* of the Farmall. With one hand on the big round red fender, he eases himself down onto the grass, now shorn close by the cutter bar. He has been haying. He does it now piecemeal, a little at a time, not like he used to, sweeping the whole wide field in an evening. He's older now and his legs give out on him pretty easily. He gave up the cows almost twenty years ago. But the haying, the mowing of the grasses on this nearly one hundred acres of grass and swampland, that he won't give up. Grass is what holds the magic for him.

Say the word "grass" to Melvin Longley and a kingdom unfolds for him, one that includes as rich a cast of characters as any Hollywood production. In his time on this earth, which is now seventy-one years and all of it spent in this town, he has come to be known as an expert on grass. If there can be such a thing. He knows grasses, as a farmer should, but he is not a botanist nor is he an herbalist nor a feed-grain specialist. The grasses he loves and about which he knows so much are the weeds, the tiny flowers of the field and the pesky harbingers of hay fever. He is simply a man who loves grasses as a bird-watcher loves the birds.

In 1988, the Smithsonian Institution acknowledged his passion and invited him to come down to Washington to be part of its Festival of American Folklife, to show off what he knows about grass and other things of country life, about which he knows as much as anyone, it seems. He went down with Louise, his wife of fifty-one years. Into an Allied Moving Van, sent to the family farmhouse on Whitney Road, moving men loaded about eight hundred pounds of Longley treasures — including tools and a workbench, flails, ox yokes, brooms — and bundles and bundles of grasses. And then he and Louise flew down together, carrying only a borrowed suitcase packed with their clothes. "Louise and I had never been off the farm for one week, to say nothing of two weeks," he said. For two weeks they held forth in a booth in a pavilion, talking about grass and crafting the rustic hearth brooms (Melvin is locally famous for these Shaker-inspired treasures) whittled in one piece from the branches of a witch hazel tree. For two weeks, Melvin Longley was more or less on display, dispersing the lessons of a lifetime to the crowds that gathered, coming in from under the shadow of the Washington Monument, curious, interested, amazed by this slight, somewhat bent man who, with his sideburns, carefully combed hair, and Western shirts with snap buttons looks more like a cowboy at the square dance than a Yankee farmer.

Melvin remembers his time in Washington with an amused smile. It came and went, a little chapter in his life that Louise tucked into his scrapbook with the other tributes from the local papers — when he stopped milking cows on the homestead (the first time there hadn't been any cows in the Longley's barn since 1643), the write-ups on the nature displays he used to put up at the elementary school when he was head custodian there, and the time the town of Shirley Center declared a day in September to be "Melvin P. Longley Day" and had lemonade and ceremonies in his honor.

Melvin brushes the hay chaff from his work pants and goes through the screen door into his kitchen. Inside his house, which sits close by this lightly traveled back road and covered with the fullness of ivy vines, Melvin can point to the room where he was born. He and Louise sit at a table he made of pine from his woods. Nearby is the bed he made from the wood of the cherry tree that he and his father cut at the edge of the hayfield. Everything here has a story. "It's a good bed for me," Melvin says. Melvin is more than six feet tall. "I can stretch right out in it."

He settles into his chair at the kitchen table, his reading place. Melvin found out most of what he knows about grasses by reading. He has Parkinson's disease, which makes it hard for him to move around as much as he used to, so he reads a lot. "Now, when I'm resting my legs, which I have to do quite often, I have plenty of time for reading," he says. "Lots of times, I wake up about half past four, so I get up, have a dish of cornflakes and read for a while. Then I can go back to bed and I can get some sleep." In these early hours, he also sometimes writes a poem, just for himself and for Louise. His handwritten poetry now fills a notebook.

It was from a U.S. Department of Agriculture yearbook that he first began to learn about the rich and well-populated world of grasses. "I've always been interested in grasses," he says. "If you stop and look, they really are flowers. Although the blossoms are minute, they are beautiful — and so *different*. The grasses that we grow commercially are only a very tiny proportion of the grasses that are self-seeded and grow here naturally. Some of them have uses and some of them have no use that I have found out. The only difference between a vegetable and a weed is that they haven't discovered what to do with the weeds. If we got really hungry, there are a lot of things growing out there that we could eat."

On his land alone, Melvin says he has identified sixty or seventy varieties of grass and fifty-eight different kinds of trees. "Grasses and trees fascinate me, even so far as in the wintertime when I'm putting a stick of wood into the stove, I really can't throw it in without identifying it first. If I don't quite know, I stick a different piece in and I wait and I think about that one."

Melvin pushes back his chair, gets up and goes into the pantry. He returns with a saucer filled partway with water. He holds out his hand to show me the seeds in his palm. "Sweet vernal seeds," he says and then empties them into the water. Like sleeping animals coming to life, the seeds start to spin in slow circles. They jump and twist in the pool. Louise watches this little sideshow and laughs. She has seen it countless times but her eyes sparkle to see it anew. She has learned a lot from Melvin. "Things that you would never dream of, you know?" she says.

"I have seen them jump up out of the dish," he says. He is enjoying this, the way Louise is. "They're planting themselves," he explains. "Each seed has two horns, hairlike things that stick out. The water twists one one way and one the other and they work against each other to make the seed roll over. In a year's time, with sunshine and dry weather, they will twist themselves an inch into the sandy soil."

And then come up, grass. He often does this for children. He used to do it at the elementary school and Louise says he must have done it a million times down there at the Smithsonian.

"No doubt other seeds do this, but not in such a spectacular way," he says. "I tell the kids how many ways there are for seeds to plant themselves. Like water lilies — the seeds form like a little boat and after they drop off the plant, it takes three days for that little boat to dissolve so they sink. By the time three days have passed, they're far enough away from the mother plant to have a place of their own."

Like so much else that he knows, Melvin read this in a book. Then he went out and looked for some sweet vernal. "There is sweet vernal everywhere in New England," he says. "People say, Where do you find it? And I say, Well, look down. Just look down!"

If you go to visit Melvin Longley, he'll want to show you the grasses but before that, he'll want to show you the church. Somehow it is that the town and the land there in Shirley Center are woven in and around the Longley family like a fine tapestry, bright with the colors of their lives and the lives of their ancestors. Melvin says that his grandchildren are the twelfth generation to live on the land here on Whitney Road. The front rooms and the hallways of his house are wainscoted with wood from the old pews and doors taken from the First Parish Meeting House (which Melvin refers to as "the church") when it was renovated and "modernized" in the late 1800s. He and his family before him have cared for that church down through the ages. The church is just a short distance from their farmhouse.

Built in 1773 and moved about from place to place, the church has been on this spot, just off the town common, since 1851. Both Congregationalists and Unitarians once used the building for their worship services but it has not had an active congregation since the 1940s. Still, it is the oldest public building in town and the townspeople have worked to preserve it for use for weddings, funerals, concerts (their Stevens tracker organ is well-known), dramatic presentations and other suitable events. On the front wall of the Meetinghouse, a plaque hangs on the front wall in honor of Melvin Longley. The steps to the old structure are worn and the interior is cool, cooler than this hot day. The stillness inside evokes stark history. There is a feeling of refuge as we enter this sacred space, the low light revealing a surprising striping that decorates the walls.

In the early 1970s the inside of the church was looking pretty bad. The walls, once bright in gay stripes of Colonial colors, had grown dingy. Long streamers of wallpaper hung from the walls, tattered and moth-eaten. At the annual meeting the chairman voiced his dismay. "He said he didn't think we needed to meet in such an awful-looking church any longer," Melvin recalls.

"And so I began," he says of his four-year project to single-handedly restore the interior of the church. There were two layers of paper to be taken off. He left the paper, where it was still decent, and razored off the rest. And then he duplicated the yards of molding paper that needed to be replaced, painting in the twenty-nine stripes by hand, using colors of blue and gray and brown that he mixed himself to match the old paint.

The ceilings are three stories high. He had to build staging to get up there. "I chased around most of the neighbors at one time or another to come and give me a hand to move my staging."

Mostly, it was a labor of love. "At first I was charging two dollars and a quarter an hour. Then I saw that it was going to be such a big project that I quit sending the bills. I did it for nothing."

That's when they put up the plaque.

Not long ago, the spire needed repair. Melvin had an idea. Hallmark once used a picture of this church on a Christmas card. He sat down and composed a letter to them. "I used my most persuasive rhetoric in the hopes they would make a contribution to the restoration of the spire." His efforts were unsuccessful. But the spire was repaired, thanks largely to Melvin Longley.

"Do you want to go way up?" he asks. The Meeting House tower is a challenge, worth it for the view. We clump up the narrow winding stairs that get narrower and steeper with each turn. Finally, an ascent like a ladder up to a hatch in the roof. My resolve weakens.

"It's nice," he says, his only encouragement as he reaches the top and pushes out the hatch that lets in a shock of light. He disappears out onto the roof. I continue on up, to the crown of Shirley Center. From that height, the little village, its large circular common ringed with historic houses, looks like a scene from a picture book. Melvin makes this climb up here quite often. "When I want to look around, ring the bell," he says. He leans over and begins to rock the enormous brass bell. It gains momentum, creaking in its wooden cradle and then DONG!, the sound of the bell pulses out across the common. A dog barks into the summer air.

It is getting into the afternoon. There are puffy white clouds skimming the edges of a very blue sky. Melvin says, "That sky tells me I'd better get back to the field."

WHEN WE GET BACK to the house, though, he decides that the haying can wait. He wants to take me to see the grasses. In his Ford sedan we start off across the flatness of the field. He used to walk out into the fields to collect the grasses.

"Too far for my legs now," he says. "For years I dreamed of walking to Ohio and stopping to work for a week or two and then moving on." He laughs mildly. "I'll never do it now."

We move along, the grasses gently brushing the underside of the car, a steady stroking sound. At the far side of the field, he stops the car and turns off the engine. "Most years, there's a lot of nice grains and sedge in here. But there's also poison ivy so I think you'd better let me go in." He pushes open the big door of the old Ford and moves into the depth of the grasses, which ripple around him in the afternoon breeze like a rising tide. I follow. He slides his knife out of his pocket and opens the blade, bends and cuts a stem. It is a long-stemmed grass with several exaggerated tassels at the top. "Fringed sedge," he says, handing it to me. He points out the triangular stem with his fingernail, which is thick as a nickel. "The sedges have a three-cornered stem. That's how you can know them," he says. "Feel the sawtooth on the edge?" I pass my finger across it. It is sharp, a tiny saw. "That keeps insects from moving up and down the stems." He wades back into the grass, cutting a stem here and there as he wades along and then returns, handing me a bouquet of the grasses.

The field we are driving across is mostly timothy, but some clover is coming in. Fort Devens, a big military training base, is nearby and paratroopers sometimes use this field for drills. He mows this part of the field first so they can use it. "They put an orange arrow into the middle of the field and try to land as close to the arrow as they can. One jumper landed in the tree across the road a while ago and had to be rescued by the town's firemen." Melvin likes this story and he tells it to me in detail as he pulls the car to a stop again and gets out.

He takes me down to show me a patch of what he calls saw grass — is it useful for anything? "Nope, not that we know of." We walk through the sharp blades. He points out another grass called blue joint.

Horse mint.

He shows me fox sedge — the top is like a foxtail.

Hidden in the grass is a crowd of forget-me-nots. He points them out. And then wild iris, the blue blossoms withered into papery skins.

The earth we are walking on is marshy and looks something like a salt marsh, wide and open, veined with streams. "Back when they mowed these places with scythes, they'd wait till late in the season when it was dry. My father said that he and his father used to pole hay out of there, carry it out between two poles. Because it was so wet, you couldn't get a wagon in there. Some of the farmers used to use brackets on their horses, something like snowshoes. They've lost horses in that mud, you know, had to kill them right there."

All around us are the mechanical sounds of grasshoppers and crickets, spaced with the cheerful *hooray!* of the redwing blackbirds. Overhead, the martial rhythm of a Fort Devens chopper blade thrums closer and closer, a reminder of the other world.

Melvin Longley bends to point to sweet vernal. He doesn't say the name, but looks at me to see if I recall this morning's lesson. I do. "Most everywhere you go you see the sweet vernal," he says. "And quite a lot of black snakes," he calls back as he heads back to the car. He has gathered a bundle of grasses and bullrushes that he cradles into the back seat. He dries the grasses he collects on a screen in the old milking parlor of his barn. He ties them and tags them for exhibit. And sometimes he takes vases of an assortment of grasses over to the church for reserve, in case they don't have flowers for the altar that Sunday.

"I want to show you Paradise," he says. I follow him through tall grasses to the woods. He steps over barbed wire and goes down into a vale. Tall hemlocks guard a deep rock crevice. The height of these trees and the depth of the rock gives the place a sacred feeling. The river sluices down through a V of solid ledge, smooth like the sides of a porcelain basin.

"This is what we Longleys call Paradise," Melvin tells me. "For a lot more than a hundred years, they've been calling it that. The waterway is Paradise Brook." On the map, he says, the brook is called Spruce Swamp Brook and on the same map what the Longleys call Paradise is identified as Spruce Swamp. "It's just as well. If they called it Paradise on the map, more people would come. Enough come as it is."

Back in the car, he starts the engine and pulls it into gear. We roll again out onto the prairie. "I like the meadow sweet and the hardhack, the steeple bush." Alongside the car is what he calls buckthorn. He slows. "They used to use that to make yellow dye," he says. And he identifies for me a familiar grass, low-growing with a tint of red. A crop of it can give the roadside a reddish hue. I've seen it all my life but have never known the name. "Red top," he says.

There is also yarrow and milkweed and goldenrod. He pauses over a waving stem. Sometimes now, he forgets the names of things, has to stop and think. At last, the words come. Balm of Gilead.

There are others, so many others. This is just a scanning of the commonplace, a quick tour on a summer afternoon. If we had more time, we'd see yard rush. Rabbit's foot sedge. Canada rush. Yellow foxtail. Bog rush. Red dock. He stops to tell me this: Redwing blackbirds tie two or three stalks of red dock together to make their nests. Purple vetch. Tussock.

Louise walks out into the field. She likes the grasses too and knows some of them by name now.

"I want to find the heavy-fruited English blue grass for her," he says to Louise. "I know there is some in here."

Her eyes sweep the landscape. "I'd recognize it if I saw it," she says.

Melvin and Louise roam through the yellows and greens and lavenders of the mid-summer meadow. "I've got it," he says and they respond together with muted cries of pleasure. Melvin Longley moves toward it and cuts a stem of the blue grass, holds it up, the showy seed pods waving like small flags.

August 1991, Yankee magazine

FOR MANY YEARS, *Melvin Longley suffered from Parkinson's disease. He amazed everyone with his ability to keep the disease at bay by remaining active. Melvin Longley passed away on November 24, 1997. The Longley Homestead, the last dairy farm in Shirley, was put into conservation in 2003. The seventy-three-acre farm, including the house and the barn, was acquired by the town of Shirley, which is responsible for its care, custody and control. Melvin's wife, Louise, died on August 1, 2009, after a treasured life. Melvin's son, Stephen, and his wife, Mona, live next door to the homestead. Stephen continues to hay the fields and bale the hay for sale to benefit the Longley Acres Conservation. He also sometimes reads Melvin's poetry aloud on special occasions, as he did at the dedication of the farm into conservation, an event Melvin surely would have loved to attend.*

Finding Venus

It is 1968 and in the dark back room of St. John's Church in Portsmouth, New Hampshire, a young black woman is seated at a small table, bent over the parchment-like pages of the church's records which date back to the 18th century. This is not the beginning of Valerie Cunningham's search but it is the beginning of her success. As she runs her finger down the yellowed page, which offers a record of various births and baptisms in, as well as contributions to, that church during the year 1807, she stops at this entry: "Contribution Xmas day, Venus – a Black – $1"

Venus. She knew she had encountered this name before. She turned back the pages of her notebook and scanned her notes. Back a few pages, she found the connector, an entry she had copied earlier from the same church records. *Baptism in 1747 of Venus, child of Dorcas Bradford.* She had written that down because of the name, Venus, which she thought might be the name of a slave child. This 1807 entry seemed to confirm that.

Even when she first encountered it, Valerie knew that the name Venus was likely that of a slave, since names of this sort — neither African nor Christian — were often given by whites to separate the enslaved from both their African families as well as from proper society. So she could be reasonably certain that Venus was a slave. But the fact that Venus did not have a last name meant that Venus was no longer in the care of a white slave owner. Valerie knew then that Venus had been freed. And so, here was Venus, alive in 1807, a freed slave in Portsmouth, New

Hampshire, receiving the generous contribution of one dollar, no small sum in those days.

It was just a smidgen of knowledge, that seven-word entry in the otherwise voluminous records of that church but for Valerie, it was a huge triumph, an affirmation of all that she had begun when she started looking to find where the history of the black people of that port city might be hidden.

"Once I found Venus, that meant I had to keep going," Valerie says.

Now in her late fifties, Valerie Cunningham has never stopped looking. Since that small moment, at which time she was married and the mother of a toddler and an infant daughter, Valerie has acquired enough such information to fill a two hundred and sixty page, three-ring binder and to guide those interested on a walking tour that leads around Portsmouth to forty different sites — from the place where slave auctions were held to the house where a freed slave once lived. The book and the tour, both called *The Portsmouth Black Heritage Trail,* are the culmination of nearly a lifetime spent in search of what it's all about for the minority of blacks who live and work in Portsmouth.

In the years that she has been looking, she has discovered there were some six hundred fifty-nine slaves in the Portsmouth area between the years 1645 and 1800. "Slavery was never abolished in New Hampshire," she says, matter-of-factly. "The thirteenth amendment took care of that. Still, other New England states adopted resolutions about slavery, but New Hampshire never put it into writing. It is that 'Live Free or Die' attitude, whatever that means!" she says, with a knowing laugh.

Valerie's research rested in her notebook, known only to herself, until she met Mark Sammons, the former director of research at Strawbery Banke. Soon after Mark came to Portsmouth in 1989, he heard about Valerie. He read a short article she had published about black history and also went to hear her speak. He was impressed and had wanted to meet her, but it was Valerie who eventually approached him with her idea of putting together a brochure and walking tour. With this in mind, in 1995 Mark wrote an application for a grant that would enable him to explore the city's black history. Under the auspices of this grant, Mark and Valerie began work on their brochure.

"Our work extended far beyond the scope of that grant," Mark says. "It became a labor of love for both of us. We would have meetings that would turn into six-hour marathon sessions — there was so much to put together of what she had discovered over the years." They eventually found an intern to work with them, and when they were done, "we found that we didn't have a brochure anymore." Out of their work came the trail and the book, which is now in every school in the city as well as on reserve at the Portsmouth Library.

VALERIE IS A strong-looking woman with kind, cinnamon eyes, light skin the color of coffee and cream, and a cloud of russet hair. It is a breezy warm day and we are sitting at an outdoor café in Portsmouth's Market Square. Across the street, the great soaring steeple of North Church rises above us, and young, smartly dressed men and women mingle on the brick sidewalk. The air is full of the rich smell of coffee and sweet breads. Lunch time, and everyone has come out to sample the warm air and the good food. A shiny red-black-and-yellow trolley trundles by — *ding-ding!* — and the tourists on board lean this way and that as they survey the historic buildings all around. In all, a happy, prosperous scene that shows a Portsmouth transformed. Two centuries before this moment, just steps from where Valerie and I are sitting, Negroes were publicly flogged. Valerie, the only black person in sight, is likely the only person present in this busy scene who is aware of this wild contrast.

Valerie Cunningham was born and grew up in Portsmouth, where she graduated from Portsmouth High School in 1959. She was the only child of Clarence and Augusta Cunningham, who came to Portsmouth from, respectively, North Carolina and Virginia. Growing up black in the

1940s and 1950s in Portsmouth was different from, say, growing up black in North Carolina, but it was not devoid of pain. "We saw it all on television, the civil rights struggles that were going on down South," Valerie recalls. The racial obstacles that Valerie encountered in Portsmouth were muted but nonetheless present. "It wasn't as if people went around calling me 'nigger.' It was much more subtle than that," she says now. "And the Ku Klux Klan was active here at that time."

She credits her parents and the small but tightly knit black community for shaping her into the person she is today. Though she has traveled widely — her husband, from whom she is now divorced, was in the Air Force and they lived on bases all over the country and in Guam and the Philippines. Portsmouth is Valerie's choice of where she wants to live. She knows the city intimately, its every layer of history.

"Portsmouth was a nice place to grow up," she concludes. "My mother is a smart woman. She wanted to be sure that I knew that I was black. She is fair-skinned and can pass (for white) but she knew that wasn't what it was all about. She wanted me to understand what it means to be black, what our heritage is, and who we are."

In high school, Valerie worked at the library every minute of her spare time, afternoons, weekends, summers. She liked being in a place where it was quiet and information could be discovered. At the time, Dorothy Vaughn was the head librarian. Dorothy Vaughn spearheaded the efforts to preserve Strawbery Banke, the city's impressive historic district. But what *was* the history of the blacks of Portsmouth, the young Valerie began to wonder. Even though blacks have represented only one percent of the population of New Hampshire for more than two hundred years, Portsmouth was different. As much as five percent of its population is black, a figure that held true in Colonial times as well. She knew that in her church, a vigorous community of Portsmouth blacks, there was an oral history that was very much alive. But where was this written down? And if it wasn't, why wasn't it?

Valerie's hunger for this information did not diminish. It grew. After she married into the Air Force, Valerie got used to moving and finding what she could of the history of her people. About a year before she had found Venus, Valerie found a book that legitimized her search. Browsing in the back stacks at a library in Delaware, where her husband was then stationed, she came across a book called *The Negro in Colonial New England*. "That was the first book on black history I had ever found. It told me for sure that there had been slavery in New England and it specifically mentioned Portsmouth." In her developing journey, she had just taken one very important step.

Whenever she came home to Portsmouth, on leave or else for brief stints at Pease Air Force Base, Valerie would ask her mother to take care of her children and she would return to her task. Her early work at the library had taught her how to research things and she learned of other sources for early history, such as the records at the old churches and in city hall. Valerie needed only to have the door cracked and she was inside, scouring the records, searching and searching for those unusual names. The records were in varying conditions, heavy books with crumbling spines, the pages often thick as parchment and everything written in longhand, sometimes hard or impossible to decipher. Her eyes strained to read the names, but in time, she found Cesar and she found Prince and she found Pharaoh, Quam, Cato, Nero, Romeo, names almost cruelly inappropriate. She wrote it all in longhand in her growing notebook of information.

Eventually, Valerie went further into the stacks, into the old newspapers, which were stored in the library on microfilm. Turning the crank and peering at the gauzy screen, she flipped by page after page of the *New Hampshire Gazette*. There she found ads for runaway slaves. These gave her physical descriptions, which thrilled her, to have these people, to whom she now felt wed, become more than just names, more than just the property of a white man.

In the May 11, 1764, edition of the *New Hampshire Gazette*, she found this ad:

> Ran-away --- Negro Boy named Fortune,
> age 16, wearing a red jacket and canvas
> trowsers.

Based on this and other information Valerie had gathered, Mark Sammons wrote in *The Portsmouth Black Heritage Trail*: "We will never know what incident triggered Fortune's departure, perhaps an argument, a scolding, or a blow like that delivered a dozen years earlier to the ship's captain's slave. But the underlying cause was the condition and nature of enslavement. The tasks at the tavern may seem routinely domestic but slavery was never benign. While white youths were formulating visions of their future, Fortune had few choices in life and little hope of improved status."

This reading of the old *Gazettes* on microfilm was a hypnotic task that absorbed Valerie so thoroughly that one night she was locked into the library. "The custodian found me late that night. It's so quiet back where I was working, they didn't know I was there. And I didn't know what time it was."

Valerie notes in her book that running away in 1764 left the unhappy slave with little choice and few places to go. "The thirteen colonies combined had only a few thousand free blacks, with no community large enough for a runaway to disappear into." Aside from that one ad, Valerie found no more references to Fortune. She felt a kinship for each slave she discovered. "I always had a hard time when I read about the children being taken from their mothers. That still is hard for me to read about."

Without records of births or deaths, marriages or baptisms, slaves were an invisible presence, easily forgotten. In her search through the old newspapers, Valerie found many ads for runaways. "It's ironic that that was one way they made themselves known to me, through these ads or through something else that would make the newspaper. Otherwise, there were no records of them at all. Unless they misbehaved, they simply were not accounted for."

The ads offered her clues she did not expect. For instance, she was struck by the colorful clothing the slaves wore. Cromwell, age forty-five, who ran away from Henry Sherburne, Jr., wore a blue cloth coat and breeches, and a scarlet cloth jacket with metal buttons. Jean Paul, a French Creole, who ran away in 1764, wore an earring, a red handkerchief on his head or in his pocket, a blue jacket, striped overalls, and large buckles on his half-boots. Scipio, who ran away from James Dwyer of Portsmouth in 1793, sounds exotically dapper. He was described as wearing a "Saxon blue Frize jacket Lin'd with baize, slash sleeves and small metal buttons, a brown Fustian jacket without sleeves, a pair of scarlet everlasting breeches." The colorful attire, the earrings and buckles, all indicated to Valerie that the slaves may not have retained their African names but they retained their African love of color and style. "A lot of the slave owners would give their old clothes to the slaves and be surprised to find that they would use the colors so differently, combining stripes and plaids."

Valerie grew up in a house just steps from Stoodley's Tavern, one of the showpieces of Strawbery Banke. Stoodley's Tavern was known as a place where Paul Revere had stopped in 1774 to announce the news that the British were on their way from Boston to New Castle, an announcement that prompted the sole military action during the American Revolution on New Hampshire soil. In her research, much of which is now used by Strawbery Banke, Valerie discovered that Stoodley's Tavern had a darker history. Just ten years earlier, the building had been the site of public slave auctions. She found several dozen advertisements in Portsmouth newspapers that read like this one: *To be sold at public vendue at the house of Mr. James Stoodley, Innholder in Portsmouth, on Wednesday the seventh day of July . . . three Negro men and a Boy. The conditions of the sale will be cash or good merchantable items.*

Ironically it was in Mark Sammons' former office on the second floor of the now restored Stoodley's Tavern that he and Valerie collaborated on the creation of *The Portsmouth Black Heritage Trail.* Through this work with Valerie, Mark came to know that this famous tavern was not only the place where Paul Revere came — the kind of history we enjoy remembering — but it was also the place where Frank and Flora, both slaves, helped to unload the ships for auctions, which included their young compatriots from Africa — the kind of history that has been, for the most part, ignored. Mark deeply admires Valerie's contribution to Portsmouth's unusual history, still emerging. "She is a community treasure," he says. "She not only has the gift, but she shares it."

Across from Stoodley's Tavern was the wharf, where the young Africans were brought in. "Often they were sold right off the boat," Valerie explained. "Most households in Portsmouth accommodated only one or two slaves, which accounts for the fact that slave ships did not, as a rule, dock in Portsmouth. Instead, the Africans came as part of another shipment, cotton or rum or sugar. Often, merchants would put in an order for a slave to outgoing sea captains and so, when they were in West Africa, buying other goods, they would kidnap a few children to take back with them. Most households preferred to have the slaves come in as youngsters, old enough and strong enough to be useful but still young enough to be trained in the way they wanted them.

"A lot of people seem to think that slavery in Portsmouth, or in New England, was somehow more benign than slavery in the South," she continued. "They will say to me, 'You don't mean *real* slavery, do you?' Of course. Slavery was slavery and there is no indication that the slaves who lived and worked in Portsmouth were any better treated than they were elsewhere."

Aside from the public floggings, which were common enough, Valerie discovered that in 1695, Nathaniel Keen of Kittery, Maine, beat his slave woman to death and was charged with murder. But afterwards the charge was reduced to cruelty and Keen was released after paying a fine.

Valerie's quest is not so much to find such injustices, though there are many to be found, but rather, to find the past, the past in whatever form. One of her most important finds came while searching the microfilm, a tedious, eye-wearying task. Inside a paper dated November 12, 1779, she came across a petition, signed by a group of twenty Portsmouth slaves, including Prince Whipple. The petition read, in part, "*that through ignorance and brutish violence of their native countrymen, and by the sinister designs of others . . . and by the avarice of both, they, while but children . . .were seized, imprisoned, and transported from their native country, where they were born free, to a country where they are compelled to drag on their lives in miserable servitude. Thus, often is the parent's cheek wet for the loss of a child, torn by the cruel hand of violence from her aching bosom; thus, often and in vain is the infant's sigh for the nurturing care of its bereaved parent, and thus do the ties of nature and blood become victims to cherish the vanity and luxury of a fellow mortal. Can this be right? Forbid it, gracious heaven.*"

The petition was presented to the Governor of New Hampshire and the state legislators and the *Gazette* was required by law to print the slaves' plea for their freedom. However, at the end of the petition, the editor of the *Gazette* had seen fit to add his disclaimer: "*for the amusement of the reader.*"

"It made me sick, when I read that," Valerie says now. "It made me angry and furious but most of all it made me *sick.* I knew what was happening at that time so it wasn't really a surprise, but I was deep enough into this history to know that these were real men, and this was their sincere plea. And they were living in a time when white men had just finished a war for independence, and these slaves wanted their own independence as well. And they were being laughed at."

She copied the petition by hand into her notebook, her only recourse at the time.

Perhaps this petition had more of an effect than the editor had thought, perhaps other factors prevailed upon the powers of the time to see that slavery was wrong. Valerie's research shows that the last slave was recorded in the US Census in New Hampshire in 1840, though the custom of slavery had pretty much died out early in that century.

It is a shadowy, one-dimensional history that Valerie has brought forth, but a history just the same. Perhaps it will never be anything but vague. She would give anything if there were photographs for her to see, diaries, or something more tangible than single names entered into old records. "I am working with limited information. There is perhaps only so much that I can know."

There is a serenity about Valerie Cunningham. She has an almost regal countenance as she moves about Portsmouth, her sandaled feet on the solid ground of her native soil. When she speaks of all this, her words bear no bitterness nor even anger. She believes it's wrong that New Hampshire still does not celebrate Martin Luther King Day but she knows how time changes things. "It's going to happen. The state does celebrate the holiday. The only place that doesn't observe it is the state house. There are some legislators who still don't get it, who don't want to get it. But they are not going to be there forever."

For Valerie, the events of the past speak for themselves. She regards history as a tool of self-affirmation that helps her to understand who she is and who she is not. She lives here and sees the past among the present, as if through night-vision goggles. Where the Gap clothing store is now, once was the Negro Court where injustices were tried. Where rhododendrons grow beside North Church, black servants were once whipped. Just a block from where the Bank of New Hampshire has its nice brick fence, there was the big Negro cemetery. When the city was putting in sewer lines, about a hundred years ago, workers dug up bones, and neighborhood children went out into the street and played with the bones. These were the bones of some of the slaves who lived in Portsmouth. Perhaps they were the bones of Venus or Prince Whipple. The fact was noted and the construction continued. There are houses there now, on top of the old slave cemetery.

But Valerie does not regard this with anger or defeat. She simply continues doing what she can do. She keeps looking — for Venus, for Fortune, for the past most everyone else would rather forget.

February 1999 Yankee magazine

VALERIE CONTINUES *her work researching the identity of faceless slaves in early Portsmouth, working wherever and however she can to give the memory of enslaved Black people the dignity they deserve. In 2004,* Black Portsmouth: Three Centuries of African-American Heritage, *which Valerie co-authored with Mark J. Sammons, was published by University Press of New England. Many of the slaves whose names and histories Valerie researched so painstakingly, such as Prince Whipple, are brought to life in this book, underscoring a particularly hard-to-find social, political, economic, and cultural history that underlies Portsmouth and its environs. The book follows the paths of their descendants "who built communities and families, found institutions, and contribute to their city, region, state, and nation in many capacities."*

One ongoing project Valerie will see through to the end is the construction of a memorial park to commemorate the African cemetery on top of which houses have long since been built. In 2000, the burying ground was identified as one of twenty-four historic sites on the Black Heritage Trail, now a popular Portsmouth attraction for which Valerie is largely responsible. When a broken sewer pipe was being replaced in 2003, thirteen burials were revealed within the excavated work area on Chestnut Street. Five intact caskets remain beneath the sidewalk, undisturbed. Eight burials that were damaged as a result of the sewer work had to be removed but will be reinterred upon completion of the memorial. Great care was taken to remove the remains with respect. The skeletal remains and teeth were analyzed by archeologists in an effort to identify any of them by using DNA. Much information was gathered, though no personal identities were revealed. Because of these discoveries, work on the memorial park has been delayed considerably. Vigils are held on the site to remind city officials that this memorial needs to be completed and the ground needs to be sanctified, at last. Valerie has been told that more than a million dollars are needed to complete the park. Fund raising is ongoing. Once complete, this will be a diamond in the necklace known as the Portsmouth Black Heritage Trail, of which Valerie is founder and president. For more information, go to www.pbhtrail.org. (Along with the rest of the country, New Hampshire now observes Martin Luther King Day.)

Bernard McLaughlin Builds a Cathedral

DIAGONALLY ACROSS THE STREET from Bernard McLaughlin's garden is a leather tannery with a stink that's a sore topic in town. But in the garden the flowers triumph. Especially when the lilacs are in bloom, Bernard says, people drive by and pull over, occasionally causing traffic snarls. They are lured by the incredible fragrance. "Sometimes it's so much, you have to hold your nose," he says, forcing back a smile.

Every year hundreds of people pull off busy Route 26 on their way through South Paris, Maine, and prowl through Bernard McLaughlin's backyard. Last year he had more than eight hundred visitors, ten or twelve a day, come from all but ten states. He says he often cannot take the time to show them around. "I take the time if I have it, and no one should be offended if I don't." They come in groups — garden clubs, botany classes, delegates of the American Iris Society — and singly, old friends as well as people he's never seen. Some of them know the garden as if it were their own and others stumble on it by surprise. It is all word of mouth. For those who ask, there is advice from a man who's kept his garden like a fine painting for the past forty-seven years. It's a canvas he can't stop daubing at, and of the faithful, he says, "My garden is always open. People come and I guess they get a lot of free advice. I don't mind. I'd be a poor gardener if I did."

Bernard McLaughlin is a small man with a smooth unlined face and blue eyes the shade of his delphiniums. Though he looks much younger, he is nearing his eighty-sixth year. In this long stretch spent in his garden, he says he has learned to know peace. He has, in fact, created it. His home exists like a period piece on a road now lined with fast-food restaurants and gas stations. His front door isn't more than fifteen feet from the fast lane, but to step behind his hedges is to leave behind the squeal of cars and the hoot and clank of freight trains that waddle past his fir tree border.

Within the acre or so that Bernard has coaxed into bloom, there are only perennials, some of them as old as the garden. "For the work involved, I prefer perennials. Annuals are so expensive." Some have called his expanse an arboretum, others have likened it to a cathedral. To call it a garden is an understatement. There are grassy lanes edged with ferns and leafy borders. There are hedges of lilacs that have grown up like walls to enclose rooms full of bloom and color and fullness. There are gardens within the garden — the wildflower garden, the rock gardens, the rows and rows of iris, the vegetable garden — yet all are of the whole. Though he says he doesn't keep track, others hold that he has the largest collection of ferns in the state and the best collection of sempervivums (hens and chickens) anywhere. He's amassed one hundred different kinds of lilacs, three hundred different kinds of iris, one hundred and fifty different daylilies, and fifty different kinds of peonies. He estimates maybe fifty different kinds of ferns. "But I'll bet twenty-five of them were here when I got here," he confides.

In his northern climate, he shrugs off convention and keeps two magnolia trees in the lee of the barn, one of them pure white. "A lot of things they tell you can't grow up here in Maine, but if you followed the book, you'd never try anything. You have to experiment." He has been called the best gardener in Maine, but to that he says, "I don't know if that means anything, but I once had a lady tell me that Maine was lucky to have me for a gardener. I kind of liked that."

Over the years he's tried just about everything and gotten rid of what he doesn't want. He keeps no fruit trees, no berry patches, no rose bushes. "Too much trouble," he says. What's evolved for him is a garden of ease. "I used to have glads and poppies, but the care and the winter storage is more than I want to fuss with. As you go along, you have to discard some."

He treats that area of Maine to its first blooms, the hepatica, of which he has ten different shades, and the magnolia, which unfold in April. There is unending bloom from then until the helenium and late-blooming daylilies go brown with the first frost in late October or early November. "It's a symphony of color," he says. "I've planted it so that anywhere I pass, at any time during the summer, there will be color. Nothing splashy. Just color."

If South Paris and the road that passes by his house have offered changes, then Bernard has not been one to accept them. He lives in a house passed down through the family and uses the tools that were there in the barn when he got there. Many of his plants are old-fashioned and no longer available. His gardening know-how is mostly common sense, nothing new-wave or gimmicky. Throughout his life there have been patterns of repetition.

When he was a boy growing up in Aroostook County, Bernard kept a border of bright flowering perennials. Against the brown-green landscape of his father's potato farm, this big colorful strip must have been like a flag. "People used to stop to admire it on their way to town," he recalls. Even back then he'd work in the fields all day and come home and work in his flower garden, taking only four or five hours to sleep. He keeps that same schedule to this day — the life of most farmers, but not most gardeners.

Unlike most New England seniors, Bernard says he got Florida dreams out of his system by working there for ten years after he got out of college. In the thirties, he was a cook at The Breakers Hotel in Palm Beach. During his off-hours, he used to walk with his soon-to-be wife through the lushness of the hotel gardens and he'd say, "Rena, someday we'll have a garden we can walk through." Shortly after that, in 1936, they were married and returned to Maine, to Rena's grandfather's house, a small farm just outside of South Paris. In town, Bernard had gotten a job at a canning factory that made fig pudding for the servicemen. He had no interest in farming, but he did want to put in a strip of perennials, a border along the front, like he'd had on his dad's farm. "I planted what I thought I'd like, some lilac and a line of phlox." And he planted some fir trees to block the road. "But the hay field would dry up and turn brown by July," Bernard recalls of the land behind the house.

He turned up another bed and pressed daffodil and iris bulbs into the soil. Behind the barn he started a compost pile and brought manure from neighboring farms to enrich the thin soil. He let some rogue oaks grow up, hoping for a bit of shade. He brought fiddleheads down from his father's farm. He dug up lilies from the roadside and combed the woods for lady's slippers. In the summer he and Rena would take motor trips whose routes were charted by the different nurseries they favored, ones in Connecticut and in Vermont. In the trunk, they'd bring home flats of primula and sempervivums, a copper beech seedling. He joined the American Iris Society and become one of its noted growers. "It all just kept growing," he says. "Everywhere I looked, there was a new possibility." The years passed and the gardens grew. Pretty soon, Bernard had a garden he and Rena could walk through, in a place as far away from Palm Beach as might be possible.

THE TICK-TICK of Bernard's mattock can be heard, clawing weeds from the soil around the hostas in the bed with the bleeding hearts. Bernard has invited me to supper. Though Rena died two years ago, cooking was not a sudden mystery to him. Most of their married life, Bernard did the cooking. Now he cooks for himself and Cyril. Cyril is coming around from the far side of the house, where he has spent the afternoon up on a stepladder, lopping branches from the lilac hedges. Cyril is Bernard's cousin, and for the past six years he has come to stay with Bernard in the summers to help him weed and trim and prune. "I used to ride my bike eight or ten miles a day. You have to do something at my age or else you deteriorate. Now I work the gardens," Cyril had told me as he pruned. It is a symbiotic relationship: Bernard needs the help and Cyril enjoys the work, is enchanted by his workplace. Cyril is retired from the paper mill in East Millinocket where he worked all his life. He still lives up there in the winter, but around February he begins to think about the gardens. "I used to think a rose was a rose and a lily was a lily. Bernard has shown me that there are so many and they're all different. I still don't know a lot of them, but it's the greatest pleasure to come out here every day and see the flowers coming. First, in May, it's just the grass and the tiny buds, but you watch it, slow, and pretty soon there's an explosion of color."

Suppertime comes along at 4:30. Bernard decides we'll eat in the garden and he goes inside. Cyril wipes down the green painted table where we will eat. "Not long ago," he says, "an elderly man from New Jersey came. His daughter brought him and he sat there in that chair by the barn for quite a while. He said he'd never experienced such peace, such quiet. Finally he got up and he offered Bernard a five dollar bill. Bernard wouldn't take it, and so the man reached into his pocket and offered him a cigar. Bernard said, 'No, thanks, I don't smoke.' For Bernard, I think it's enough that people come here and appreciate what he's created." Cyril spreads a cotton tablecloth with a pattern of faded yellow flowers. "There's flowers everywhere, even out there behind the brush pile." He hustles me down a shaded path to where the garden ends. We pass through the tall grass and come to the brush pile, high as the tool shed. He points to a clump of lilies, blooms rich as lemon pie, and a cluster of purple phlox. "I say, 'Bernard, how'd these get out here?' And he says, 'Oh, the birds must've put them there.' But I think he planted them. I think he wanted them there as a surprise."

We walk back down the lane. Bernard has brought out the dinner plates out on a tray and Cyril stops just short of hearing distance and lowers his voice. "Bernard's garden is his own expression of himself. I go to the art shows sometimes, and after a while I can tell the artist without looking at the names, the way they use the colors, the things they chose to paint. Bernard's garden is like that."

Though Bernard doesn't often include meat in his menu, tonight he has fixed pot roast, boiled potatoes, and mashed turnips, with a pitcher of lemonade instead of the usual ice water. During the afternoon Bernard had taken me for a ride to see some of the local gardens he admires. One was a broad lawn turned up into squares planted with petunias and bachelor's buttons and marigolds. Though he enjoyed the color and admired the work that went into it, he despaired of the soil, which was dry, the color of cocoa. Weeds were creeping in everywhere. "It just made me tired to look at all that witchgrass. And there wasn't any body to those beds, just spots of color against the soil." He pauses from his pot roast and looks out across his gardens, where, even if some weeds had started in, it would be hard to notice for all the ground covers he's mixed in with the flowers. Where the soil is evident, its richness is reassuring. "Of course, everyone's garden is different. I garden the way I feel. I like what isn't so ostentatious. Some people go into a garden and like what jumps right out at them — the blooms that are showy. But there's so much beauty in things that are almost inconspicuous, the lichens and the mosses."

He offers broad-based advice for the beginner. "I don't go according to Hoyle. If I did, it wouldn't be mine. When you're starting out, buy a few things that you like and add to them. Don't buy too much at once. Also, don't buy at supermarkets or shop for bargains, like offers on the backs of magazines for so many plants for a dollar." Bernard's face contorts into horror. "You don't even know what you're getting! Buy from a nursery with a good reputation so you'll know the names and how to care for them. Then you'll have something that'll last. Good soil and good plants. You'll have no trouble."

He says diligence accounts for much of his success. "People see the size of this garden and they say, 'Isn't that a lot of work?' Well, it is a lot of work. But it isn't work to me. I never let my garden get ahead of me. I try to make use of all my time. In an hour, I can get the rock garden weeded."

In spite of the size of the garden, Bernard does not use a garden cart or a garden tractor. "I'm like a Chinaman," he says. "I do everything by hand." He has two wheelbarrows, one that he figures is a hundred and twenty-five years old. It has wooden sides and wooden handles that are worn shiny, as if they'd been waxed. He has another one that is metal, with an iron wheel. "That's the modern one," he points out. "I got that during World War II." His tools are simple — spades and forks, a scaled-down shovel, and a mattock he wouldn't weed without. He keeps the handles painted red to preserve them and make then stand out among the foliage. Most of the tools were hand-me-downs from Rena's grandfather, but he never leaves them out, and the toes and the tines and the tips are kept polished by the rub of the earth. If it weren't for the fact that you can't get them like that anymore, you'd think they were new.

After supper Bernard returns to the garden, culling the dead blossoms from the stems of the rhododendrons and azaleas. A young man with an old lady, who uses his elbow to support her slow steps, pass down the aisle from the road, stopping to admire the snow-white peonies that drop, in their fullness, into the path. A few steps further: "Look," he says to her, "the baptisia has come into bloom this week." Though it's a two-hour drive, this is the man's eighth visit this summer. "I study this garden like a book," he says. "I'm hoping to open my own perennial nursery next spring and if I can learn from Mr. McLaughlin, I have a better chance of success." He brings his grandmother with him, he adds, because to her it seems the same as going to church.

Many people say that coming here is a form of worship. Bernard stops and raises his hand to them, a full wave, his hand full of withered blooms. He turns to me and says, "I once thought about charging a fee, but the other day a group came down from the nursing home. A lot of them were in wheelchairs and everything was *ooh* this and *ah* that. No, I could never charge. This is my gift."

September 1983 Yankee magazine

AFTER THIS ARTICLE APPEARED, *Bernard McLaughlin's South Paris garden gained wider and wider recognition. In his later life, he became known as the "dean of Maine gardens." Bernard McLaughlin died in 1995 at the age of ninety-eight. He worked in his garden almost to the end. A close friend of his, Betty Ann Cushman, who often worked with him among the perennials, told me that Bernard wanted very much to die in his garden. "We had conversations about this. But, for a lot of reasons, that didn't happen. He did die in his home though and for that we are grateful."*

At the time of Bernard's death, the future of his house and gardens was in jeopardy. Bernard had not provided anything for its preservation. "He didn't think it was worth much. He was a humble man," Betty Ann explained. "I was one of the eight or so who fought to save the gardens and created the Foundation. It was quite a struggle. There was a lot of opposition." They called themselves 'the cowgirls' and went to battle, scouring the countryside in search of funding. They succeeded. The McLaughlin Foundation, a nonprofit organization, was formed to preserve Bernard's historic home, barn, and his extensive gardens. "He shared his garden with so many and inspired some who never cared much about gardening to become gardeners," she said. "His steady quiet work had that ripple effect: his garden grew way beyond his own."

Bernard's gardens are open to the public and frequent horticultural workshops are held in his historic barn. For more information, go to www.mclaughlingarden.org. In addition, I'm sure Bernard would be bemused to know, you can find his gardens on Facebook.

The Mushroom King

There are old-world mushroom hunters, Italians and Poles, who pick mushrooms in the last, hot, damp days of summer and on into late fall. They do not always know the tongue-twisting Latin botanical names, but about their own mushrooms, they are experts.

Around where he lives in Millers Falls, Massachusetts, Tony Anzerino is known as the Mushroom King. He picks Italian mushrooms, the vernacular for mushrooms that Italian people favor. According to Tony, Italians pick only tree mushrooms, never their stemmy little cousins that look like toadstools. These mushrooms resemble undersea coral and are sometimes confused with fungus. They grow at the base of hardwood trees and stumps (and occasionally on pines), and at their peak they bloom with layers of thick petals the color of cream and butterscotch.

I first discovered Tony while reading the *Greenfield* (Massachusetts) *Recorder.* There was a photograph of a man holding an enormous ruffled mushroom in his lap. The caption said, simply, Mushroom King, Tony Anzerino of Millers Falls. Curious, I called the editor of the *Recorder* to ask who this man was and why he was called the Mushroom King. "Oh," he said, "that's Tony. He picks big mushrooms and when he gets a particularly big one, he calls us to see if we'll come down and take a photograph. We put him in the paper now and again. Everyone knows who Tony is."

So I called Tony and told him of my interest and suggested I might go out to hunt for mushrooms with him sometime, maybe I could learn a few things. "Come on down," he said, "I can show you a thing or two."

He told me that around late August he starts to go out for mushrooms — just checking, he says. But by September the mushrooms are out in earnest and, "I'm out almost every day, cruising my routes, bringing home mushrooms." He keeps hunting through late November, often right up until the first snow. "Late in the season," he says, "the mushrooms are very tasty, even if they're frozen to the tree." By the first snows, except for an occasional rogue, the hunt is over. Last year, a particularly good year, Tony estimates he gathered close to three hundred pounds.

And so I picked a day in the fall and I drove down to visit with him. Tony lives alone in a two-story house on the main road in Millers Falls. It was a sunny day after rain from the night before and a strong sun coming in. Tony was in his driveway, beside his pickup truck, the bed loaded with what he said was about forty-five pounds of mushrooms. At seventy, Tony is a small, wiry man with an unlined, expressive face accented with a bandit mustache and a full head of silver hair that stands up like a plush carpet. His smile is warm, somewhat mischievous. "This is going to be a good year," he said, as he leaned over the rail of his truck and admired his catch. "In seasons like this, when the conditions are good, this can happen three, four, possibly five times."

I looked in awe at this truckload of mushrooms. "What do you do with all of these?" I said. "Do you sell them?"

"No, no, never," he said. "But I give away lot."

"Look here," he says, hustling me across the driveway. Two chest-type freezers stood in the asphalt courtyard outside Tony's back door. Each one is as big as two coffins. He opened both to show me the inside. Frosty packages were marked: venison, rabbit, beaver, blood pudding. Pushing aside a variety of garden vegetables he put up himself, Tony burrowed down and pulled up a whole pig, cut up in parts. And bags and bags of mushrooms. "What I don't give away or stew up for my friends, I freeze in one-pound bags." He sorted through everything, telling me the history of the meats and the vegetables, how he came to have what he has.

"I have always been a hunter. I come from a family of eighteen kids. My mother would wonder where the food would come from. We ate what we could catch — lots of coon and woodchuck. My brothers and I used to get blue jays and blackbirds with our slingshots and she'd stew the meat up in the spaghetti sauce. Always, on my way home from school, I'd hunt for mushrooms."

When he was done showing his bounty, he had disturbed the order of his freezer universe enough so that he had to push and rearrange things, like an interlocking puzzle, so that the chests would latch again. Then he invited me in.

The house, small with a steep pitched roof and abbreviated farmer's porch in front, was crammed to the rafters with what he has not been able to part with over the years, combined with what he has collected. Aside from the belongings of a lifetime, the house was filled with the produce he has gathered from the fields of farming friends in Whately and Hatfield. "Once the farmers have made their harvest," he explained, "I go down and take the rest. They leave a lot of good vegetables on the ground." Bags of potatoes, onions, winter squash, cabbage, the spoils of a good year, waiting to be made into winter meals filled his bathtub, the hallways, and were piled on top of the kitchen counters. "I only go to the grocery store to buy toilet paper," he said. He stood in the midst of this as if he were seeing it all for the first time and threw his hands in the air. "Someone once called me a pack rat. I had never heard that word and I got offended at first. But then he told me it meant someone who keeps everything. I guess he's right! I can't throw anything away," he confessed.

When Tony cooks these mushrooms, which he did for me on the day of my first visit, he spikes them with pork fat, garlic, fresh basil, and an herb whose name he doesn't remember. In his crowded kitchen, he worked like a galley cook on board a cramped ship, expertly moving the cut-up mushrooms around in his well seasoned black skillet, using the small space left on the counter with expert economy. "Some people, they are afraid of any mushrooms that don't come from the grocery story — can you imagine?" he said as he removed the skillet from the burner, lavished two thick plates with his concoction, and granted each plate a napkin and a fork. We made our way, down a narrow path of bags of potatoes and piles of newspapers and magazines, some with datelines twenty years old, into a room similarly filled. He stopped to move a few things around and make room for another chair. He keeps only one there, for himself. With the gracious air of a gentleman, he gestured to the newly established seat for me and he took the other one. "I don't often have company," he said, shyly. He took up his fork and pointed to the pile of Mushrooms a la Tony on his plate. "Mangia, mangia," he said with a chuckle. Aware that this was my journalistic duty, I took my fork and cautiously sampled the fare. The mushrooms were chunks, they could have been meat or some kind of squeaky cheese but, for me, they had the taste and texture of Italian sausage.

"You are nervous," he said, observing the cautious way I was eating. "Don't worry, they are safe. I've been picking mushrooms since I was six or seven years old."

Tony's early years were spent in a tough neighborhood near Providence, Rhode Island. "I used to go out to outlying patches of woods with my grandfather. He grew up in the hills of northern Italy, and knew a lot about this kind of thing. Later, I went out with my mother." It was from them that he learned to know a good mushroom from a bad one.

Tony has never picked a poisonous mushroom — it isn't something he worries about, he's so confident in his ability to spot his own kind of mushroom. But he remembers his mother's rule: "If you think you've picked one that might not be good, set it to boil with a penny in the pot. If the penny turns black, the mushroom's bad."

Tony calls the mushrooms by the names of the trees under which he finds them — the maple, the elm, the acorn (oak). "The best-tasting mushroom is the Prince. I find it on the acorn. The maples taste sweet, a little like maple syrup; the acorns, like acorns. They all have a different taste and color. Some, though, are too tough — you might as well eat crow. They grow anywhere from one pound up. I once found one that weighed forty-two pounds.

"We look for our own type of mushrooms. The French have theirs, the Poles have theirs. Those Polish mushrooms — I know them when I see them because I have friends who pick them — but to me they are slimy, *awful!*" Tony raised his eyebrows in exclamation. "I would never *touch* them!"

(A good friend of Tony's, who is of Polish descent, also carries on the tradition of picking mushrooms in the fall, but he picks Polish mushrooms, which more resemble the common button mushrooms we find in the store. He also is emphatic on the difference. "Tony's mushrooms? I wouldn't go near them. They would be *poisonous* to me!")

Although he lives alone, Tony loves to cook for his friends, and with the abundance of mushrooms he gathers each fall, there is never a shortage of raw materials. Last year, on the day before Thanksgiving, he gathered a bucketful of "maples" and stuffed them with a mixture of breadcrumbs, eggs, ground venison, and herbs, baked them on cookie sheets, and took them down to Alan's, his favorite neighborhood bar. "In two minutes, they were gone," Tony reported with pride. Some nights he will pack a grocery bag with fish or beef, vegetables, tomatoes, lots of mushrooms, spices, and herbs and go on down to Alan's. He will set this meal — possibly mushroom stew or mushroom-tomato sauce to serve over fish — to simmer, and then join his friends at the bar. One afternoon I joined him there. His friends were lively, sitting in the darkness at the curved bar, while the sun, outside, shone brightly. Periodically Tony got off his stool and pushed through the swinging doors that led to the bar's kitchen where he fiddled with his concoction, adding a pinch of marjoram, a bay leaf. His recipes are his own and he's at a loss to recite them. "I can't remember the names of half the herbs I use, but I know them by smell." When he was satisfied, he served up generous portions to everyone around the bar, who received this like hungry men, waiting for their dinner, something they have come to expect and enjoy. "It's a way for me to cook for my friends. It doesn't cost me much. Nothing in this world really costs me very much."

Like hunters and fishermen, mushroom pickers are territorial. While competition these days is not so stiff, back when he was growing up in Providence, when the ethnic tradition was strong and territory was more scarce, Tony remembers, "You'd catch sight of a good mushroom and go for it and someone would holler, 'Don't touch that tree! It's in my territory.' And you kept your hands off."

In Millers Falls and the brick-mill, lunch-pail towns that surround it, Tony has his territories. Since the tradition of mushroom picking has waned, he feels secure in his crown of Mushroom King. His biggest rivals these days are cordwood dealers and kids. "The kids kick the mushrooms around just for fun. I can't say I blame them, but it makes it hard for me to wait for a mushroom to get really big. And a lot of my trees have been cut down lately for firewood. For a year, maybe two, after a tree has been cut, you get mushrooms, but never again."

Tony's trees are on the edges of cemeteries, in parks, near playgrounds. He will often spot a small mushroom and take the gamble to leave it to get big. "You can just about watch them grow, like cucumbers or zucchinis." Many of his trees are in the yards of friends, who often guard the mushrooms for him and call him up when they look big enough to pick.

"CINDY, SHE'S GONNA keep an eye on that one for me," he says, pointing to a small, coral-like growth that emerges from the junction of tree and earth at the base of a shade tree. It is in the yard of a white-trimmed Cape on a quiet, tree-lined street.

Tony is taking me with him on his mushroom hunt. We are in my Honda, Tony riding shotgun, turned sideways, scanning for quarry. Yesterday, he called me up to tell me that the mushrooms had come out early so he's making a sweep. "I went out just to check up on some of my trees and there they were, in a big ring around the acorn tree in Turners Falls." He came home with fifty-three pounds of the creamy mushrooms, ready for cleaning, bagging, and generous distribution.

As we ride, Tony's eyes are glued to the scenery. "You don't have to go so slow," he says to me, as a stream of cars passes us. "I could spot one of my mushrooms if you were going ninety miles an hour." He peers intently at the thick-trunked trees that flash past us. "My trees start giving me mushrooms when they begin to die a little. If you look at the tops of the trees you can sometimes see some dead branches. I don't really know where the mushrooms come from, but I've got a theory. I think the tree drinks up the water and it goes up into those dead branches and then runs back down under the bark and — *poof* — out comes a mushroom. What do you think of that?"

He directs me down suburban roads, past kids on bicycles, old men snoozing on porches, geraniums still bright in the autumn sun. Most of the trees we check are fruitless. Tony shrugs and says, "It's too early yet." Finally he gestures to the left: "Swing down here a minute. Let's look at one last one." I turn onto a narrow street bordered with a row of tidy houses. He tells me to pull over. We get out and climb up a steep bank beside the road to a children's park where swings and seesaws are set in a clearing edged with several good-sized oaks.

There it is, like a bouquet. The hunter reaches deep into his jeans pocket. He ceremoniously opens his weapon. With his Boy Scout penknife, Tony cuts the hefty Prince, flush with the ground. It is the size of a volleyball. We get back in the car and he sets the mushroom in his lap like a prize.

"That tree, she's given me a lot," he says, shaking his head with pleasure. "But I'm still looking for a mushroom like the one I found a couple of years ago. I had to pick that one with a shovel! The fellow from the Greenfield paper came down to take my picture with that mushroom. It was as big as a bushel basket. I stood right next to the scale so you could read the weight — forty-two pounds! But," Tony says, as his eyes take on a sparkle, "I cheated a little. I wet it down before he came."

October 1982 Yankee magazine

AFTER THIS ARTICLE *was published, Tony was delighted to tell me that he had received one proposal of marriage and several letters of interest from available women, all of whom lived in Florida. I know that with one, there was an exchange of a ring. But the marriage did not come to be. He kept in touch with me for a long time and then there was silence. Arithmetic alone makes me sure he is no longer alive. I used to enjoy passing by his house on my way elsewhere, the front porch crammed with things, windows blocked by all that the small house contained. It's a wonder it didn't sink into the ground from the weight of it all. It used to make me think of a great big bundle, tied in string and I wondered who on earth would unpack it when the time came. But, passing by a few years ago, I noticed a big change. The driveway was clear of old trucks and freezers. The house was newly and brightly painted, curtains in the windows, and flowers in a box on the porch rail. For me, it was like an announcement: Tony is gone. The passing of an era.*

The Ballad of Tony Burke

When Tony Burke came to this country from Ireland in 1965, he did not expect that thirty years later, having worked hard, saved diligently, and having bought his own home, he would spend five years living like a squatter in a boarded up, condemned building.

But that is the story of Tony Burke, a local legend in Amesbury, Massachusetts, where his tale is sung in local pubs and his tenacity has brought large real estate conglomerates to their knees. Thieves and lawyers be damned, Tony Burke doesn't give up his principles easily.

"It's not hard to be tenacious when you've had everything taken from you," he says now, hardly a note of his musical Irish brogue diminished, though more than half his fifty-four years have been spent here, in the United States. A victor with the spoils, Tony sits proudly at his kitchen table, the bright white walls freshly painted, the wood floors polished, dishes in the cupboard, gossamer curtains in the windows, a poster of the verdant hills of his homeland on the wall beside him. Be it ever so *humble*, there is *no* place like home. He reaches across the table and touches the cream-colored envelope with a lawyer's logo in the upper left-hand corner. "This is it, the story is finally over," he says, his sharp blues eyes smiling.

The story begins in 1988 when Tony went looking to buy a house for himself. It was time. In all the years he'd spent in this country, which included two years of service in Viet Nam in the 1960s as well as more than twenty years sorting mail for the U.S. Postal Service, he'd managed to save up $40,000. At last, he had decided it was time to make the great investment.

The first thing he did was talk to a man who will remain nameless. Tony's had enough trouble. He does not want to name names. Let's just call him Tony's so-called friend. But at the time, there was no so-called about it. They were close, old friends. "He arrived here from Ireland the same time I did," Tony says. "We became friendly through the Irish pockets around Boston. We socialized, double-dated, and I was an usher at his wedding. I used to like to go over to his house and play the accordion. Yes, I'd say we were very close."

While Tony had worked for his wages at the post office, he watched his friend grow wealthy in real estate. He thought maybe he could learn a few things. For starters, Tony wanted advice from his friend on this house he had his eye on. "I asked him and he said, 'Let's go have a look,' so we hopped into the car and went out to see it. But he advised me not to buy it. He thought it wasn't built right. Instead, he said, 'I'll show you a place over in Amesbury.' So we drove over there, and he showed me a condo and he talked it up, and then he took me to a bank that I'd never heard of, and before I knew it, the whole thing was a done deal."

This place where Tony had just bought his little piece of America was called Camelot, a village of one hundred twenty-six Tudor-style, half-brick condominiums — of which Tony's friend was a partial owner.

On that afternoon in August of 1988, Tony wrote out a check for his life's savings. The rest of the $82,000 selling price, he financed on a mortgage. He was nervous. "It was the first time I'd ever bought anything, and the $30,000 I gave him was nearly everything that I had."

A couple of months later, his friend talked him into buying another one of the condos, explaining to Tony that this was the way to make money, not just tread water with the mortgage payments. "You rent it out," he explained to Tony. "You be the landlord!"

"I really didn't want to, but he was a good talker and he was saying about how Seabrook was going to be opening up and there would be a lot of new people coming to the area and I'd make good money and so on." So Tony spent the rest of his savings and went even deeper into debt.

Tony rests easily in his chair as he tells his saga. He's a solid man, built like a brick, and when he wants you to know what all this has meant to him, he takes off his ball cap and reveals his completely bald head. "I just want you to know what this has done to me," he says, passing his hand over his pale scalp.

Even from the very first, Tony could tell that Camelot had cracks in its ramparts. "There were a lot of people around the pool during the daytime. I could tell that people weren't working. A lot of them, I found out, were on welfare. I *did* have an uneasy feeling. The only thing that gave me an easy feeling was that I trusted my friend so much. He was so successful. I was following in his footsteps. This was my first purchase. I figured he wouldn't lead me astray."

Gradually Camelot began to erode. "I saw little signs here and there. The pool closed down. They said they didn't have enough money for the upkeep. Then they closed the office. Then MassElectric started sending letters saying they were going to shut the electric service off. It came to be known that they were owed $38,000."

He wasn't aware of all of this at the time, because he was at work most of the time, but there were periodic power outages and the garbage piling up. "I'd mention this to my so-called friend, and he'd always tell me, 'Ah, don't worry about it, Tony. Everything's going to be fine.'"

But his so-called friend knew better, much better than that. He was one of the owners, along with a dozen or so others, and they had stopped paying their condo fees. Which is why he was so anxious to sell the two units to Tony. He wanted to get out from under what he knew was a failing operation.

In September of 1991, MassElectric shut off the power to Camelot. As a result, the town condemned the complex because the smoke detectors no longer worked. After that, the town shut off the water. "That's when everybody started moving out," Tony says. "Everyone except me."

Since everyone else in Camelot was a renter, Tony was the only tenant who stood to lose anything by moving out. If Tony moved out, he could see only too clearly, he would forfeit his life's savings. And he wasn't about to do that. "I knew that I had been taken. I had no idea something like this could happen. I couldn't believe it. I still can't. I was mad. Oh, yes, *I was mad.*"

And so began Tony's long dark night of the soul, a five-year stint he likens now to fighting in a war. Others might simply call it hell on earth. Once the power was turned off and the water main closed, the buildings became silent. Weeds grew high around the walkways. Stray cats took up residence in the hallways. All the windows of all the buildings were boarded up, and a chain link fence was erected around the perimeter. As conditions worsened, barbed wire was added around the top. Meanwhile, Tony hunkered down in his bunker on the second floor.

The day the complex was officially closed, Tony went over to the flagpole, lowered the stars and stripes into his arms, and carried it up to his unit. From the railing of his wrought iron balcony, he refastened the flag under which he'd fought on foreign soil for a country he'd chosen to belong to. "I wanted to let them know that I was an American and a Vietnam veteran, which I'm very proud of. Mostly, it was pride that made me do it. I wanted anyone who saw the flag to know that there was something American going on here, that there was a story behind this and I hoped that they might respect that. Most people did, except for a few lowlifes and thieves."

The lowlifes and thieves became Tony's next challenge, as the condemned buildings became a magnet for drug addicts and vandals. Thieves broke into Tony's apartment and stole his TV, his VCR, his radio, even his telephone. Now he really did have nothing. The only thing he replaced was his telephone and he replaced that six times as they continually battered him. He continued to work his job at the post office, but the thieves seemed to know his schedule. Sometimes he would come home from work to find the walls of his apartment scrawled with taunting messages. *Tony, you're too nice to us. You make it so easy to get in!* the punks would write in Magic Marker on his wall. Once, they even sawed through the roof with a chainsaw.

"They wanted me to pack me little bag and walk on down the street but every time I was broken into, that only made me more determined not to leave."

Instead of packing his wee bag, Tony spent his spare hours replacing broken glass and wrenched padlocks. In fact, Tony's cold and lifeless flat was so fortified, it took him several minutes to unlock all six padlocks, refasten them on the inside and then barricade himself back inside, setting steel bars in place.

Tony carried water in jugs from the faucet at the gas station nearby. In the summer he discovered he could collect water from the downspouts of the gutters that rimmed the buildings. This water he used to flush his toilet. For brushing his teeth and shaving, he had special bottles of spring water. On his way to work, he'd stop and shower at the gym. He ate fast food or with friends. "You would not want to eat in my apartment. The smells were pretty bad," he says. But he slept there, a steel bar within reach.

The weeks and months and years that passed only made his vigil all the more desolate. "It was a big empty place. The wind would howl through those long empty hallways. I didn't feel lonely but I felt alone. There is a difference."

In his youth, before he came to America, Tony studied to be a priest and he thinks now that helped him through this. "I've always had a belief in God. Prayer helped a lot but I actually didn't go to church very much during that time. I was ashamed of how dirty I was. At work, people knew my circumstances and they were understanding if I didn't make it to the gym. But I didn't mix around very much. I didn't want to be thought of as, well, homeless."

After he'd endured this life for three years, his co-workers took up a collection for him. It was not only that he was living like that, but by then he was also up to here with lawyers' fees. One day, his colleagues presented him with a check for $2,000 and an engraved plaque, which honored "Tony's unfailing cheerfulness in the face of grave adversity." Aside from the poster of the rolling green hills of Ireland, this plaque is all that adorns Tony's living room wall today.

"It helped," he says. In addition to his legal fees, Tony never missed a mortgage payment on his "home," all of which left him literally penniless. Not just the money but the recognition from his friends at work meant something very special. "There were days when I'd go into work and I probably looked like I was homeless. They were good to me."

Other people helped him out. The people who ran the gas station offered him water from their faucet. The folks behind the counter at the Burger King got to know him and so did the people at the laudromat. "They all understood my position," he says. As a result of all the burglaries, Tony got to know the police quite well, and they were good to him. "Even now, when I pass one of them on the street, we trade salutes."

The health department turned a blind eye as well, a fact that probably provided Tony with the eye of the needle through which he passed. "If the town had decided to take a harsh view and force me out, of course, I would have had to leave."

Meanwhile, Gary Shane, a local songwriter and, ironically, a real estate agent, took note of Tony. "I'd drive by and see he had the American flag hanging upside down, which is a distress signal in the military. I had read about him in the local paper. One day I stopped by and introduced myself. I told him I wanted to write a song, and he liked that idea." What came of that was "The Ballad of Tony Burke," which Gary began to perform in local pubs like The Grog in Newburyport. As the story expanded, he'd add new verses. He took the act to Boston and played it in the clubs there. "One night Tony showed up, and he came up on stage and played his accordion. They loved him. He was wonderful," Gary recalls.

In 1995, in a deal with the bank arranged by one of his lawyers, Tony paid off his mortgage — an additional $25,000, which made him the proud owner of two condemned, rodent infested condominiums in that desolate place still known as Camelot. "I didn't want to pay it. I'd already paid so much for a place that was no longer habitable. But, now I am glad that I did." He now sees that this was about the only good advice he was given by a succession of lawyers about whom Tony can only say, "Shakespeare was right." (". . . let's kill all the lawyers," *Henry VI,* Part II).

"There was no point at which I said to myself that I would give up. I have many many good friends and I had been offered many nice places to stay but I was keeping a vigil. I determined that I would die first, before I'd leave. I served in VietNam. I knew what it was to put my life on the line."

In 1996, everything began to change. A new real estate group bought Camelot and began to renovate the weather-beaten structures. For two years they worked and every day when Tony came home from work, he could see the difference, a gradual transformation, something like the sun rising.

In 1998, with the interior completely renovated, painted a deep pink and new mauve carpeting in the hallways, Camelot came back to life, transmogrified into Birchwood Pointe, a tidy complex that bore little resemblance to the old place.

ON A SPRING DAY in 1999, the window of the unit where Tony's American flag flew for five years is covered with Easter decorations. Instead of a barbed wire, there's brightly painted white post-and-rail fencing. The security system inside each building is so well programmed that getting past it can be challenging. Smoothly dressed young men and women emerge from the units, climb into sleek cars, and head toward Boston. The grass is green and well-trimmed. Birds sing on the wires. The swimming pool is being readied for the coming summer. Tony's padlocks and his water jugs are gone. He has sold the second of his two units and has completely done over the one he kept. "I had to throw out all the furniture. The smell was just too strong," he says.

Gary Shane is working on the last verse to "The Ballad of Tony Burke." "It has a pretty good ending," he said recently.

"Yes, that it does," Tony says. "My only bitterness is with my so-called friend who sold this place to me. He's still, you know, living the life of Reilly. He never suffered from any of this. I'm trying to use everything within my belief, the good upbringing I had and the good parents that I had, to forgive him. And I'm having a *lot* of trouble doing that. I haven't done it yet. I surely don't think that I'll ever forget him."

Neither is it likely that Amesbury will forget the Irishman who came to Camelot and would not leave, come hell or no water.

September 1999 Yankee magazine

OUR SEARCH *for Tony came up empty but when we went to his condo in Amesbury, we talked with one of his neighbors. She told us that Tony got married a few years ago, sold his condo and they moved to Maine, where they live, hopefully, happily ever after.*

Tin Can Man

IN A SMALL WHITE HOUSE on a side street off a side street in the seaside town of Portsmouth, Rhode Island, there lives a village, so lightweight, a child could pick it up and carry it away, but strong enough to lift the weight of the world off the shoulders of Bill Souza, who created the village and its bridge and its river and its train station and its horse and rider.

"Don't expect too much," Bill says as he parts the heavy drapes which reveal the silvery village, shimmering in the light of the overhead fluorescent. "It's only scrap aluminum and beer cans," he says with a mischievous glint in his eyes. The village that Bill built is in his basement, on top of his pool table. He hasn't played pool in decades and he doesn't drink beer but this is what he's created, the bricks and mortar being the cans he's picked up beside the road, thousands of them, maybe millions. Although he has been working on this little town for some 15 years, it isn't finished yet. "There are still some details I want to add," he says.

Bill Souza is now seventy-four years old, fit and trim with a golfer's tan, but back when he was forty, he had a hard time sleeping. He was working as a boiler man for a cotton mill. It was hard, physical work and he needed to sleep, but sleep would not come. He went to his doctor and the doctor said, "Get a hobby!"

"So I was reading the Sunday paper one day and I see this article about this woman in a nursing home who was making furniture out of beer cans, just for something to do. So I says, 'Ah, that seems easy enough. I think I'll try that.' That's how it all began."

The first thing he tried was a rocking chair, cutting the top off a beer can and then cutting the sides into strips, bending and folding. "I figured out how to peel them down and curl them up and pretty soon I had a rocking chair. I made a bunch of them. My wife's friends went nuts over these. I put pink velvet on the seat and gave them away like crazy. Then I wanted to do something more challenging so I started making ships, you know, little sailing ships, beer-can-sized. I made hundreds of those and gave them away to everyone and his brother."

Bill laughs to recall the early days of his nascent artistic career, which was a complete departure from anything he had ever done in his life. After the cotton mill closed down, he went to work as a maintenance foreman at Raytheon. He did that for twenty-three years. But at night he had his other world in the basement of his house.

"It was kind of progressive. After I'd made just about every piece of furniture I could think up, I wanted something that was really challenging, so that's when I started to make the cars."

Bill has never used plans. He works from photographs. "I just look at a picture of the car and then I start putting stuff together, gluing it. I use epoxy, that's the best glue for this. It's strong as a weld."

While he was in his car phase, he made dozens of them, including a 1905 Daimler Benz touring car, a 1963 Corvair, in honor of his favorite car of all times, a WWI Sopwith Camel, and a replica of the Newport trolley that he remembers riding when he was growing up. He gave a lot of them away but even so, he had twenty-two cars and airplanes around the house. "I didn't know where to put them anymore." The problem was easily solved when the Preservation Society of Newport County asked if they could have them to put on display at Green Animals, the historic house and gardens of philanthropist, Alice Brayton. And so he donated them all to the historic site, which is just around the corner from his house. "But that left me without anything. I had to start something new."

The village began with just one house. Bill was eighteen when he fought in World War II, an infantryman in France and Germany. Later, he was sent to Vienna. The ornate architecture of the buildings there captivated him "Them opera houses, man, they were something," he says now. Maybe he was thinking back to those buildings when he started the house that started the village. It's ornate, with frilly trim and an arched front door. With Frank Sinatra playing gently in the background, Bill spent night after night in his basement, making the shingles for the roof, cutting and folding and scoring the pattern into each fingernail-size shingle. "So then I'd get them done and I'd be all thrilled and then it was time to shingle the roof so I'd do that for a week or more."

And so went the evenings, the weeks and the years — one shingle, one door latch, one fence post at a time. Peer inside the tiny windows and you'll see the furnishings, complete with fancy fireplaces, a grandfather's clock the size of a child's finger and chairs the size of raisins.

"When I finished the house, I felt like there was something missing. I realized that it needed a fence around it, just to give it a finishing touch. That's how it started. After that, I thought that a garage would be good. Then there had to be a car in the garage. Then I felt like a greenhouse would be good. Then came the train station and the chapel. You see? One thing leads to another. You get me down here and I'm in my own world, believe me, I'm in my own world."

The train that sits at the village station is a wood-fired steam engine. He found a picture of it in a book that tells the history of the railroad. "Some people have told me that the back is wrong but the picture only showed the front. I couldn't see the back. I had to use my own judgment."

Bill sits down in the worn stenographer's chair he keeps down here and pulls himself up to the table. Snippets of aluminum litter the floor at his feet. He takes a shiny piece of can, smooths it with his big, rough hands, and then starts to score and fold. His fingers move quickly, and almost instantly he holds up a square post. "See, that's how I make the columns. I can do them any size." The columns on the house porch are decorated with tiny curls of gingerbread. "You know why I do that fancy trim? I cover my mistakes that way!" he says, rolling out a good belly laugh.

Bill thinks little of the skill it has taken for him to create what he has. He is somewhat bemused by the response he gets from people who come down into his basement to see his work. "They are amazed, especially old folks and children, they go bananas. I see it all the time, so it doesn't seem like much to me. You know, it's nothing much for me to make this stuff. If it doesn't work out, I throw it out and start over again. It's only beer cans, you understand?"

He estimates that the house alone consists of four or five hundred beer cans. He can't even think about how many cans it took to make the entire village. Nor can he estimate how many hours he might have put into their construction. "I never stopped to think about how much time it took because I have all the time in the world. I could have sold a lot of my stuff but the thing is that then it would be a job and I'd have to put a time on it — how much time it takes to make and how much each hour is worth. That's not why I'm doing it."

Along the way, Bill made most of the tools that he uses for this unique craft. A friend gave him some special scissors that the phone company uses to cut aluminum. For the miniscule curlicues, he has small rods that he wraps the shavings around. To get the effects that he wants, putting treads on the tires and patterns on rugs, he has had to improvise, using small metal blades and long slender bars, whatever works best.

Bill does not think of himself as an artist, in fact he chuckles at the very idea. When people say his work is folk art, he doesn't understand what the term means. But he knows what he loves.

"You know, I can do anything with aluminum. I can't tell you why. I just can. I just love to work with it. You know what I love best about this? I come down here and I don't know what I'm going to make. I start working and it just comes to me and pretty soon, I've got something.

When I get finished, I look at it and I say, 'I made that out of nothing.' I didn't have any plans, I just used the stuff that I have here, you know what I mean? I get a big kick out of that. It's something out of nothing, something made out of trash. Yeah," he says, "I like that!"

March 2001 Yankee magazine

BILL SOUZA'S CARS *are still on display inside the museum at Green Animals Topiary Park in Portsmouth, Rhode Island. The Preservation Society of Newport, which owns Green Animals, also has his village, which they display on special occasions at some of their other historic houses — often at The Elms at Christmas time. Further information can be found at www.newport mansions.org*

The Power of One

THE RISING SUN brings veils of mist out of the damp soil, and the rain-swollen stream tumbles jubilantly behind Doris Haddock's Dublin, New Hampshire, home. Into this new morning, Doris steps from her front door, her walking shoes on, the long sleeves of her denim shirt buttoned at the wrist to discourage biting insects.

"Which way shall we walk?" the five-foot-tall great-grandmother asks. I've come to walk with my neighbor, Granny D, our local hero, the ninety-year-old woman who recently returned home from a very long walk.

When she was eighty-eight, Doris said she'd walk across the country to call attention to campaign finance reform, the effort to stem contributions that slip through not-quite-illegal channels from corporations and special interest groups into the pockets of political candidates. To Doris, this so-called "soft money" is the root of all that is wrong with our democracy. Starting in California, she planned to walk ten miles a day, for one year, and to enter the nation's capital on her ninetieth birthday, on foot. Like many women her age, she had arthritis and she had emphysema, but this did not stop her. Her son (and next door neighbor) Jim, said, more than once, "She'll die trying," for he knew better than any of us her stubborn spirit.

With Jim's guidance, she began to train for her journey. On our back roads, we'd encounter her, this diminutive lady, a heavy pack on her back. For months, she walked the winding, hilly roads of Dublin, logging nearly a thousand miles. She slept on the ground to prepare for what she imagined might lie ahead. All the while, she was trying to get newspapers and magazines interested in her mission.

"No one seemed to believe that I could do it," she says now, as we begin our walk down the gravel road.

The idea had come to her when she was visiting with Jim in Florida one year. "We were driving through the Everglades, and I saw an old man walking along the roadside. He was carrying a bag in one hand and a cane in the other, and it looked as if he had all his worldly possessions with him. I said to Jim, 'What on earth do you suppose he is doing?' And he said, 'Well, Ma, it looks like he's on the road.' and I said, 'You mean on the road like Willie Nelson?' And he said, 'Yes.' 'Like Jack Kerouac?' 'Yes!' So we discussed this for a while. My husband died in 1993. He had Alzheimer's for a long time, and I took care of him. After that, I just wanted to go, go, go. To *get away!* And so I said to Jim, 'Haven't you ever wanted to walk across the country?' And he said, 'Well, yes, but I have to earn a living and you're too damn old!' And I said, 'Says who?'

"Jim knows me pretty well. You get to a certain age and your children start to act like they are your parents. So he thought about that for a while and then he said, 'Well, you can*not* go across the country without a cause.' And I said, 'Well, what do you think I've been working on for the past two years — campaign finance reform!' And he said, 'Oh my God.'"

Doris was a long-time member of what is known in these parts as the "Tuesday Morning Academy," an informal gathering of older women who come together on Tuesday mornings to focus on literature, art, and politics. For the Tuesday Academy, Doris had researched the issue of campaign finance reform, and the academy had been following the weak attempts Congress had been making to fix the problem, rather like trying to change a flat tire while the car is still rolling. This was long before the issue had become a common phrase on the nightly news. When Doris returned from Florida, she announced to her "classmates" that she would be making this walk. She mapped out her trip and members of the Academy helped link her with friends in towns where she would be walking. Soon she had an itinerary, with a star next to towns where she could be assured of lodging. For the towns where she knew no one, she contacted the local police and hoped to convince them to let her sleep in an empty jail cell. She herself knew nothing about computers, but her grandson, Joey, designed a website for her. They called it www.grannyD.com and with that, she hoped that anyone who was interested could follow her journey.

Her rhetoric poised, Doris Haddock began trekking on her eighty-ninth birthday, January 29, 1999, in Pasadena, California, where she had hoped to strike up some attention by walking in the Rose Bowl Parade. To her surprise, they banned her from walking in the parade, because she was walking for a cause. That was her first tussle with authorities. Disappointed but undeterred, she walked after the parade had ended, wearing a high visibility jogger's vest, a gardener's straw hat, sturdy boots and carrying a twenty-five-pound pack on her back. On her shoulder, braced like a soldier's rifle, she carried a big flag she had stitched that said, simply, "Campaign Finance Reform." Those first days were slow going.

Jim kept in constant touch with his mother and joined her when he could. Friends from Dublin and members of her Tuesday Morning Academy flew out to walk with her. She walked through Pasadena and Colton and Redlands and into Twentynine Palms and then into Arizona. Through Parker, Bouse, Salome, Wickenburg, she trudged her way. She rose early to beat the heat but in the Mojave Desert, she collapsed. Severely dehydrated, she spent four days in the hospital. A sympathetic supporter named Dennis Burke took her back to his house and he and his wife helped her recuperate.

Now, as we walk beside the bog near her home, Doris remembers this time in the desert as a kind of turning point. "Dennis decided I needed a camper, something I could sleep in at night. He went to a used car dealer and convinced them to 'lend' us a camper for two weeks. That was the start of it."

Her collapse in the desert had attracted attention in the news media. Doris Haddock's campaign had truly begun. "It gathered a certain momentum," she says now, perhaps an understatement from a woman who was subsequently listed by the magazine *George*, alongside Madeline Albright, Hilary Clinton, and Elizabeth Dole, as one of the twenty most fascinating women in politics.

Shouldering her yellow flag, wearing T-shirts and khaki shorts in heat, and heavy woolen pants and sweaters in cold, Doris marched like a soldier, ten miles a day, one day at a time, through Los Lunas, New Mexico; Dalhart, Texas; Hooker, Oklahoma; Kismet, Kansas; Mack's Creek, Missouri; Odin, Illinois; Versailles, Indiana; Chillocothe, Ohio; Clarksburg, West Virginia; Falls Church, Virginia; and all the little towns and big cities in between. In all, she walked through more than a thousand miles of desert, climbed the Appalachian Range through blizzards and when the going got tough, she strapped on a pair of skis and covered more than a hundred miles that way. She finally strode right into our nation's capital, just two months late. She began in obscurity and arrived on the other side of the country a national phenomenon.

Doris never had to sleep on the ground or in a jail cell, and she never missed a meal. Her arthritic pains left her and her emphysema all but vanished. "I had an inhaler when I started," she says, "but I don't know what happened to it. I must have lost it."

On morning walks along the familiar roads near her house, Doris' child-size feet track at a good pace. She dislikes hills, and when the road steepens her breath quickens and she recalls the "worst" part of her journey: West Virginia. "It was cold," she says. "And there were lots of hills."

Eventually, Jim bought a used camper for his mother to use. On the back he had printed: *CAUTION! Ninety-year-old walker ahead! Support Campaign Finance Reform!* The camper is now parked in Jim's driveway, a bright reminder of Doris' triumph.

When Doris arrived home, the bands played and Dublin threw a big party. The invitations for her to speak seemed endless. Most of us who had bid her good-bye were amazed to find that, thirty-two hundred miles later, Doris looked stronger, younger, more alive. She not only walked thirty-two hundred miles, she also delivered hundreds of speeches, nothing she had ever done before. In Toyah, Texas, she told the crowd, "We didn't send our young men and women off to fight for a government of, by, and for the corporations." In Nashville, Tennessee, she said, "We must provide a public financing system for candidates. Otherwise, the candidates are not honestly offering themselves to us. They are already sold." In Texarkana, she said, "It's obscene to have to raise that kind of money (the millions funneled to campaigns) when children are going to bed ill and old people are eating pet food. It's simply insane." Radical words for anyone but Granny D. In Parker, Arizona, she was welcomed by the Marine Corps Marching Band. Along her way, politicians fell in and out with Doris Haddock, trying to set their feet on her untarnished path.

Granny D walked through four pairs of shoes, staunchly refusing the Nike contract offered her, in spite of her very real need for money to keep her walk going. She exhausted four sun hats and dozens of walking companions. She walked the walk and talked the talk through two hundred eight towns in thirteen states. At her welcome-home party in Dublin, she said, "I am thankful to New England for raising its children with businesslike severity so that we might be a little tough and more courageous and become, after long lives here, great connoisseurs and critics of beauty and community. . . .Wherever I went across America, people wanted to shake my hand and wish me well, not because they thought I was something special but because I was someone like them. Americans are not selfish. They are kind and full of great spirit."

Two months after she arrived home, Doris returned to Washington D.C. to once again call attention to her cause. Surrounded by supporters, Doris stood in the rotunda of our Capitol building and read the Declaration of Independence. As she read, police arrested her for demonstrating.

They put her hands behind her back and cuffed her. She and her supporters, (including her son, Jim, and several of her elderly lady friends from the Tuesday Morning Academy), were taken by bus to the police station to be booked. She was released and a month later came before the court in Washington D.C. to answer charges. She faced the judge and read her statement: "Your honor, the old woman who stands before you was arrested for reading the Declaration of Independence in America's Capitol building. I did not raise my voice to do so and I blocked no hall. . . . Your honor, we would never seek to abolish our dear United States. But alter it? Yes. It is our constant intention that it should be a government of, by, and for the people, not the special interests. . . . In my ninety years, this is the first time I have been arrested. I risk my good name, for I do indeed care what my neighbors think about me. But, your honor, some of us do not have much power, except to put our bodies in the way of injustice — to picket, to walk, or to just stand in the way. It will not change the world overnight, but it is all we can do."

The judge could have imposed a six-month sentence on Doris and charged her five hundred dollars. Instead he charged her ten dollars, an administrative fee, and praised her for acting on behalf of the "silent masses." He told her to "take care, because it is people like you who will help us reach our destiny."

Our walk this morning has been brief, a mere three miles. Tomorrow morning, she will address the Rotary, and the next day, she will be at a rally in Boston. Just the week before, she sat on a podium alongside Jane Fonda and Ted Turner at Emerson College and together, the three of them received honorary doctorate degrees. Next week, she will be addressing the graduates. It's the neverending story of Doris Haddock.

In Doris' back bedroom, big golden keys to dozens of cities across the country adorn the bureau and the closet pole sags with all the T-shirts and hats given her along the way. A bulging scrapbook holds the texts of all the speeches she delivered as she made her way across the country, including one on the floor of the United States Senate. Before her eighty-ninth birthday, Doris had never given a public speech in her life.

But now she is pushing ninety-one, which apparently to Doris does not mean the end but the beginning. "It's the power of one," she says. And then she adds, "Only in America!"

November 2000 Yankee magazine

GRANNY D's *historic walk in 1999 was only the start of her political career. Few on this earth can claim that the last ten years of their long life were the most significant but that was the case for Granny D. In 2004, she wrote a book about her walk,* You're Never Too Old to Raise a Little Hell, *and she ran for U.S. Senate in the same year, at the age of ninety-four. Reasoning that few knew who Doris Haddock was but many knew of "Granny D," she officially changed her name to "Granny D" for the campaign. She won thirty-four percent of the vote against the incumbent Republican, Judd Gregg.*

Ironically, just before her one hundredth birthday, the Supreme Court ruled that corporations are the same as private individuals, essentially invalidating the campaign finance reform laws showcased by her long walk and her many talks. This was what she had to say about that: "The Supreme Court, representing a radical fringe that does not share the despair of the grand majority of Americans, has today made things considerably worse by undoing the modest reforms I walked for and went to jail for, and that tens of thousands of other Americans fought very hard to see enacted. . . .The Supreme Court now opens the floodgates to usher in a new tsunami of corporate money into politics."

Doris "Granny D" Haddock died of respiratory failure two months after her hundredth birthday surrounded by friends and family at her son's home. She was active nearly to the day she died. At her funeral, small straw hats were passed out in memory of her ever-present sun hat with the colorful woven band, a turkey feather stuck into the band. She wore this straw hat whenever she was out walking. One of these miniature hats is in the photo on the cover of this book.

The Curious Odyssey of Doctor Littky

Although the consequences could not have been foretold, when Dr. Dennis Littky first came to Winchester, New Hampshire, in 1978, he came for a retreat, to spend time alone in a cabin in a remote part of town known as Pudding Hill. He was thirty-three years old and had spent the past six years in a prosperous Long Island town creating a model middle school that attracted upwards of two hundred and fifty visitors every year from all over the country. "It had been a unique opportunity," Dennis says. "I started from scratch: I hired all the faculty, developed the curriculum. I even picked out the curtains. But usually I put in seventy-five to eighty hours a week. That's how I do things. My work is my life and I needed to break that."

It was to be a dramatic change for a person who is most easily described as gregarious. The man whose energy seems to electrify even his red hair and his beard came to this small town at the junction of Vermont-New Hampshire-Massachusetts borders with only a few belongings packed into the trunk of his aging yellow Karmann Ghia. The car could not even begin to climb the rutted, rocky pass that led up to the three-room cabin that hangs off the hill so precariously that if it were in California, it would be swept to the base with the first seasonal mudslide. He had enough money saved to live frugally for two years, and then he planned to go to Bali.

Dennis had been to New Hampshire only once before in his life. He was a city boy, born and raised in Detroit, handsomely educated with two Master's degrees and a pair of Ph.D.'s in education and in psychology. After a brief practice as a clinical psychologist, he'd begun his career as an educator during the racially tense sixties in Ocean Hill-Brownsville, an explosively tough section of New York City. From all this, he'd gleaned little about trees or insulation or woodstoves or gas lights or outhouses or below zero, the very things that would preoccupy him for the next couple of years as he came to know first himself and then a town unlike any he had ever known.

In the town of Stony Brook on Long Island, Dennis had been something of a celebrity. His accomplishments had been written up extensively in local newspapers as well as educational journals. As the principal of Shoreham-Wading River Middle School, he had been enormously loved by students and teachers, and when he left, they threw a party for him and presented him with a scrapbook that must weigh twenty pounds, pasted full of snapshots and letters from teachers and students, unshy in their admiration of the wild-looking man. "How you live, what your outlook is, and how you treat us is really great!" gushed an eighth-grader. "I love coming to work . . . you offer me a home," wrote a member of the faculty. "I learned one thing: Don't think people are smart because of what they wear. Dr. Littky is very smart, even with jeans on," concluded a sixth grader. Though Dennis cherishes that scrapbook and the sentiments inside, he wanted to come to New Hampshire fresh, without that image trailing him. "I just wanted to be Dennis, not this cool principal with the Ph.D. So I didn't tell anyone who I was. That was the fun part."

There weren't very many to tell. His quest for solitude was quickly granted. Though he got to know the Amarosas who own the hardware store in town and his nearest neighbors, a mile away, these were casual and brief encounters. Most of his days were spent alone in a not-very-varied schedule of splitting wood and carrying water and food up the long hill. He traded in his Karmann Ghia for a Jeep, which made getting up his road easier in the summer, but not in winter when the road was closed, the snow not plowed. He spent hours every day reading books about people who lived alone, people enduring great odds in alien and harsh climates. When he'd finish, he'd write long letters to the authors. He also wrote long, undated entries in a journal he kept in three-subject spiral-bound notebooks, which, as the months went by, piled up like chapters of a book. Some entries sound just like another: "Read, wrote, split wood. Ate dinner." But others were more contemplative: "I'm up on the mountain in some ways making myself stay, putting myself through something. I don't know why, but I think it's important. Sometimes it's very hard, with just the sounds of gas singing through the mantel and a single battery telling me what time it is."

He had come on this cabin by accident. He was going to look for land and a camp in Maine, a place he could use in the summer to get away. The mother of a friend offered him their family's cabin in Winchester as a stopover. He took the keys with him and planned to stay one night on his way up. But he stayed the whole week, never going to Maine. Before he left, he wrote a poem to his friend's mother, exalting the camp with the three-state view, and left it on the kitchen table. The next year Mrs. Hearne told her daughter she'd decided to sell the camp. "I want to sell it to the man who wrote that poem." He bought the cabin and seven inaccessible acres for thirteen thousand dollars.

"I didn't know what kind of town Winchester was. I just bought the place up in the hills. I didn't know how wild it was," Dennis recalls.

He'd go into town nearly every day to get his mail, and then he'd stop off at the hardware store to visit with the Amarosas, who often took phone messages for him. "He was so friendly, so appreciative. I didn't mind. I had four children, what was one more?" Winnie Amarosa says. "I had no idea how educated he was. I thought he was just that sort who wanted to live rustic. One day his mother called up, asking for *Dr.* Littky. My husband said, 'Doctor Who?'"

Dennis would stay and chat with Winnie and Frankie and the occasional customer, watching the comings and goings on Main Street through the store's big window. The nature of the town began to dawn on him, like haze lifting.

Winchester's thirty-six hundred people live in a wide, rectangular tract of land rounded off by soft green hills that rise like bread loaves from the flat center of town. Though it's a town of subtle enough natural beauty to have once been considered, a couple of centuries ago, as the home for Dartmouth College, today it's one of the poorest towns in a poor state. A few years ago, a New Hampshire newspaper referred to Winchester as "a little piece of Appalachia," and if anybody objected, they didn't write in to say so. A lot of people work at the shearling tannery in town, others at the paper mills down by the river, and according to county welfare figures, quite a few don't work at all. The high school was said to have a dropout rate of 20 percent, but those inside the school say they knew it to be much higher.

Along the main street, which is a north-south state highway, the covered sidewalks offer a tempting spot for townspeople to sit during the day and often on into the night. Such a scene is probably what provoked the popular description of Winchester as a "cowboy town." Or maybe it is the unbridled nature of the town where frustrated police chiefs and town managers come and go with remarkable speed. The summer that Dennis came to town, local youths, perhaps trying to bait the overzealous new police chief, enjoyed the habit of sitting out on the porch of the local tavern, smoking joints and drinking beer. Or inscribing zigzags and doughnuts in the pavement of the four corners with the rear wheels of their fast cars.

This is what people would see, anyway, when they'd pass through on their way somewhere else — the sidewalk sitters and the tire marks in the pavement and the shirtless youths leaning on the hoods of their cars. That was enough — they didn't want to explore any further.

"Winchester was thought of as kind of a joke," Dennis said recently. "I'd go somewhere and people would laugh: 'You actually *live* in Winchester?' And I began to see that people in town made jokes about how crummy the school system was: 'Oh, you can't spell? You must have gone to Thayer!'" Education was his specialty; he thought maybe he could offer something, so he joined the PTA, which at the time had fifteen members, all of whom were women. It was the beginning of the end of his retreat.

"I COULD SEE that one of the worst things about Winchester was the people's self-image. Everyone I met was really a good person, yet because of the power of that negative image, these wonderful people didn't come through." The regional daily paper rarely featured news of Winchester, which ego-bereft Winchesterites took to mean, "Who cares?"

In his journal, Dennis wondered more and more about starting a community newspaper as a way to alter the image and bring the people in touch with each other. Would it work? Would anyone else think it worth the effort? He announced it at the PTA meeting and posted signs around town for an organizational meeting to resurrect the *Winchester Star,* which hadn't been published since 1917. Fifteen volunteers showed up. They got together two hundred dollars, and three weeks later, on the floor of Marcia Amman's living room, they pasted up the first issue of the *Star,* largely by guesswork. None of them had ever worked on a newspaper before. A one hundred percent pure Winchester product, the writing and photography were down-home and rough around the edges, and the columns were sometimes crooked. But it was all about Winchester. Each month there were crossword puzzles put together by teenagers, cartoons drawn by kids, and profiles of local farmers and tradesmen written by housewives. It was by the people, for the people. One cover had a checkerboard of photographs of all the babies born in Winchester that year with a scramble of names for the reader to match up the chubby faces. "When the first twelve-page newspaper came out, we had a party," Dennis recalls. "We stapled the *Star* to trees along the route to show people how to get there. We had champagne. It was special. I believe you have to make things special for people."

A strictly volunteer effort, it still cost money to put it out and there was none. Girl Scouts went door to door for contributions. They applied for a five thousand dollar grant Dennis knew might be available and they got it. That bought the *Star* a year's rent and an expensive typewriter.

Dennis was back to work. He put in long hours and was paid nothing. "I didn't start the newspaper to make money. I didn't care anything about the newspaper business or know anything about it. It was to build the town, to pull it together and make people feel good about themselves, to respect what they have." In an additional burst of energy, Dennis ran for a seat on the state legislature and won. Using this as his foot in the door, he worked to try to change tax laws that adversely affected the school system. The imbalance was this: while Winchester residents paid higher taxes than almost any other town in New Hampshire, the schools received less money than any other. Some in town say that it was after he became a legislator, sending friendly and informative notes to keep all residents up to date on what went on in Concord, that people began to take him seriously.

Through the *Star* and the PTA, Dennis got to know Marcia Amman and Judy Knox, two women very concerned about the school system because their children were in it. Marcia had grown up in Winchester and had graduated from Thayer, class of '65. Shortly after high school, she married and moved to Massachusetts. When the kids were toddlers, the Ammans moved back to town. "Deep down, I felt I'd had a good education and a wonderful childhood here. I wanted to raise my kids here. But when I came back, things had changed. I subbed one day at the school. I hadn't been back there since I'd graduated. Kids were walking all over the tables. They were lounging through three-hour study halls without a book. I went home in tears." Dennis showed Marcia a movie of his old school, something that had been put together to show at other middle schools. "I said to Dennis, 'Well, that's wonderful, but those kids have so much. My kids aren't ever going to have anything like that.'"

The inequity didn't escape Dennis who says, quite simply, "It's just so unfair. A lot of the kids on Long Island would go to Europe for summer vacation and college was taken for granted. Some of these kids have never been outside Winchester, even for a weekend." He knew that for the kids at Thayer to have a chance they would need an education not just adequate, but one that was appropriate, geared especially to the circumstance of rural poverty.

In spring of 1980, the Thayer principal resigned. Judy and Marcia and others in town urged Dennis to try for the job. By that time they not only knew the extent of his background, but also had witnessed the effect he'd already had on the town. Judy put ballot boxes around town, asking for the townspeople's opinions of what the high school needed and urging Dennis as the town's choice.

He was a conspicuous figure in his jeans and baseball cap, driving his Jeep, his state legislator's license plates splattered with mud from his rough road. Nearly everyone who knew him, liked him. Nearly everyone who didn't know him, had a theory about him. One downtown merchant called him a Communist. Others speculated that he was an FBI agent.

When Dennis showed up for his interview with the school board, he wore the same corduroys and short-sleeved shirt that he usually wore when he dressed up for PTA meetings and to go to Concord for sessions with the legislature. "I knew these people. I saw them all the time. I would have felt *stupid* getting all dressed up." While he was sitting in the hallway, waiting for the interview, the candidate ahead of him came out. He was wearing a three-piece suit and carrying an attaché case. "I really wanted to know who the final candidates were, so I went up and introduced myself. The guy wouldn't give me the time of day. I think he thought I was some guy off the street. In the interview, the school board asked me about a dress code, and I asked them if they meant for me or for the kids. They said, 'For you.' So I said 'What you see is what you get.' The next day I heard that line all over town. It almost cost me the job.

"I wanted the job so badly. Once I started thinking about it, the possibilities were very exciting. I knew the school was in horrible shape, but it was *my* town. I think I would have been hurt and embarrassed if I hadn't gotten it."

The vote on the school board was close, three to two, giving Dennis the job. He took a salary of twenty-two thousand dollars (that was equal to his first job out of college and eighteen thousand dollars less than what he'd made at Shoreham-Wading River) and plunged in.

Even before he'd set foot in school, Dennis made the magnanimous statement to the local newspaper: Thayer was going to be one of the best schools in the state.

THAYER HIGH SCHOOL was built in 1922, in the style of almost every other school built in this country during that era: a square, two-story brick building, barren of adornment inside or out. Except for the junior high school addition, there have been no substantial alterations made since 1922. The classrooms are large with tall windows and high, pressed-tin ceilings. The hallways, with exposed plumbing strung overhead, are lined with olive drab lockers that make it hard for three to pass abreast. When Dennis first came, the walls needed paint, especially to cover the obscenities written all over the bathroom stalls. Attendance was poor, the dropout rate higher than twenty percent, and the class that graduated the June before sent only four of its forty-eight seniors to college. There was no comparing the kids at Thayer to the well-off students that Dennis had captained on Long Island. At Thayer there were pregnant girls even in the ninth grade; other kids had no apparent home. Broken homes were nearly as common as whole ones.

Judy Knox, whom Dennis hired to start his innovative apprenticeship program,* recalls, "When I walked into this school for the first time, I just had to steel myself. Everyone was so *angry*. Kids were running up and down the halls congratulating each other on how many F's they'd gotten."

The soul-searching entries in Dennis' journal vanished, replaced by long lists of What Needs to Be; high on the list was communication between parents and school and town. He scheduled conferences with parents, something that had never been done before, and private bets were placed among veteran Thayer teachers: "He'll never get parents to come through that door," they wagered. But, even if he had to go pick them up, he got nine out of ten of them there to talk about what they wanted for their kids. Likewise, he scheduled talks with every kid in the school. "I asked each one of them what they were going to do after they got out. Most of them said, 'Get a job.' But when I asked them what kind, none of them knew. They didn't have the faintest idea!"

He sniffed around town for people with the kind of qualifications he looks for in a teacher, namely, excellence. He couldn't attract the kind of teachers he'd hired at Shoreham-Wading River, not with salary offers starting at ten thousand dollars. But he found that there were teachers willing to sacrifice pay; the gap was bridged by Dennis's enthusiasm. For instance, Dennis had heard that Richard Lawson had moved to town. Richard had quit after seventeen years teaching science at a Massachusetts high school. Burned out, he said he'd never teach again. Dennis called Richard up one night at 10:30, offering him a job at Thayer. They met and talked it over and Richard agreed to go back to teaching,

---

*Editor's note: At that time, Thayer's apprenticeship program was completely unique. Using federal grant money, the school was able to place students in local businesses during the school year. Students spent an hour every day working at places such as the bank, a drafting company, and a truck repair garage. This not only offered job opportunities and sometimes careers but it also created community interactions that yielded positive results. Today programs like this are fairly common in high schools and colleges but Dennis' initiative at Thayer in the early 1980s was groundbreaking.

accepting four thousand dollars less pay than he'd been making. "The kind of energy that Dennis has is contagious," Richard says. "I knew it was going to be entirely different working with him."

Though state funds available to Winchester were paltry, Dennis knew that there were grants available, that they need only apply. He trained teachers to fill out the tedious grant proposals and did many himself. "What they're looking for when they're giving out grants are good ideas and I'm never short on ideas."

"The apprenticeship program provides about fifty thousand dollars worth of free instruction for the school," a *Star* volunteer assessed. "A lot of what Dennis is aiming at is designed to bring things to the school that don't cost the school anything. He does it by enlisting the aid of the community."

Indeed, one of Dennis's strengths is that he is able to get money out of nowhere. "We can get it if we believe we can. People say, 'God, how did he do that?' And I sometimes get criticized for my budget because the way I move money around seems almost mysterious. It would be great if we had resources within the school. But we don't. So we can gather resources through the apprenticeship program, for one. We have apprentices at a drafting company with facilities we couldn't hope to have. But there are other things, like our library is very inadequate. Also transportation, especially with the comings and goings of the apprentices, is a real problem. I bought a car, a used station wagon, for the school. It helps tremendously, moving a couple of kids around when you don't need a big bus. But I was criticized for that."

Last year the school heard about a building that could be had for free. "All we had to do was move it," Dennis says. A crew of students and teachers took it down and rebuilt it behind the high school. It is now the science building, complete with furniture and its own heating plant.

A visitor to the school might see Dennis hugging students or rooting for them like a cheerleader. He's not their buddy but a friend, and they know that. His first year, when everyone in town knew him as Dennis, he had to impress on them the importance of everyone in the school calling him Dr. Littky. Everyone does. He has a sternness that comes out at the appropriate times, his playfulness evaporating.

At Shoreham-Wading River, there was virtually no vandalism. At Thayer it is a big problem, but a diminishing one since Dennis took over. Enlisting a lot of student help, Dennis fixed up the building the best he could with money available. "The girls' bathroom was really the pits," Dennis assesses. "I got the girls together and told them I was willing to fix it up, but if it got bad again, I'd have to hire a monitor. So they cleaned it, they sanded it, they painted it. It was a process everyone was involved in. It's *their* bathroom."

In a school where the dropout rate was high and attendance a problem, in some cases simply because the parents keep the kids out for their own convenience, suspension and expulsion are not adequate disciplinary tools. "I don't have great things over them. I can throw a student out, lower his grade, but we've got to *make* things important. If a kid has skipped school, what good does it do to keep him out of school? A lot of parents aren't even home during the day. That's putting them back on the streets. I'd rather keep them in and work with them. When I start to see that I've done everything possible for a kid, offered him all kinds of breaks and options and the kid still doesn't respond, and I see that it's hurting the atmosphere of the school, then it's time for that kid to step out."

Dennis is presently checking into the possibility of setting up a work crew to which offending students can be assigned, working on town roads, town projects.

"Everyone at Thayer feels a part of a team effort," points out an observer. "By making every member of the faculty feel that his or her role has a significant impact on the school, Dennis has created a very cooperative, strong staff that cares very much about what happens to Thayer."

DENNIS IS AGAIN putting in seventy-five or eighty hours a week for his school. This fall will be his fourth year. He is often at school ahead of the janitor at seven a.m. and is still answering the phone after supper. Sometimes, in the deep of winter, he stays in a cottage near the high school to avoid the hours needed just to get in and out, but most of the year he still lives in his cabin with no electricity, no plumbing, no phone, no running water. Last year he had a well dug, but he hasn't gotten around to hooking it up to the house. "I guess it really doesn't matter to me," he confesses.

Not everyone backs him. Some blame the problems that still hover over Thayer on Dennis. Some people still grump about his appearance. But this year sixteen members of the graduating class went on to college, more than four times the number that went the year before he came. The dropout rate has slowed to five percent. And the Apprenticeship Program is to be the focus of a conference that will be held in Winchester in October, when once again educators from around the country will come to see what Dennis has done.

Dennis' proclamation that Thayer would be one of the best schools in the state wasn't something said in a fit of exuberance. He repeats it today and explains: "We won't by any means send the most kids to college or have the highest SAT scores, but it will be the most appropriate place, it will be an example of what education can be in a rural area like this. It will be looked at as another kind of education. Thayer will be the best."

Marcia Amman, among others, wonders if Dennis will stay long enough for that to happen. "He applied for a White House Fellowship when we were working on the *Star* and we almost lost him. Winchester is so lucky to have him. We could *never* have attracted anyone with the kind of credentials that Dennis has. It's just that he was here. The town was sleeping and he walked in and he's just touched everyone. My worry is that he won't stay long enough for all the pieces to fall into place."

"I won't leave until the job is done," is Dennis's answer to that. "But it will probably take more time than I'd thought."

He's patient that way. Dennis has always wanted to learn to play the piano. While he was working on the *Star* he heard about a piano for sale for twenty dollars and he jumped at the chance. He borrowed a truck and got five or six men to help him move it up to his cabin. It was summer and the truck went up the hill all right, but the road doesn't back right up to the cabin, so they had to grunt and sweat the big upright the rest of the way. They got it to the porch only to find that it wouldn't fit through the door. "Dennis didn't hesitate," recalls one who helped in the move. "He said, 'Just a second!' and went inside and returned with a hammer and a crowbar and proceeded to tear out the door. When it would fit through, we carried it in and left him there with his door all apart."

That was four years ago. His door is back together and the piano is still tucked in across from the woodstove. Dennis bemoans the fact that he hasn't had the time yet to learn to play. But to learn, it takes time and a piano. This is clearly a matter of time because, as he points out, "*Surely* I can't learn to play without a piano."

October 1983 Yankee magazine

IN 1992, *a TV movie (*A Town Torn Apart) *was made about Dennis and Thayer High School and a book* Doc: The Story of Dennis Littky *was published. Attempts were made to fire Dennis but he survived and eventually left Thayer in 1994 on his own terms. He then moved to Providence, R.I., to join Ted Sizer, a leader in educational reform. In 1995, Dennis cofounded The Big Picture Schools, based on his philosophy of education: to design small, personalized schools for the underserved urban student. This network has now grown to sixty-three schools in the U.S., seven in Australia, twenty-seven in Israel, and fourteen in the Netherlands. In 2007, The George Lucas Education Foundation selected Dennis as one of the twenty "most daring educators in the world." Thayer High School closed in 2005 and students from Winchester now attend a consolidated high school in Keene, N.H. Dennis still owns his cabin on top of Pudding Hill in Winchester, which he uses for retreat.*

Ted Ames' Grand Adventure

On an afternoon last fall, sixty-six-year-old Ted Ames was working away on his computer in his office, a chockablock affair in one of the front rooms of his house, which sits up on a ledge of granite overlooking the picturesque Maine fishing village of Stonington. For long stretches over the past forty-five years, he'd navigated his fishing boats out into the big ocean from working harbors like this one, looking for fish. Since the mid-1990s, he had been spending most of his time looking for where the fish had gone. A crisis had befallen the fisheries of the eastern Gulf of Maine, an appalling situation that had rocked his life as well as the lives of countless other Maine fishermen. Quietly, over the past two decades, the cod and haddock had vanished and the fishermen had too. From Monhegan Island all the way to Grand Manan, "No one's home," was Ted's succinct conclusion.

The idea that this ancient livelihood might be on the verge of extinction disturbed him greatly. Ted first went to sea at the age of six with his grandfather, a retired lighthouse keeper, in boat powered by a little gas engine. They lived on the island of Vinalhaven, settled by his family in 1754. That day, they were out for codfish but Ted became seasick, as he often did when he was younger, and they returned home. But not for long. In time, the nausea left him and the sea became his second home. Ted Ames has spent the better part of his life poking up and down the Maine coast, shrimp fishing, scalloping, lobstering, groundfishing, you name it, he went for it. He once navigated himself home in a blinding snowstorm without a compass and has had an enormous fish-hook pierce his ear while dragging out on the Banks, but these situations were nothing compared to what he was facing at that moment last fall. In 1990, with the fisheries up and down the Maine coast declared virtually bankrupt, Ted reluctantly sold his dragger, the *Dorothy M.,* a forty-five-foot, twenty-ton affair that he referred to as his "pocket battleship." To make do, he taught school and ran a water lab. A bad fall had left him with chronic back pain and a diminished capacity to operate a boat. He continued to fish for lobsters, which remained plentiful, but even with all this to cope with, the conditions of the fisheries were what troubled him most.

Everyone, environmentalists and state and federal agencies alike, agreed that the fish were gone. But on how to manage the fish that remained or, even more speculative, how to bring them back, there were vigorous disagreements. A handy solution seemed to be limiting the number of days a boat could be at sea and the number of federal permits issued. In other words, shutting down the waters. But how can that keep the fishermen alive? Ted wondered.

Ted was not only a fisherman but a scholar, having earned a master's degree in biochemistry from the University of Maine. He had studied spawning, habitat and fishing patterns in the Gulf of Maine. In addition, he had chaired many regional and statewide fishing organizations. Soon, he hatched a plan: He'd interview as many retired fishermen as he could — the ones who had fished in the 1930s and 40s. They knew where the fish had once been — information that might lead them to where the fish might return. "If we could find out where the old spawning areas were, we could restock them," he says.

Ted picked out twenty-eight of the best inshore cod and haddock fishermen that he knew of and, throughout the mid-1990s, he interviewed "some of the most wonderful bunch of old codgers you could ever imagine." He obtained grants, just enough to cover his expenses. Mostly he did it for the love of and the hope for the future of the Maine fisheries. Using his marine biology skills, he mapped the information he gathered, which showed the spawning grounds identified by the old-timers and overlaid it on a map of the spawning grounds from the 1970s. "It fit like a glove," he says.

Now that he had identified the historic spawning grounds, he felt that the fisheries could be recovered, if only the laws could change. Currently fishermen can harvest groundfish anywhere in the Gulf of Maine for a limited number of days a year. "The system has been broken and the only way to get it back is to have a different type of management from what we have," Ted says. "Boy, I'd love to see it happen. But every time I've made my proposals, I've been told where to go and how to get there in the most vivid descriptions imaginable."

And so, as he sat there in front of his computer last fall, his fishing days pretty much in his past and his hopes for changing the fate of his beloved Maine waters hanging in the balance, the phone rang. A man from the John D. and Catherine T. MacArthur Foundation said he was calling about a fellowship. Often referred to as "genius grants," these fellowships are unique in that they come without warning or application. Anonymous recommendations are made for worthy candidates and from this pool, fellowships are awarded. At first Ted thought this call was about someone else, for he knew many he thought deserving of this honor. But the man was not calling Ted about someone else, he was calling to tell him that the fellowship, worth five hundred thousand dollars, was to be awarded to him. Ted, in their view, successfully "fused the roles of commercial fisherman and applied scientist, in response to increasing threats to the fishery ecosystem."

Since 1981, over seven hundred writers, musicians, physicists, chemists, physicians, educators, and artists have been endowed with the coveted MacArthur grant. But this was the first time that a fisherman had been given such an honor.

SIX MONTHS LATER, over a haddock sandwich in the café in Stonington, Ted recalled that life-changing day. "It was right out of the blue and willy-nilly. Here I was, already at a kind of turning point in my life. Well, gosh, it blew me away," he says. There has been some time now for reality to settle in. For Ted, it's back to the business of saving the fisheries.

Ted is wiry, built like a fighter, with the green eyes and peppery, steel-wool beard of a pirate. Quite often, a mischievous grin sneaks through as he tries to explain the complexities of area management, which are second nature to him.

"The combination of modern electronics with large fishing vessels has created a technology too powerful for fish stocks to withstand," he explains. "Balance no longer exists." Even within a profession known for independent thinking, Ted has bucked authority where he thinks it's needed — which is just about at every turn. When asked if he is a maverick, he says, "I suppose, though I never think of myself that way." But the government, damn it, has got it all wrong.

"At the moment, no fisherman is allowed to go out to fish more than fifty days in a year. The result has been disastrous," Ted says. "It has bankrupted Maine's groundfish fleet."

The battle is hard fought as the economics squeezes more and more young men out of what is already a tough and diminishing enterprise. Out of the remaining twelve to thirteen hundred fishing boats in New England, a mere fifty land eighty percent of the fish. These are the mammoth, two-hundred-fifty-foot, multimillion dollar boats that haul out of New Bedford, Gloucester, Boston, Portsmouth, or Portland. Under such a restrictive code, small boats way downeast in the little harbors like Stonington don't have a chance — the giant boats race out to the spawning grounds and drag the bottom for all the fish they can get. "Is it more appropriate to have fishermen as stewards of the resource or should we just give it all to the biggest hog who can sweep up the most and the fastest and never mind about tomorrow? We are suffering the consequences of that method right now," Ted says.

Ted sees the government's strategy as a negative approach, pessimistic, forcing many fishermen to simply sell their boats and go to work elsewhere. "We don't need fewer fishermen! We need every one of them that we can get!" Ted advocates an approach that will not only help the fish to recover but will also help fishermen take charge and husband the fishery on their own. "To say, 'you're catching too many' simply doesn't give the fishermen a constructive course of action. Protecting local spawning habitats and nursery areas provide the key."

To formulate his method, Ted looked to the past. "What people are usually not aware of is that the lobster fishing in the 1930s was basically dead. Fishermen would go out and come back with twelve, fifteen lobster. They figured out that they were basically raiding the nursery so that the fish could never really reproduce. The lobstermen themselves initiated a whole series of management measures that were effective: protecting habitat, protecting juveniles, protecting brood stock. From that time on, because of these measures, the population of lobsters in Maine has gone continuously up." Ted, who has recently launched a lobster hatchery in Stonington that will function to replenish stocks in their small fishing zone, understands exactly how well this system has worked for the lobster fishermen. As a result of these methods, lobstering is the only thriving fishing industry left in the eastern Gulf of Maine.

Ted would like to see a similar system put into place for groundfishing. "We need to fish smarter. We need to create a system where stewardship becomes important to the fishermen. The way to change it is to take those critical habitats in each section and make a special management zone where you put stringent rules on how, when, and where you catch fish and by doing that, you create an opportunity for the stewardship that allows for people to profit. Then it becomes meaningful."

He also sees as vital an educational system that includes fishing and its ecology so that the young people can understand the entire economic picture of fishing, not just the end result of selling the catch to the highest bidder.

It's hard not to become nostalgic about fishing in these waters. A longing sets in for things to return to the way they were. In his research, talking to so many old timers about their experiences at sea, Ted talked with Roger Beal, Sr., of Jonesport, who recalled the great Machias Bay codfish run of 1942. In detail, Beal recounted to Ted the day when he and his father went out and hauled in seemingly endless nets filled with thousands of cod, some as tall as a man. No such haul has been recorded since. The tale is poignant to any fisherman who remembers fishing in the days of plenty, when fish were as big as men, but tragic to fishermen who are aware that for years they have been ruining spawning and feeding grounds by dragging heavy equipment along the bottom of the sea, breaking up all the habitat.

Ted knows from firsthand experience how seductive trawling is. "God bless it, it's the dominant fishing technology today, dominant because it catches everything. Haul it in, dump it on your deck, and from the pile of stuff, pick out what you want and discard the rest. It's an incredibly comfortable, easy way to catch fish.

"But what you're doing is cleaning out the chicken coop before the eggs hatch. And at this point, the ground rules are such that if a fisherman has access to a spawning area and he knows when the fish are there, and he knows that other people know the same thing, he has to get there first. And the race is on. The government has created a self-defeating situation. The government is responsible for this. The fishermen are not."

Because he understands the natural world, Ted remains hopeful. "You have the potential for thirty, forty, fifty million pounds of fish a year being taken from eastern Maine and today you have squat coming in. We don't really know if the system would come back the way it used to be but we do know that if we provide the conditions where it could happen, there is a good possibility. I really believe that if you can get the system functioning again, we'll have fish coming out the wazzoo."

He considers the recovery of Maine fisheries to be within reach. An additional and sizeable contribution to the reduction in the fisheries has been the existence of the many dams on the rivers fish have historically used to spawn. "Right now, the fisheries are very depressing but, jeez, they removed a dam at the mouth of the Penobscot and a couple of years after that, we started seeing fingerling cod in the upper part of the bay, in areas where we had not seen cod since the 1930s! Which means, *da-dah, da-dah, da-dah*, there *is* the mechanism that will bring back these coastal stocks!"

This is what Ted Ames calls his "grand adventure" — the fishing, the research, the winning of the MacArthur grant, and now the possibility of recovering the fisheries that have fed his family's line since the mid-1700s.

"The waters of eastern Maine could be a sport fisherman's paradise, a tourist's dream come true," he says. "The economic bang for improving this system just takes my breath away. It's so obvious, I can almost taste it. This is sitting there like a ripe plum for all of us to take advantage of, if we could just get our act together."

The MacArthur grant is given with no strings attached. If he wanted to, Ted Ames could spend the entire sum on a mansion or take his family on a cruise around the world. When he was awarded the fellowship, he was asked what he would do with the money. "I told them, 'I'm going to do just what the old fisherman did when he won the jackpot. I'm going to keep doing exactly what I've always done and when I run out of money, I'll figure out some other way to go fishing!'"

He laughs, an explosive burst of energy and emotion. "This MacArthur fellowship has given me a bully pulpit. I've rattled the cage at every corner on the same issue, which is to create a mechanism for fishermen to get smaller without paying a terrible price." He knows he has his work cut out for him. "At the turn of the century, it was fish, fish everywhere, and today, not a fish in sight. If things go well, it ought to look once again like it did back then, but we'll have to do a little fishing for something other than fish to get there."

This he has done, fearlessly navigating the shoals of government red tape.

A year ago, he wondered where he was headed now that his fishing days were mostly behind him. Now he has many fewer questions and many more possibilities.

He takes me down to the Stonington docks and shows me, with a flourish, a big old derelict building, once a lobster buying station. Teetering on the edge of the dock, it looks ready to fall into the harbor. This, he explains, will become their resource center, a place where fishermen can meet with researchers and state and federal regulators, sharing information and resources. The center will have archives and a museum, to ensure that the information gathered can be used in the future. And it will be a place where the young people in town can learn about the marine trades and about the environment, learn how it all fits together in its intricate mix and how the fisheries can be taken care of so that they will still be there for future generations.

It's hard not to share Ted's enthusiasm; no doubt, he's the captain of this ship. "If we take care of it, we'll have a fishery that can be fished hard or easy and we can fish forever and our kids and grandchildren will have it too. That's what I would like to see. Oh, boy, how I'd love to see that!"

November 2006 Yankee magazine

According to Ted, *the lobster fishery in eastern Maine is in very good shape, at least in part due to the success of his hatchery. "We were producing 100,000 lobsters a year. In fact, there's an overabundance of lobsters right now. We started the hatchery because fishermen wanted to learn whether we could raise lobsters to replenish these areas," Ted says. "In just a few short years, we have learned we can do that." The hatchery has been mothballed and, when it reopens, it is Ted's hope that the University of Maine will take over its operation, with students working and learning at the facility. His hatchery is regarded as the most successful operation of its kind in the United States.*

The Penobscot East Resource Center, of which Ted is a founding board member and of which his wife, Robin Alden, is executive director, has expanded from a staff of two (Ted and Robin) when it was founded in 2003, to a full-time staff of seven as well as interns. It has also moved from offices in the old Stonington schoolhouse where they were when I visited in 2006, not into that old derelict building where Ted envisioned expanding broader programs for local residents and fishermen — there were too many obstacles to that idea — but instead into a beautifully renovated building nearby, also on the Stonington waterfront. This 7,129 square foot space includes staff offices, intern work spaces, meeting rooms, and a public education area. In addition, there is a fishermen's room that allows off-hours access to fishermen, and a coffee pot perpetually on brew. This substantial gift from local businessman, Donald Sussman, will enable the Resource Center to bring together fishermen, scientists, local businesses, and members of the community, affording a variety of programs and facilities. Included now in their programs is a Community Supported Fisheries, which operates in the same way as Community Supported Agriculture, so popular now in rural areas. Community support for building the fisheries and the marine trades has only increased. All part of Ted's dream.

Ted reports that, in the four years since this article was published, the condition of the fisheries in the Gulf of Maine has not changed significantly. But he's confident that these many new programs being put into place will eventually have a positive effect on the vital fish stocks of the Gulf of Maine. "We have great hopes," he says.

Stepping into the Limelight

THE TEMPERATURE has been zero and below for most of the week. Michael Chute is fitting split lengths of wood into the box stove, tight, jamming in one last thin split before closing the cast-iron door, which is warped and leaves a thin crescent opening that glows bright orange. The sun has left that side of the house, and ice crystals have grown like blooms on the face of the single-paned glass.

Carolyn is in the bathroom. She has just done a wash in the galvanized washtub that morning, and she is wringing the clothes by hand and pinning them to the baling twine that's strung over the tub — the winter clothesline. She has draped her gray cotton prairie skirt over the back of one of the rockers to dry next to the stove, and she comes out now, her long, thick hair clean and brushed out soft, and feels the waistband of the skirt: "'Well, I'll have to wear it wet."

Carolyn is getting ready to go to one of her first book signings, at a library up north in Lisbon, where she will read from her book and greet her new public. She takes the skirt into the bathroom and comes back out shortly, wearing the calf-length skirt and a well-worn red plaid flannel shirt. She sits on the edge of one of the rockers and pulls on her felt-lined boots. They are big, bulky. While she laces them she says to Michael, more to herself: "All the reporters say I've got big feet, but I don't. It's just these boots that are big. My feet are small inside." The boots are one of the necessities she was able to buy with the seven thousand dollars she was given in advance of the publication of her first novel, *The Beans of Egypt, Maine,* which was published just four days before this day in January.

For the past month there has been a steady procession of newspaper reporters and photographers — from New York, Washington, D.C., Hartford, Boston, Chicago — finding their way to Carolyn's home in Gorham, Maine. Some days there has been one reporter visiting in the morning and another in the afternoon, an extraordinary showing for a first novelist.

On the kitchen counter is a huge bouquet of red and yellow roses sent to her by her editor at Ticknor & Fields — though the book has only just been published, it is already in its third printing, a nearly unprecedented occurrence. A spokesman for the publisher had said, just two days before, that demand for the book had caused them to ship more copies of a single title than they had ever shipped to Maine. Nationwide, forty thousand copies had sold pre-publication, and it has been predicted that sales will top one hundred thousand, enough to make it a best-seller. Carolyn is expecting to earn a dollar on every book that is sold, but to date she has not received any more than the advance, which she got almost a year ago. At the time she wrote to her agent: "Got the check today. It was like a dream. We all took turns holding it. Even my neighbors."

"Oh, my Gawd," Carolyn says and starts up out of the rocker and races into her room. Once it was one of the two bedrooms in this tiny tract house but now, with workspace made from plywood and 2x4s, it is Carolyn's study, where she started but was unable to finish *The Beans,* the multitude of reviews for which lie buried in a pile next to her beat-up manual typewriter. She will be reading from this book tonight for a gathering at the Lisbon Falls Library, which is about an hour's drive north. She starts to page through the book. "I might have gone without it."

From outside comes the uneven tempo of dogs barking. "Red's barking again, Pa," Carolyn says to Michael. "Doesn't he ever get tired?"

Outside the window of this room, almost close enough to touch, is the neighbor's dog, Red, an Irish setter who is tied to an iron stake by a chain the length of a man. "All day long. Bark, bark, bark, bark, bark, bark, bark." Carolyn joins in as she flips through the book and marks off pages. On the cover is a painting, done in primitive style, of a young woman in a calf-length prairie skirt, her long hair blowing in the wind. She is standing in a clearing in a forest. An angry looking baby sits on the ground beside her. The woman, it should be noted, is wearing a pair of brown tie shoes, not big boots.

Michael shrugs on another heavy wool shirt over the one he is already wearing and tucks it into his pants, which are made of wool and thick as a blanket. Over this he puts on a heavy denim jacket, the cuffs worn to a fray, and his green felt crusher hat, which he wears with the brim turned down all the way around. He has never missed one of Carolyn's readings, even from the early days when she was a little-known writer of short stories. He checks the stove one more time and then picks up Toto, a football-sized dog with a coat like an unmown field, cradles him, and says, "Let's go."

CAROLYN CHUTE's novel has already been reviewed favorably in newspapers all over the country. Nearly every review has compared her work to William Faulkner's, but she says, "I can't understand that. He writes big long sentences and he uses big words. I don't even *know* any big words. We both write about poor people but if that's what they mean, well, *gee*!"

One review, in *Publisher's Weekly*, has left them angry: "The review said nice things about the book, but it insulted poor people real bad. I don't think he even read the book — he said that Earlene and her father lived in a shack and they didn't — they lived in a nice house. And he said that Beal had been laid off from the mill — what mill? Beal worked in the woods — he was *working* and he was poor! So, what's that called? Speed reading?"

Earlene Pomerleau and Beal Bean are characters from her book, characters who intertwine inside the poverty-stricken landscape they share growing up in the fictitious Maine town of Egypt. The Beans of the book live across the right-of-way from Earlene and her Daddy. Earlene's Daddy calls them "predators, uncivilized animals." But Earlene finds them fascinating and somewhat irresistible. She watches them out her picture window, absorbed, like a child at the TV. Eventually, even though her father has enforced a lifetime of Biblically inspired discipline trying to keep Earlene safe from the Beans, she gets pregnant by Beal and marries him. *The Beans of Egypt, Maine* is the bitter and tragic story of Earlene, who fights to stay alive in a world with no choices.

The book has also spawned a certain amount of indignation, presumably among people who would rather not see the conditions of rural poverty examined in such excruciatingly real and vivid detail. The day before, Carolyn read a letter to the editor in the *Maine Times* from a woman who objected to the *Times* calling Carolyn's book "brilliant" and "truthful." The letter upset Carolyn and has been on her mind since.

Carolyn, who is thirty-seven, began the rough work on this novel nearly twenty years ago and has worked on it off and on since then. She grew up in working-class surroundings in neighboring Portland, the daughter of an electrical parts salesman. She left high school when she was sixteen, pregnant, and married; the marriage ended in divorce eight years later. The mother of a small child, a woman without skills or a high school education, Carolyn found herself sliding into the grinding and endless cycle of poverty. To earn a living, she picked potatoes and worked scrubbing floors, earning minimum wage. She collected food stamps and got a high school diploma from evening courses. Afterwards, she began to take courses at the University of Maine, one, two, three courses at a time. She took writing courses, and with her new skills she got a job at the local newspaper as her town's correspondent.

After the divorce, she was able to retain their house. It was a tiny house on a little squeeze of land that shared a right-of-way with other houses, all tucked in together like shingles on a roof. It was a conventional design, but Carolyn transformed it. There weren't enough windows, not enough light, so holes were cut in the walls and windows made from scrap wood and glass. There were no shelves for her books and plants and bottles and figurines, so the walls were strung up with boards, plywood or pine, whatever could be found at the dump that week. On the bathroom wall, using the clear-colored poster paints that children love, Carolyn painted a picture of a window, a huge picture window. She painted in curtains, and the scene was a field full of cows, grazing contentedly.

Other conversions were less deliberate: the plumbing disintegrated so there was no running water. It had been years, anyway, since she'd been able to afford hot water. The money ran out so there was no way to buy oil for the furnace. Many times the electricity was shut off.

Tired of being a single parent, Carolyn became restless for a mate. The year before, she had made out lists of what she wanted in a man: she knew the kind of clothes he would wear, the kind of truck he would drive, and that he would love both guns and animals. She knew he would work in the woods. And she knew enough about how he would look to paint a picture of him that is startlingly similar to the looks of Michael Chute. Then, accompanied sometimes by her grandmother, she set out in search of him, cruising the back roads, stopping and investigating when she heard the sound of chain saws or passed a truck with fish or deer decals on it parked by the side of the road. It was on one of these pilgrimages, at a turkey shoot in Sebago, that she met Michael Chute. Once she got to know him, she was able to check off every item on her list as fulfilled.

After she and Michael married, work on the novel intensified, and her stories began to sell to small literary magazines, which usually don't pay more than $50 a story. "I never did send my work around. Mostly, other people did it for me," she says. "Ollie, oh . . . ," one of her stories, was selected by Anne Tyler to be included in *The Best American Short Stories of 1983*.

Even so, the novel was still not done, and in the midst of all this they suffered a new surge of cruelty: a baby boy, born dead. They named the boy Reuben, which is also the name of the "biggest, baddest, meanest Bean." Carolyn dedicated the book to their baby, a dedication which reads: "In memory of real Reuben. Who spared him this occasion? Who spared him rage?" It is a dedication which has caused some confusion. "Even years back, I had this character Reuben because it has always been one of my most favorite names. And then when I got pregnant, I thought, 'I like that name, but I hate to use it because this guy's a *villain* in the story.' But at the same time I felt why should that stop me. There's a lot of other Reubens around, so we called him Reuben, in spite of Rubie Bean. But then he died, so I thought I'd dedicate the book to him and ask the question of who caused his death (Carolyn feels that there is inadequate medical care available to people on public assistance and that this contributed to the death of her baby), and how he was actually *spared* because we are poor and there's times when we feel like giving up. I kept thinking of how he was *spared* from perhaps being someone like the made-up Reuben Bean, from being so frustrated and *mad* at the way everything is all the time."

Carolyn and Michael, who is unskilled and works when he can, in the woods or in the junkyard or in the fields, knew instinctively that selling the novel was the only way to break the poverty cycle. "Michael has no skills and the only thing I can do is write. I knew it was our last hope. I can't write at the house — there's too much going on. So a friend of mine lent us her camp in Vermont, and Michael and I went there and I worked *solid* for three months. I worked ten hours a day, seven days a week. Michael had hoped to get work there, but he couldn't find any. We applied for food stamps, but they wouldn't give them to us because we own a house in Maine. We lived on potatoes, onions, and water for the last month."

Though Carolyn's novel appears to be seamless — indeed, it reads very much the way she talks — she says that she has rewritten it many times over. "I cook it till it's done," she says. "Until it's just right, it's just lousy."

Six publishers turned it down. But oddly, unlike other writers waiting to hear, Carolyn says that she was not concerned about whether or not it would be taken. She says she always knew it would be, but her concern was *when*. "We were getting scared. We didn't have any heat and I wanted to *really know* when it was going to be published, so I asked Mary Howell, a psychic on the radio over in Portland, *when* is this going to be published and *how*? Mary Howell told her that she saw good things for the book, that it would be accepted in March by a house that would give her "phenomenal publicity."

And so it was. A few days before February turned to March, Carolyn's agent sent her a mailgram with the news: Ticknor & Fields had bought the book.

Though he does not read or write, there are ways that Michael Chute should share the byline of *The Beans* with Carolyn. "Sometimes we'd act out the parts together," Carolyn says. "And more important than anything, when I'm writing, I have to kind of disappear into this little made-up world without coming out of it, and Michael was *willing* to get into this made-up world with me. We'd sit at the table and talk about the characters like they were real people."

It was Michael who sat in judgment over the technical parts, the parts about guns and cars and logging trucks. "I messed up on one part," Michael admits. "When Roberta was lifting the hood on March Goodspeed's Lincoln, I should have told Carolyn that she wouldn't have been able to open the hood from the outside like that. Those Lincolns have a hood latch on the inside."

In his gun cabinet, which was made from scrap lumber and two old barn windows, Michael keeps not only his rifles but a collection of books and magazines in which Carolyn's stories have appeared. She has signed the title page of each one: To Pa — and then she draws the shape of a heart — my best friend. From Carolyn. In here he also has a manuscript the size of a New York City phone book, one of the original *Beans* manuscripts which Carolyn says he insisted he must have. This, too, is signed, and Carolyn has drawn a cover cartoon: bean-shaped circles, lots of them, with eyes and noses drawn in.

"I could never have written the book without Michael. Never, never, never." When she got to the end of certain sections, she read them out loud to Michael. "A lot of people who don't normally read books have read this one, and I think Michael helped there, too. I knew he would not be reading it himself. I wanted it so that he could *picture* it, clear as a bell."

It is this picture-perfect detail that has made the book draw the attention that it has. Like a series of photographs, it presents the interiors of lives rarely examined. Though there is nothing political about the story, Carolyn had politics on her mind when she wrote it. More than anything Carolyn would like the book to honor the poor. "A friend sent my book to Reagan and a copy to Meese. I signed them. I said, 'If you can even just ask Americans to look at poor people with more respect and stop tromping on them.' We live like rats — some in even a lot less pleasant surroundings — and *survive*! I think that's something to look up to! It is amazing to me that anybody can make it through poverty and live to be old."

MICHAEL FINDS his way to the back of the library. Sixty folding chairs are set up, leaving only sidling room in the aisles. Michael settles into a chair in the front row and Toto sits, alert, in the chair next to him.

A young man with a wispy beard and wire-rim glasses comes in, carrying a dog-eared copy of *The Beans*. He takes a seat in the front row near Michael and leans his elbows on his knees, giving Michael a look of admiration. Finally he says, "Aren't you Carolyn's husband?" Michael nods, shy. "Ayup." The young man says, "I recognize you from the picture in the paper. I heard you guys on 'Maine Things Considered,' you know, on National Public Radio? Did you get to hear it?" Michael says, "No.

We don't have a radio. Well, no, we do have a radio but it isn't a very good one. It runs when it wants to and anyways, it only gets AM." Toto, who has had his share of publicity as well, eyes the newcomer uneasily. "That's Toto, right?" the young man says. "Can he do that trick?" Michael smooths the dog's topknot. "Toto," he says, "what do you think of Reagan being in the White House?" Toto's black eyes look out from under his mess of hair. He lets out a low growl. "That's right, Toto," Michael says. "Now, what do you think of Nancy Reagan's ruby slippers?" Toto draws in a sharp breath and snarls more deeply and then snaps — two piercing barks.

The room is filling quickly. People are pressed against the walls and there is no way to get in or out of the two doors, which are clogged with people. It is decided to move the reading to the Episcopal Church, four doors down.

Outside, the wind lashes out at the crowd, which moves like a single beast down the main street of Lisbon Falls. The church and the chapel quickly fill, and dozens of people are left to stand. Michael finds a single chair left at the very back of the chapel. Toto sits up in his lap, attentive.

After she has been introduced by the librarian, Carolyn comes out, her big boots squeaking on the polished floor, and walks toward the lectern, which has been set up in front of the altar, still decked with Christmas poinsettias. A TV cameraman comes in, making a racket with his enormous load of camera equipment. Carolyn picks up the book, holds it directly in front of her face, and starts reading in the pouty voice of a little girl who's got something to prove. "It's Saturday morning. All clouds. Very cold. When Daddy's downcellah busy with his lathe, I go to the edge of our grass to get a look at the Beans. The Beans' mobile home is one of them old ones, looks like a turquoise-blue submarine. It's got blackberry bushes growin' over the windows. I scream, 'HELLO BEANS!' About four huge heads come out of the hole. It's a hole the Bean kids and Bean babies have been workin' on for almost a year. Every day they go down the hole and they use coffee cans and a spade to make the hole bigger. The babies use spoons." The crowd breaks out laughing and Carolyn cracks up with them and then continues. "One of 'em wipes his nose on his sleeve. They blink their fox-color eyes." She stops and puts the book down. "Now I have to tell you guys something. In New York there've been some reviews of this that act like these people are really, like real *scroungy* or something. Well, all kids *I* know do things like dig holes and wipe their noses. Really, I don't see anything scroungy about these people except the ones that lose their tempah. Some of the people in New York that have done the reviews have been *appalled* by what goes on up here. I think they must lead very sheltered lives — they don't go outside? They don't know anybody? I'm not even being funny — some people think that everybody's warm and they've got plenty to eat. Well," and her voice turns low, "it isn't true."

She picks up the book and continues to read, the audience laughing and applauding at the humor she has brought to this tragic subject. And as she goes on, Michael, in the back, is listening like it's the first time he's ever heard it.

THE BLONDE-HAIRED cameraman aims his lens at Carolyn and works the focus ring, getting his footage for the evening news. The woman reporter has dyed blonde hair and her face shines with makeup the color of canned salmon. She sticks a long microphone toward Carolyn's mouth. The woman's voice has the lilt of an overly polite receptionist. "How has all this changed your life?"

Carolyn squirms. "Well, I used to be shy . . . Well, you know, I'm not rich!"

"Well, but you're going to get some money, no?" The saccharine voice persists.

"Yeah, I imagine. Yeah." Carolyn tries to smile.

The woman with the mike looks pressured. "How has all this changed your life, really?" She pokes the mike closer in toward Carolyn, like a prod. Carolyn shoves her hands into the pockets of her jacket and turns sideways to the camera self-consciously. The cameraman moves to keep her in focus.

"Well, I'm a little busier. I can't write anymore." Her voice comes out uncharacteristically small.

The woman moves in closer, cocks her head coyly and asks, "Are you afraid that all the money and success will change your life?"

"The only thing is that it takes up time. That would probably be the only thing."

The reporter keeps the mike at Carolyn's mouth and raises her eyebrows, silently asking her to say more. Carolyn looks at her, cornered, and then breaks out in a grin: "You mean like make me dress better?" And she flaps the jacket open and closed with her hands still in her pockets.

"Now," the woman doesn't miss a beat, reading her questions from a pad, "is the book really about you and your life?"

Carolyn's eyebrows scrunch together. "*No!* No! It's a made-up story. It's *fiction*."

"Uh-huh. Well, what do you hope that people who read the book are going to get out of it?"

Carolyn cuts in: "Hey! Guess where I'm going tomorrow? *Egpyt*, Maine! A reporter from the Lewiston paper is going to take us. I didn't even know that it existed — I thought I was making it up. You know that signpost that says Paris, Poland, Denmark, whatever? Well, Egypt wasn't on there, so I figured it didn't exist . . . But, there it is. We're going up to see them tomorrow."

"Are you afraid that this change in your life is really . . ." Carolyn starts to laugh and roll her eyes, but the woman persists and keeps her face dead serious. "I mean, there was a certain knowledge of a certain kind of life that enabled you to write this wonderful book — are you going to *lose* something when you get money!"

Carolyn reels back as if she wants to break and run. Then she grins. "You mean poverty? I hope so."

"Well, I was just wondering, you know, if it could be some sort of *intangible* thing you could lose — I mean you're going to be associating with different people now. Will you still keep the same friends?"

Carolyn wraps her jacket around her with both hands as if she has suddenly been hit with a cold blast of air. "Yeah! Of course! Sure will."

There are other questions and finally the woman says, "Thank you, Mrs. Shoot," and Carolyn says, "Chewt — *hard* ch like chicken."

When they get home, they will not watch the interview on TV. They traded their TV for a set of snow tires last fall. The house is as cold as a barn, but the plants still look alive. Michael sets a fire in the cold stove and Carolyn sorts through her mail, which now comes to her in such quantities that she sometimes has to pry the stack free from the mailbox.

The room begins to warm and Michael keeps feeding the stove with the precision of a machine. Carolyn brushes her teeth at the kitchen sink, rinsing her toothbrush under the homemade faucet: a length of garden hose with a spigot attached with a clamp and black tape. Though Carolyn has spent the evening amidst admirers and signed hundreds of copies of her book after the reading, and though she is excited about going to Egypt, the woman who wrote the letter to the *Maine Times* is still on her mind. In the letter the woman said, in part, "No one need go without food in Maine if a man is able to have a garden, or without heat if he is able to cut wood . . . it is sad to think that people in Maine are living like the characters in this book." Now she says to Michael, using the toothbrush as a wand, "You know what, Pa, we ought to write to that lady and ask her if we can plant a garden on *her* land or cut down some of *her* trees." The lot on which Carolyn and Michael's house sits is barely big enough for the house and the pen for the geese and chickens. There are less than a dozen trees.

THE GUNNING of the engine of the big truck parked in the driveway next to their bedroom window wakes them up the next morning at 6:30, as it always does. As they rise, the smell of exhaust seeps into the room. Michael sets another fire, his breath coming out in clouds. The thermometer reads eight below zero. While Michael goes outside to feed the geese, Carolyn makes instant coffee and toast. She put two pieces on a plate for Michael and two for herself and sits down at the table, crowded with the unopened mail. Michael comes back in with an armload of wood which clatters into the woodbox as he lets go.

"Michael, we aren't going to get back until late. How are we going to keep the place warm?"

Michael pauses, his nose cherry red. "I think it'll be okay."

"Maybe," she says. The toast eaten and the woodstove jammed once again, they bundle up. Michael scoops up Toto, and says, "Here we go again." And into the cold dawn, they set out for Egypt.

April 1985 Yankee magazine

THE BEANS OF EGYPT, MAINE *became a best-seller, selling 350,000, and was made into a movie entitled* Forbidden Choices. *Carolyn Chute's subsequent books cleaved to the same theme of the plight of the rural poor, which continues to be at the heart of Carolyn's life. Soon after* The Beans *became a best-seller, Carolyn and Michael had a house built in Michael's hometown in southwestern Maine, where they still reside. In spite of her success as an author, their living conditions remain much the same as they did in her house in Gorham: no running hot water, water delivered to the kitchen sink by garden hose, tin-roofed outhouse, and wood heat. In 1995 Carolyn and Michael founded the 2nd Maine Militia or, as she likes to call it, the "Wicked Good Militia." She invested in an industrial-size copy machine and devoted herself to sending out information packets to friends and sympathizers, manifestoes on revolution and the intricate ways government has of championing the rich and keeping the poor in their places. She describes her militia as "no-wing" and says that this country is not about Left vs. Right but instead, about Up vs. Down. She calls the militia members, of which there are more than four hundred, a mix of many types. "There are libertarians, secessionists, anarchists, progressives,*

Greens, an economics professor, a pediatrician, a rocket scientist, not exactly people who need me to speak for them, though some articles have made it sound that way," Carolyn explains.

In the meantime, Carolyn has published four more novels. In 2008, School on Heart's Content Road, *was published. She started writing this novel in the early 1990s and the manuscript grew to 2,600 pages. Eventually she decided to publish the book in parts, which she frequently refers to as her "five-ogy."* School on Heart's Content Road *is the first of the five. In its review,* The New York Times Book Review *said this: "Like a ferocious bulletin from an alternate universe — tumbling, pell-mell, brilliant and strange — comes this explosive and discomfiting fifth novel by Carolyn Chute."*

She does not take kindly to having her work described as "political."

"I'm more about questions than anything else. Humanity is, was, and forever shall be clever but not wise. I do not think of my work as political because I don't see any political avenue as a fix. Mostly, I write what I see."

Carolyn continues to live her life like a character in her own novel, living in the rural part of Maine, among many who have been disenfranchised and cast aside by the fast, affluent pace of the 21st century. She is their advocate and their defender. In spite of the AK47 she sometimes brandishes, her words are her most accurate weapon.

The Story of Ruth

Every once in a while, when the 21st century seems too close, I like to drive way Down East on the coast of Maine to the little fishing village of Cutler. When I'm there, I stop to visit with Ruth Farris. Ruth's house is near the harbor, the kitchen is always warm and she's always got a story to tell. If I can't make the nine-hour drive, I can read her column in the *Machias Valley News Observer.* She tells her stories there and she keeps us up to date on what's happening in Cutler — who came to visit whom, how many loons she spotted while out rowing her boat, what's up in her garden, what the weather might be. Ruth's columns are like the very best letters from home, full of news, advice, and lots of love.

Since 1961, Ruth has been writing for the paper. She doesn't think of herself as a writer, nor even a reporter. She is more like the keeper of the town. Often there is eloquence in her simplicity, poetry in her words.

There is a fallish feeling as I start off my items for this week. Last evening the moon gave a glow across the water as it slowly went down. It was the color of an orange.... As I rowed in to the beach one day, one sand peep flew out. I wonder how long it will stay.... What a change to the outer beaches where seas had pounded those places. It is interesting to see how the rocks have moved to form different shapes. Also, the ocean at times looks so blue. (September 1994)

Ruth is a hardy woman with circles of rouge on each cheek, little rising suns and lines on her face — worry lines, laugh lines, life lines that run deep, like roads on a map. Ruth has not traveled much, but she has a grip on her town, on her place here at the end of the American coastline. She doesn't mind sharing this with you, all the little events that make up a life in a small town, all the tiny miracles she observes in a single day.

Ruth Farris grew up Ruth Corbett, the daughter of the keeper of the light out on Little River Island. There were eight children, four boys and four girls, living in the red-roofed farmhouse beside the light. The island was big enough for a garden and there were boats to row. "We always had a good time," Ruth says, remembering back. The island is still in her view, very nearly, from her dooryard. If she steps out across the road, it's there, and if she puts her boat in and rows, as she does every day that the weather is nice, in twenty minutes or so she is back on the island. The light is automated now and the farmhouse boarded up, but it's all pretty fresh to Ruth, who is seventy-five but strong, her hands as big as a fisherman's.

Ruth lived on the island until she was twenty-four. She moved to the mainland, to Cutler, when she married Glen Farris, a lobster fisherman. Over these many years, from the windows of their house, Ruth has watched the great tides in Cutler harbor heave and sink, heave and sink, like a great timepiece that lives inside her — she can close her eyes and know where the tide line rests, the phase of the moon, the temperament of the wind.

Among other things, Ruth predicts the weather for her neighbors. In her column on September 17, 1985, she wrote: *What a warm week this has been! Almost too hot to stay outdoors...with these high tides, lucky not to have a storm. Having such hot weather could feed a hurricane up this way.*

Two weeks later, the paper featured photos of the devastation wrought by Hurricane Gloria.

Like the moon, there are many phases to Ruth's life. In her kitchen little painted figures line the shelf behind the big cast iron stove — pieces she has carved in the dark part of the winter, little gulls, wings out, and lobster buoys, white with deep red rings around them. In the summer she sells these carvings to tourists. In the back room is her desk, where she writes her column in longhand on a yellow pad. Beside the couch in her living room is a fine button accordion. She taught herself to play many years ago and now she plays for the Grange meetings and on evenings when she feels the need for a tune to cheer her.

The last time I went to Cutler, Ruth was at the sink, cutting up a big cod. Her son-in-law had caught it in his traps and brought it over when he got in to the dock. He often does this. Ruth, the daughter of the lighthouse keeper and the wife of a fisherman, cannot remember ever having bought a fish. Glenn died seven years ago but her son-in-law fills in on that score. In this house there has always been fish. He also brought her a lobster claw. She put the claw into a saucepan and set it on the hot part of the stove. The room was filling with the sweet steam of the lobster cooking. The cod, she was preparing to dry.

"Do you like dried fish?" she asked.

I told her I was not sure.

She took a jar from the shelf. It was filled with chunks of dried fish. She shook one out into my hand. I put it on my tongue. Ruth took one and popped it into her mouth like candy. The fish was soft and the flavor of fish was strong but not unpleasant. "Some people don't like it," she said.

She set the fillets in the bottom of a turkey roaster, covered them with a layer of salt and carried the pan to the shed. In a few days she'll set them out to dry. She took off her apron and hung it on a peg. "We'll have a row, if the wind will let us," she said, looking toward the harbor.

Ruth's boat is a big dory that her husband bought for $10 at auction many years ago. It was a boat from the island, sold off by the Coast Guard while they were keeping the light. "It's been a wonderful boat," she says. It is painted gray on the inside, bright blue, stem to stern. It bobs on the mooring just off the rocks across from her house. To get to it, she rows out in a little pram that she keeps on the beach. The tide is full, slack tide.

"I love to row," she has told me, many times. Now, as we settle into the craft, shipshape, and set out for the island, she says,"I can row just about as I did when I was young, better maybe. Rhythm. It's the rhythm. I love dipping those oars, feathering those oars, row and feather, row and feather, row and feather, skimming over the water."

Saturday evening I took a row in the calmness of the harbor. Such a beautiful sight to watch the sun set from a boat. The clouds were bright rose and how the trees stood so lovely against the clear sky and the peacefulness of the day. It was soothing to my mind. There were two ducks swimming out from the rocks and a blue heron standing in the water by the seaweed ledges. (July 1985)

Ruth pulls on the oars. The water around us moves swiftly. A wind has kicked up. The boat spins a little. "No," she says, "we're not going to move." If there is anything that Ruth knows about, it's the water in Cutler. We head back to the mooring.

If she cannot row, Ruth walks. She takes me up to the point of land beyond her house. It is woodsy and smells like a Christmas tree. On the way, she pauses to observe. Great clusters of berries hang on the mountain ash. A lot this year, she notes. "The crows eat a lot of them. They make an awful rumpus. They get drunk on those berries and sing and carry on."

Halfway up she stops beside a ledge that looks down onto the sparkling water. "This is my leaning tree," she says, putting her hand against the smooth bark of a big mountain ash. "Do you have a leaning tree? See, it's got a slant to it." She leans her full weight back against it, and seems at peace. "I love to hear the water slapping. A boat slicing through the water makes a lovely sound. I love it in the wintertime, when there's no leaves. I can look up and see the clouds. It's wonderful to come out and be by yourself. The noise of the world gets you all jangled, all worn out. Go out there and look, look at the little things and then come back to your house and you'll find you've rested your mind. It's worth a thousand dollars."

When her two daughters were small, Ruth used to take them out for walks on weekends. Sometimes they would camp. "We had an awfully good time together, my girls and I. Every weekend we had things planned, where we were going to go, what we were going to do. We would go camping, stay in there nights, sometimes in an old camp, different places where we would go hiking. My husband wasn't much for that. After he came in from the sea, he liked to come home and stay. So we'd take off."

Ruth's older daughter, Delia, is writing a book about her mother, a collection of Ruth's columns and memories of her mother. She may call it *The Book of Ruth*. "I guess it'll be the book of Ruth, all right," Ruth says, laughing, her warm brown eyes squeezed shut at the thought.

From a distance, the sound of a boat engine grows steadily closer, coming down the harbor. Ruth is still on her leaning tree, eyes still closed. "My son-in-law," she says.

"You know the boats, without looking?" I ask.

"Yes, I know the boats. That's him. Good boat. He built that boat. He's built a lot of boats. He's going out to lobster fish. I know that engine. Yes, I can tell."

Delia Farris spent this past weekend at home with her parents. She told us of her great trip to Cape Cod over Thanksgiving. (December 1985)

"Whenever I arrive back to Cutler, I close my eyes and just listen. Mama tells me about her garden and the things that we share in common." Delia Farris lives in Warren, mid-coast, about three hours from home. Delia comes home when she can, more so perhaps now that she is writing the book. When she was in her twenties, she left home and stayed away. Now she is in her forties and she is back. Delia has seen something of the world, has lived in different places, and she knows enough to know that her mother and her aunts and her uncles, all of them, are a disappearing tribe, the passing of a culture. She has come this weekend in time for the supper, one of her mother's bean suppers up at the church.

Outside the church, the foghorn moans. Inside, down in the basement where the tables are set, smells of baking beans and casseroles rise. Ruth is in the kitchen. It's steamy and warm. She's slicing brown bread. Delia is too late to get a chair at her aunts' and uncles' table so she and her friends sit two tables down. The Corbetts and the Cateses take up two whole tables. The rest of the town has eight to fill and they do, quickly, tucking their knees under the long tables, setting the napkins on their laps and waiting for the bowls to be brought so they can dig in.

"This is my best day," Ruth says of the monthly supper day. She has been up since dawn. Ruth has managed the Cutler suppers for nearly 50 years, since she was a young bride. Last night she made two pies, blueberry and apple, and set the beans to soak. This morning, she started the beans early in the big canning kettle. She uses a big bean, kidney beans or Jacob's cattle, and molasses, sugar, onions, pork ("not so much pork as I used to"), and vinegar. "The vinegar is what gives them so much flavor." She cooks the beans at her house until early afternoon, when she carries them over to the church, which is just a short walk from her back door. They continue to cook there, in the big church oven. In the meantime, she made a chicken casserole and found time to row out to the island. The weather was warm, and she saw loons. Her best day.

Ruth fills big bowls with her beans and the young ones ferry them out to the tables, along with baskets of biscuits, plates of steaming brown bread and an endless variety of casseroles. This is also her best day because it is when she is together again with her brothers and sisters. Two weeks ago, her brother, Neil Corbett, and his wife, Allie, celebrated their 50th wedding anniversary right here in the basement of the church. They squeezed 250 people in down here. "There were so many cars parked out on the road," Ruth told me, "it reminded me of the Fourth of July." The Fourth is a big holiday in Cutler, perhaps as big as any in the calendar year. Tonight, there are not that many but there is a good crowd because the suppers always bring people in from out of town. Neil and Allie are here, of course, and after they finish eating, they go out into the kitchen and help wash the dishes. So do Ruth's sisters, Kathleen and Florence. For all the preparation, it's over before you know it, the last of the diners scraping their plates for the last of that apple pie essence, sitting, sipping their coffee, and talking over the month's events.

They filter out, a group at a time. Purcell, Ruth's oldest brother, gets the broom and starts to sweep. He sweeps over to the piano and puts the broom down and settles onto the bench. A sad sweet song rolls out. Delia sneaks up behind her Uncle Purcell and snaps a picture, the flash lighting up the room like summer lightning. "I want to remember this," she says. "It won't last forever." She surveys the scene, her mother and her aunts and uncles wiping the dishes in the steamy kitchen, the piano music, the laughter coming out in small waves. "It's the companionship, you see, the companionship. It's not like this everywhere."

How I remember the foggy spells on the island. The bell a-banging night and day, the sound of the sea splashing around the ledges, seabirds calling, but we couldn't see them, the night hawks call and frogs singing in the swamp. Early in the morning, the gulls crying. It would be so thick, you couldn't see the call of nature. (June 1988)

Delia has made a difference to her hometown, even though she lives now at a distance. Six or seven years ago, she and Jasper Cates, an inveterate local fisherman, the family as ingrained and entwined in Cutler as the Farrises, broke the spirit of a developer who had come into town lusting after their coastline, the last of the completely undeveloped stretch of coast before Canada. He wanted the headlands, the magical pink granite bluffs that rise up high and protect Cutler from the blast of the open ocean. He wanted the headlands for house lots. Delia and Jasper worked tirelessly to defeat this man and his plans. In the end, they pretty much talked him out of it. The man had come from New York and planned to put an airport up on Western Head. His vanity license plate read "Skyscraper." Could there be any worse vision for Cutler? Delia thought not and on the eve of the sale, she sleuthed about, looking for that easy-to-spot license plate. She saw it parked at a motel in Machias and knocked on the motel door. He was in his skivvies. He had a map of Cutler spread out on his bed. She told him about the fog, how it sometimes comes in and sits in Cutler for days, as thick as chowder. "You won't be able to land your plane very often," she told him. The man went home to New York and came back with his wife. It was a terrible day, spitting snow. They tried to walk out onto the Head. Delia and Jasper don't know if they ever made it but they came back to their car and drove home. The deal was off. The land was subsequently acquired by the Maine Coast Heritage Trust, and now there is a trail up there to the headlands, a trail that Delia loves to walk, a trail in which she rightly takes a great deal of pride.

Delia has a passion for saving these places of natural beauty. It is the same passion with which she is writing *The Book of Ruth*. She has been working on the book for three years now. Many times, working on the book, she's cried for what's gone by. In the time since she started the book, eighteen of the old folks of Cutler have passed away. "They're leaving us," she says. "Pretty soon they'll all be gone."

No amount of talking can change that.

Do you know how I got through the change of life? I went out and built a camp from driftwood on the outer shores of Cutler. (June 1985)

The camps that Ruth built are mostly gone now, taken by time and wind and weather. It was something she did, building camps for herself and her girls. The camp she made out of driftwood washed off the seawall and she rebuilt it and then that one went over too. She pitch-poled it up on higher ground and it stayed, but eventually, it rotted. She and her grandchildren took it down not so long ago.

Susan Dowley, an artist in Lubec and a schoolgirl friend of Delia's, is working on pen and ink drawings to illustrate *The Book of Ruth*. She's known Ruth as long as she's known Delia. They are bent over a drawing of Ruth in her boat, pulling on her oars, the island in sight beyond her right shoulder. It doesn't quite look like Ruth, the lines on the face aren't right, the mouth is not Ruth's, somehow. They agree to use a photograph instead. "Sometimes, that's the only way," Delia says.

The other drawings are evocative. Ruth bent with a hoe in her garden. One of Ruth's camps, trees growing up close around it. Ruth raking blueberries. Ruth cutting fish to be dried. Another dilemma: Ruth dries her fish on the steps of a stepladder, setting her ladder in the sun in the shelter of her garage. She and her brother Purcell are the only ones left in Cutler who dry fish. Purcell nails his fish to the wall of his shop. Susan had a photograph of Purcell's fish, hung against the cedar shingles, a lovely composition. But it isn't the way Ruth dries her fish. Still, they like the image of Purcell's method better. But what would Ruth say? Delia studies the photograph. She thinks it over. "She'll say, 'It's all right, mine dry better anyways.'"

For the book, Delia has gathered what columns she can find. It hasn't been easy. The *Machias Valley News Observer* is a weekly and no one keeps back issues, least of all Ruth. Her columns are like conversations, gone tomorrow.

Ruth didn't start out to be a writer, never thinks of herself that way at all. "There was a woman, Corice Maker, who used to write the news of Cutler. When she wasn't able to do it any longer, I started in," Ruth recalls.

At first she followed Corice's lead, reporting on the town's comings and goings, who had visited with whom and who was in the hospital, in need of a card. Gradually, she felt more comfortable and began to include memories of her growing up years on the island and her observations of the natural world all around her. In Cutler, and beyond, she became known as Mother Nature. "Children gave me that name," she says.

People from away, summer folk, began to subscribe to the paper, just to read Ruth's column. Ruth spends one evening a week and sometimes part of the next morning putting the column together. She takes notes during the week about things going on in town. On Tuesday she sits down to write at her little desk in the back room. When she gets stuck, she gets up and goes for a walk or for a row and when she gets back, she writes about what she's seen, the birds, the goings-on in the harbor, the weather. On Wednesday she drives in to Machias to meet her deadline. For her efforts, she is paid $10 a week plus four free subscriptions. She receives letters from all over. "People come up to me and tell me how much pleasure they get from reading my column. It makes me feel good, that I've made people happy."

My kitchen table is a great place for me. I have been putting little traps together. I read, play dominoes, and listen to my radio and many good meals are enjoyed on these cold days. (February 1994)

When the day is over, Ruth likes to sit in her rocker beside the stove in the kitchen. On the table beside her is a stack of books — the Bible, *The Old Farmer's Almanac*, birding books. Glenn's death didn't slow her. It was the first item in her column that week: *My item to you all this week is a sad one for me to write as my husband, Glenn, passed away on the 29th of May. It's very hard for me to get the words together. We all face these sad times in life and with faith can carry on. He was always ready to help people with any problems. We had forty-one years together and I am blessed with a good family.*

Her column that day was shorter than usual, carrying only news of the town and this news of Glenn's death, no observations. But by the next week, she was back, telling her readers of her wanderings. Though she misses him, her life continues on, full and enriched by all that she sees around her, by all that she has brought to her life. "I've enjoyed every day that I have lived," she has said, many times.

Ruth gets up and goes into the living room. Accordion in hand, she sits down on the couch and begins to play, simple, dreamy tunes — "Over the Waves" and "Smile Awhile." Ruth plays with a great deal of emotion, her eyes closed, the notes drawn out and embellished.

Outside there are signs of the approaching winter. Boats have been brought in from their moorings and the harbor looks a little empty. Ruth has noticed fewer out-of-state plates coming down her road. Her sweet peas, on a trellis beside her back door, are ready to be cut down. She is talking about mowing her lawn for the last time and bringing the row-boat in to shore. Ruth does not dread the coming winter. "I look forward to winter," she says. "The time goes by fast. I never get bored."

In winter Ruth walks, and sometimes in a warm spell she takes the little punt out for a row. She reads and watches out her window for the weather. Neighbors call and ask for a forecast. They are maybe a little less vigilant. They may sleep a little later. They've got Ruth, keeping watch.

August 1995 Yankee magazine

RUTH SUFFERED *a crippling stroke in 1996 and she died in November of 1997. In that last year, daughter Delia came home to help care for her. She also helped her continue to write her column. The effects of her stroke left Ruth unable to speak or write but Delia was able to help her write the news of Cutler. "Together, we would sort out the town news and I'd write it up for her. And then together we would drive the copy down to the paper, right to the door and the editor would come out and Ruth would hand the column to him with great dignity."*

Delia has kept her mother's house and rents it out as a retreat for writers, artists, hikers, birdwatchers, musicians, people who love lighthouses, and those who love the coast of Maine. She kept the house just as it was when Ruth lived there, complete with all her lighthouse memorabilia and all her books. "People love, on a foggy or damp day, to tuck down and read one of Ruth's books," Delia says.

For a number of years, Delia was a social worker in mid-coast Maine but times are hard in Maine right now so she has once again moved home to Cutler. She is still working on her book about her mother and has had a few chapters published in magazines as she works on it. Ruth's brother, Purcell Corbett, is now ninety-two. His memory of times gone by is very sharp so Delia spends a lot of time with him, recording stories of his growing up years with Ruth and their brothers and sisters in the lighthouse. She is thinking about carrying on the tradition by doing a column for the Quoddy Tides, *as the* Machias Valley News Observer *is no more. Of her mother, she says, "Cutler, to this day, still speaks about Ruth. She was a big person in this town."*

For information about renting Ruth's house (known in the listing as Ruth's Retreat), go to Vacation Rentals by Owner, http://www.vrbo.com/190109

The Meaderborough Sampler

"ONE DAY I WAS picking peas, and you know how hard it is to see the green of the pea pod against the green of the leaves." It is a damp spring day and Elwyn Meader is in his garden, surrounded by young shoots, the start of another year's bounty. He occasionally lifts his cloth cap to scratch his balding head and when he does, he reveals a line of nasty red blackfly bites across his forehead. "And my wife said, 'Why don't you change the color of the pea pod so we can see it against the plant?' Well, that gave me a thought."

Elywn Marshall Meader is responsible for more of the food we northern gardeners grow than any other single human being. Grower of the most unusual five acres of gardens in the Northeast, he is the rare father who has been able to root his children where he can roam among them and keep them under his care forever.

Here on this small parcel in Rochester, New Hampshire, can be found the Miss Kim Lilac, the seeds for which he found while walking a Korean mountainside in the late 1940s and which he brought here to introduce to the New England landscape, a contribution notable enough for Elwyn Meader to rest on his horticultural laurels for the rest of his life. Not a chance. In good time, he developed the New England-hardy Reliance Peach; the beautiful purple-podded Royalty green bean; the cucumber that revolutionized the pickling industry; a sweet corn known as Midnight Snack; a compact New Hampshire midget watermelon; three different kinds of raspberries, two apricots; one apple; and four fruits that others have named after him: the Meader blueberry, the Meader persimmon, the Meader kiwi, and the Meader raspberry. That is just a primer — in almost any seed catalog a Meader creation can be found, but it takes a horticulturalist to spot it. In all, Dr. Meader introduced more than sixty varieties, from beets to peaches to chrysanthemums. The creators of the seeds that we grow, the foods that we eat, rarely hold the spotlight, though they are to the product what an author is to a book, a composer to a symphony, a painter to a canvas.

Dr. Meader is well into his seventies, with pale blue eyes behind small, round, rimless glasses and a smile that suggests mischief. A cloud of white whiskers rims his clean-shaven face. Dr. Meader deftly deflects the adulation most horticulturalists shine his way. Among plant breeders, Elwyn Meader is not only a legend but also an anachronism, general practitioner among specialists. He began his work in the late 1930s, working alongside Alfred Yeager at the University of New Hampshire. It was just as hybrids were coming into being, and his work there gave him free range of everything that grows up out of the earth. That makes him the envy of many today. A modern plant breeder makes beans or corn his life's work, and he may know nothing of apricots or kiwi fruit, any of which Dr. Meader knows like the road to home. "I've sometimes said that when it comes to plant material, I can't let anything alone," he says.

The peas make an interesting point. What he thought would provide the solution to his wife's complaint was a pea with a brightly colored pod. Maybe purple, he imagined.

"It's common to accentuate your successes and not say much about your failures," he says, only too happy to talk about the purple-podded pea that failed. There is a slowness about him — he moves slowly through the rows and speaks with care, each word separated from the next. These are traits that are mated to his field, in which it can sometimes take 20 years to know the results of an experiment. "I worked on that probably ten or a dozen years, and finally, as plant breeders say, I put the whole thing on the shelf. Why? Because I was never able to get a *sweet* purple-podded pea."

What did come out of those trials was a green bean with a purple pod. The Royalty, which grows a regal purple on the vine and turns green the moment it hits the heat in the pot, has been a success for over twenty-five years. "My wife won't can any other kind," he says of his magical invention.

From the road, Meader's gardens look much like any other in rural New Hampshire. The gardens are not edged and the lawns aren't mowed to putting-green perfection. Dandelions prosper in the spring. Though it may seem like an ordinary homestead — Mrs. Meader is often out in the gardens, picking, or hanging up the wash beside the sequoia tree, one of the many exotic species that grow here — these five acres of fields are his laboratory, to which scientists from all over the world send samples for him to grow and analyze. The little square of New Hampshire soil is a vast sampler stitched over long years by Dr. Meader, made up of ideas, inspirations, experiments, and a few failures. The Meaders have no children but they have a host of creations as beloved as any child on this green earth. His only help is his wife, Virginia, and his laboratory annexes are the kitchen (and the indispensable kitchen range); the cellar, where he keeps root crops through the winter; and the barn, where he keeps the Planet Jr. and hoes and cultivators, wood-handled tools of all description. It is also where he keeps the seeds, in reused jam jars and peanut butter jars, lined up on shelves over the other essential, the chest freezer. He has no greenhouses and the cold frames are beginning to go soft in the corners after decades of use. His work is outdoors, where things grow, and when the forecast for first frost is made, he does not cover his crops. Though he and Virginia subsist on the incredible yield of his gardens, his purpose in growing is really not so much to harvest as it is to observe. "I want to know," he says. "I want to know."

It is all here in the section of Rochester known as Meaderborough because this is where Meader was born and where Meaders have lived since 1700. It is Zone 4, as a gardener would describe it, where severe winters, with temperatures reaching twenty and thirty below zero, are the rule, a hardiness zone that suffers when it comes to variety. Or it used to suffer, before Dr. Meader started scheming. Lots of things — apricots, peaches, sweet potatoes, peanuts, tobacco, persimmons — enjoyed by those farther south are left out. But they are not left out of Dr. Meader's garden. Much of the breeding work he has done is aimed at cold hardiness. He doesn't want to move south, doesn't care for heat. He likes it where he is, where he feels he was meant to be. "I'd rather bring the southern things farther north," he says.

He can't change the climate, but to some degree he knows, he can change the plant. A lot of his plants are Asiatic in origin, many brought back with him from a trip to Korea forty years ago. "Because that's where we get hardy materials. Plants can travel right around the globe at the same latitudes very nicely, but when you try to bring them from southern latitudes into northern latitudes you get into trouble."

Dr. Meader's mind does not move along national boundaries but along the Hardiness Zones. These should divide the world, he thinks, not Great Walls and Iron Curtains. "What I think of Winston Churchill and Joe Stalin and Franklin D. Roosevelt sitting around a table dividing up the world on the 38th parallel isn't fit to print." What it means to Dr. Meader is that there are places in the world off-limits to him, plants about which he doesn't know as much as he would like. He knows that his Reliance peaches are grown in Siberia and that Royalty green beans were being grown with great enthusiasm in Great Britain and in Africa before they were ever marketed in this country. Climbing on an arbor across the road from his house, among other kiwis, is a kiwi from Lithuania. Smuggled, he says. A very necessary part of his work, he says.

HENRY, A SLIGHTLY crazed orange cat, follows Dr. Meader wherever he goes, mewing and squeaking. A black rooster, amidst a flock of red hens, *urr-urr-r-urrrs* all day long from the pen beside the persimmons, and when he passes by, Dr. Meader *urr-urr-r-urrrs* back at him. There are bluebirds here, common as robins, and hummingbirds dart and weave, drunk on the amplitude of nectar. Orioles scheme for a break into the netted blueberry patch. Across the road Dr. Meader keeps a hive of honeybees, perhaps the most fortunate honeybees in New Hampshire. The season never seems to end, and there are blooms from one end of the frost to the other. Like a Whitman's Sampler, there is something of everything.

Outside the parameters of frost, there is lettuce. Dr. Meader has several different kinds of lettuce growing in a square in his garden. He likes lettuce. He shows off his red romaine, which was a happy accident. "I was running lettuce trials, mixing heads of romaine with ordinary lettuce, and next spring some volunteers came up in the garden." Dr. Meader goes over his garden carefully in the spring, before plowing, checking to see what came up on its own. "I noticed one that was red. So I took it up and grew the seed. There's no doubt in my mind that it's better than any red romaine in the trade. Because there isn't any other."

Dr. Meader leans over and snaps off a different lettuce leaf that is delicate, crinkly, green, and pokes it into his mouth. "This year I learned something as far as satisfying the woman in the house," he says. Breakfast is the only meal in the Meaders' house that lacks a salad. "I had a lettuce in here with kind of crumpled leaves. I brought it in the house, and she said, 'Don't bring any more of that inside.' She didn't like the color of it because she couldn't tell the color of the sand from the lettuce when she washed it. And the sand sticks in the crumples. Well. So much for that." He stoops over the next row. "Here is Buttercrunch. It's always been one of my favorites but after it rains, it's hard to get it clean." But then why, it seemed reasonable to ask, does she accept the Buttercrunch? "She doesn't accept it anymore. She now insists on this type." Dr. Meader plucks a green, smooth, palm-shaped leaf. This is called Nancy, and it's just as good eating quality as Buttercrunch but easier to wash." It is not a type he developed — he believes it came from France. "So now we plant Nancy, not Buttercrunch, because I don't like to miss my meals in the house."

There is only one thing: he wishes it were a deeper green in color. "But I could put on green-colored glasses when I eat it, I suppose."

WORKING TOWARD the perfect vegetables, the perfect fruits: it's an odd vocation. Most who are involved with it say it is as much an art as it is a science. Asked to assess Elwyn Meader's contribution to the plant world, Rob Johnston, founder and owner of Johnny's Selected Seeds, replies, "What contribution did Van Gogh make to the art world? Meader spent a life developing a multitude of plant varieties. He also has the ability to know when something is good. It's a little like being a scout for a baseball team. You have all these young talents and you can't keep everything. With plants it just goes crazy after a while and you have to make choices. Meader knows how to make choices."

Dr. Gerald Dunn, a plant breeder who worked with Meader at the University of New Hampshire, agrees that a good plant breeder has to have a good eye, and Meader has a good eye. "When Meader went to develop the Meader persimmon, he had about a hundred seedlings in pots out in the shed and come spring he dumped them out behind the chicken house and he picked out the one that had green shoots. Sounds simple, doesn't it? You have to be able to recognize a reliable selection when you see it. Meader used to walk down the aisles of the greenhouse and select the right seedlings. Meader could tell from the color of the leaf on a watermelon seedling what color the rind would be."

Meader receives no royalties for his inventions, and he doesn't patent his seeds, as has become increasingly popular among younger plant breeders. The rewards are small. One of his less celebrated contributions was straightening the neck of the butternut squash, some forty years ago. "Well, people have forgotten all about it now because everybody's got straight necks. I crossed the butternut with the Serikubi from Korea, and from that we got a strain of butternut with all straight necks. Most people don't know about that," he says. These details must be pried from Dr. Meader, who is unable to list all of the varieties of fruits and vegetables he has brought into this world. He has no list and cannot suggest a source. This does not concern him. I must consult others to compile one, and we all agree that without Dr. Meader's help, the list may never be complete but it would not be incorrect to state that there are more than sixty varieties of plants, from beets to peaches to kiwis to chrysanthemums, to his credit. And when he says, "I think I've done a few things in my lifetime to help my fellow man," he is praising his profession as much as anything.

More celebrated than the neck of the butternut is the blueberry, at least to Meader and some of his Rochester neighbors. From the half acre of blueberry bushes at the far end of his cultivated land, Meader is able to pick blueberries in time for the Fourth of July, and from then on the bounty is at times embarrassing. "It's amazing," he says, "what anybody can do with blueberries, if they pay attention to them and know the rules of the game. More people have difficulty in growing blueberries because they don't realize how much different they are from other garden culture. If we're going to talk blueberries, we ought to go down nearer to them." I am back again, on a midsummer visit, and Dr. Meader leads me past the tomatoes and through the rows of corn, past a small orchard of fruit trees — some look like three different trees banded together (a result of grafting) — down to the blueberries.

The two sides of his garden are divided, as if by equator. One is acid, the other alkaline. "When I work with the plants on that side, I'm a different man from when I get down here on the blueberries. But we agree to talk with each other," he says, dry humor crackling.

Successful blueberries are all a matter of soil preparation. Apparently the soil here was good and is good. The blueberries, some of them, are as big as dimes, sweet and juicy. Dr. Meader nabs a berry as he passes a bush laden with berries growing in great clusters like grapes. He pops it in his mouth. He stops, picks two more, and passes them to me.

He pauses a moment to share his favorite recipe. "I've come to the place where, as delicious as blueberries are with a crust wrapped around them, I'd just as soon pick some, put them in a pan, sprinkle a little sugar over them and turn the burner on low, just so it draws out the juice. Then get a spoon and sit down and be happy."

About thirty years ago the land where his blueberries are was a pine grove. He cleared the trees and planted the blueberries — perfect soil. "I never had the soil tested on it. I could just look at the plants that were growing on it and know what it was. People struggle trying to acidify soil," he says. "They may be able to find the right conditions just by moving over a little on their land to where the soil is already partly or totally acidic. Why fight when you can do it the easy way?"

The blueberry patch is covered with netting that he stitched himself, by hand, a dozen or so years ago. The frame is of cut trees. He cultivates the blueberries about twice a year and he banks their roots with pine needles and occasionally sawdust, though he finds that the sawdust can be taken away in a big wind while the pine needles cannot.

It takes five years to get anywhere with a blueberry plant. "What I suggest is, get four or six plants. Then put up nets. When people tell me they've just put in some blueberries, I ask, 'Have you got your nets yet?' emphasizing the *yet* because the birds love them. Take a patch like this. Without a net, a flock of two or three hundred starlings can swoop down and clean me out in two or three hours."

On this half acre there are fifty-two different types of blueberries — there is the Bluejay and the Collins and the VM22 and the Blue Etta, and of course, the Meader. On just one day in early August, Dr. Meader opens his blueberry patch to the public — the "public" being those to whom he has sent an invitation — for a pick-your-own. There is no limit; they can pick as much as they want or are able to within the time set.

Last year they picked three-quarters of a ton. He cautions that it is a madhouse. "Bring your shin guards," he deadpans.

THE MORNING that Dr. Meader has selected for the pick-your-own is hot and misty. By quarter of seven several dozen pickers are lined up by the porch, where they must wait until Dr. Meader gives the go-ahead. All eyes are on Dr. Meader who is standing on his porch. Pretty soon he gently lifts his hand and says, "Go on down." As soon as they go through the gate, they start to search for the bush that served them so well last year.

The dew is as heavy as rain on the bushes where the blue fruit waits —a shade of blue so particular that Dr. Meader claims he has never seen it photographed successfully. "It's a blue like the sky," he has said. A continuous stream of people come down the lawn, bearing buckets and baskets and flats. Others leave, lugging the fruit. People chat as they pick, and there is laughter moving gently through the bushes. One man, who is quickly filling his buckets, hears the laughter and says to his companion, "Everybody is happy today!"

Elwyn Marshall Meader could not imagine greater riches than that.

THE TERRIBLE August heat passes and a late October visit finds Dr. Meader on his porch, seated at a painted pine table, prying seeds from a small watermelon, as a cold rain falls from a low sky. He rises in genteel greeting. On his porch are boxes filled with fruits — a box with four Chinese pears, a package of ladyfinger potatoes — offerings from other breeders and nurserymen who hope for his critique. "I get most anything," he says as he shows me these oddities. He also sends. The week before, a small parcel had arrived at my office. In a small box that once held envelopes, Dr. Meader had nestled two Meader persimmons and a Meader kiwi into a cradle of Styrofoam peanuts.

The kiwi grow like grapes on an arbor across from his house. His success in propagating them here, so far north, prompts him to harvest most of them for their seed. He sends these seeds worldwide to interested growers. The persimmons grow on trees, three of them, beside his henhouse. Though the kiwis are exciting and the vines quite beautiful, the persimmons seem the most remarkable northern fruit. Though most cannot survive north of New Jersey, Dr. Meader has hardened these. They do not begin to ripen until the last part of October, after the leaves have fallen and there have been several hard freezes. They are his late-fall treats and only the worst weather would prevent him from going out to the trees and picking one or two for eating on the spot.

The rain of this day is not bad enough, so Dr. Meader leads me to the trees beside the henhouse. He pushes against the trunk of the largest of the three — like most young fruit trees, they have slender trunks and the branches reach outward — and gives it a shake. Bright orange fruit thump to the ground. The leaves, which are broad and exotic, litter the ground and Dr. Meader pushes among them with his index finger and comes up with a handful of the fruit and gives me two. The Japanese call these "date-plums" and that is close. They have a rich, sweet flavor, flesh with a texture like peaches. A better source of Vitamin C than citrus, the persimmons are smaller than the sort found in some supermarkets, and the skin is tender and sweet, not puckery. There are no seeds in these Meader persimmons, the only kind of which this can be said. Dr. Meader has discovered that he can go out to the tree in mid-January, pluck the rock-hard fruits from the frozen branch, bring them indoors and snack on them when they thaw.

On our way back from the persimmon grove, he shows me a pear tree with leaves that turn fire red in the fall and red-stalked celery he will put in his cellar for the winter. He shows me an apple tree that bears five kinds of apples, the branches grafted on, not with pitch but with ordinary caulking compound. He points out a burgeoning chestnut tree, one he brought from Korea so many years ago. He's sent all the chestnuts to Oregon, where they will be raised as trees. "I could have taken them down to Calef's [the local country store]," he says, "and sold them there, but I figure it's better for mankind that they become trees."

The rain picks up and Dr. Meader invites me into his kitchen, his workplace of fall, winter, and spring. The kitchen is as important as the garden. It is here that he and Virginia make the cooking trials for so much of the produce raised experimentally. Virginia often simply includes the item in question in the meals, but she won't serve just *anything*. "My wife is kind of conservative," he had told me earlier, "so sometimes I have to do a little cooking on the sly."

Dr. Meader and his wife, who is busy making something that smells wonderful, are Quakers, and the kitchen reflects this with its clean, bare walls, pressed tin ceilings, simple painted cupboards, and big black iron stove, which heats their household water and in which Dr. Meader enjoys making baked beans, spiced with an apple and an onion. The two of them, just this past week, have finished canning for the season, and in the dark cellar the reward is lined up: 300 jars. "Let it snow!" Dr. Meader exclaimed at the finish. (In addition to the stored foodstuffs, it should be noted that Dr. Meader cuts all his firewood, with hand tools.)

Beside the stove is a pine table, his desk. He offers me the rocker beside it and sits himself down. He turns on the tiny lamp and the tea-colored shade brightens the dark day. The desk is stacked with letters and catalogs — a printer's proof of an entry into a seed catalog introducing his giant kohlrabi, a catalog that lists the Meader Hardy Kiwi, an order form from a catalog that lists his raspberries. Letters arrive from all over the world, seeking his advice or asking his cooperation in studies. A great deal of his time is spent in correspondence, here at this kitchen desk, the letters done out in longhand, for he never learned to type.

Dr. Meader is nearing eighty and knows that in this field of extremely delayed gratification, he will not see the results of some of his trials. "I only wish I were fifty years younger. When you get nearer to eighty than seventy-five, you don't plan many twenty-year projects — just ten-year projects." In spite of his enormous contribution to the world of plants, Dr. Meader has never written a book and does not intend to. It would take too much time, he says, time he would rather use developing new plants. "Coming up is the Fall Bush Cherry," he says. "That's a culmination of twenty-five years' work. If I'd taken the time to write a book, there never would have been a Fall Bush Cherry."

He is often asked why he does not want more credit for all that he has given the world; he is often asked what reward there is for him, since it clearly has not made him rich or famous, and he answers, "The fun of having done it. That's enough, isn't it? Sure. Sure."

July 1989 Yankee magazine

WHEN DR. ELWYN MEADER *died in 1996, it was said to have been the end of an era. His farm in Rochester is no longer a farm, merely a house, stripped of the exotic plantings that once grew there. It can be surmised that after he died, samples of much of the plant material that Dr. Meader propagated there were shared with friends and collaborators in plant breeding. Dr. Alan Eaton, a professor at University of New Hampshire who knew of Dr. Meader only by reputation had this to say: "After Professor Meader retired, he continued to work on his breeding projects at home. His methods were a bit unconventional. Not that his breeding techniques were unconventional; it was his selection of material to retain and release that differed so much from other university plant breeders. They typically look for varieties that can benefit commercial agriculture. Professor Meader had an eye for things that would interest backyard gardeners. Since he made selections that way, he developed and retained ties with plant breeders around the world who shared that goal." But Dr. Eaton was unable to find any faculty members at UNH who had retained any of Dr. Meader's plant material or are continuing his work. It was unique.*

Those who admired Dr. Meader often spoke first of his unselfishness in sharing his work and his ideas around the globe and so many of us have his legacy growing right in our gardens, unheralded. He often said that the most valuable thing he'd ever done was to give things away.

In Love with North Adams

THE CITY SITS CROUCHED in a gap that runs through the Hoosac mountains, that great rollercoaster that starts to build somewhere west of Charlemont and doesn't end until it hits New York State. Joe Manning has come to tell its story.

"Right here, on Bank Street, it was just a little alley, it was so narrow." He's gesturing with his hands to show what isn't there when he stops, caught in an out-of-body experience. "I speak of it almost as if I knew it myself, even though I was never here."

"Here" is North Adams, Massachusetts, and Joe Manning is looking back into a past he never knew, a past he has only recently reconstructed in a book he published himself three years ago, a past that he continues to unravel in preparation for his next book. We are standing in the middle of town — an odd, open expanse that feels more like a prairie than the center of a city, a city that, over the past one hundred and twenty-five years, has morphed from a small struggling Western Massachusetts hill town (1800), to a thriving industrial city (1930s), to a depressed and empty place (1980s) to the new and exciting home of the largest center for contemporary art in the United States. A big, sprawling past for this fifty-nine-year-old Connecticut social worker to take on by himself.

"What we are walking through is the heart of North Adams. It was gutted out of here in the 1960s and 1970s, under the banner of urban renewal. This was just nothing but dirt for ten years. The carnival used to come into town and set up here because it was the biggest space around."

Starting in 1969 and over the course of three years, wrecking balls leveled more than one hundred buildings, pulverizing the heart out of North Adams. Although more than thirty years have passed since that wrenching time, to the surprise and discouragement of virtually everyone in town, nothing has ever replaced what was taken away.

"It seemed exciting at the time," Joe Manning says of urban renewal, which history, at least in this place, has proven an unfortunate misnomer. "It was like a circus, I mean, for three years, the city was overwhelmed with this activity, this show, all the old-timers would stand out on the sidewalk and watch it. And they thought that when these buildings came down, it was going to bring new life to our city. It wasn't until about ten or fifteen years later that they said, *What the hell did we do to ourselves?* It was too late by then."

Joe Manning, a trim redhead with the build of a long distance runner and the mischievous blue eyes of a leprechaun, fell in love with North Adams in a way that still mystifies him. It began as a whim in 1996 when his wife, Carole, read an article about an amazing-sounding art museum being built in an abandoned factory building in North Adams.

She read it out loud to him one evening and he stopped what he was doing and said, "I don't recall ever having been there." Intrigued, he looked for North Adams on his map and found it at the outer edge of Massachusetts, near the Vermont border. One Sunday, not too long after that, they took the two-hour drive from their home in Torrington, Connecticut.

They stopped at the Miss Adams Diner for a late breakfast and then descended into downtown North Adams. "We parked on Main Street and walked for several hours, marveling not only at the strange and haunting beauty of the city, but also at the odd lack of anyone on the streets."

The only disappointment of that day was the discovery that the museum they had read about was still three years from completion. The Massachusetts Museum of Contemporary Art, known to all as Mass-MOCA, never ceased to be of interest to Manning, but his focus shifted. That first journey was the first of some two hundred and fifty trips Joe Manning would make to North Adams, visits that culminated in the publication of his first book, *Steeples*, and the research for a second, which he has titled *Disappearing into North Adams* because that is what he does when he comes here.

Maybe it was some odd collision of his needs and the needs of this sleeping giant of an old industrial city that was slowly being awakened by, of all things, art. But around the same time that Joe happened onto North Adams, he was starting to write poetry again. He hadn't written any poems since he was in high school. The day he and his wife went to North Adams, they were sitting at the local sandwich shop, known to everyone as the Bean. It's a big, high-ceilinged place that serves sandwiches named after some of the more legendary buildings that were demolished during urban renewal. Sitting there, he thought, this would be such a great place to sit and write poetry. So he said to Carole, "Maybe I'm totally out of my element, but I want to come back here one day and see if I can write some poetry."

He thought he should come at sunrise, he didn't know why, but he got up really early one Saturday morning. It was dark when he turned onto Rt. 8 and headed north into the Berkshires. He arrived in North Adams just as the sun was rising and the light and shadows on the old storefronts were like something out of an Edward Hopper painting. He sat at the Bean and took notes and walked and walked, up and down the hills. "Within a week, I had six poems," he says.

All of these poems are in his book. He calls one of them "Elderly Housing." In his early wanderings around the city, he discovered a place called St. Joseph's Court, an elderly housing project located in the old grade school. Most of the residents, he discovered, had been to school there many many years ago.

"I was sitting across the street and looking at the building and wondering what it was like for people who went to school there to be there now. I started thinking about an old woman living there and how she might feel."

And so he wrote the poem, based on this old woman of his imagination. After he wrote the poem, he took it to St. Joseph's Court and showed it to the director and asked her what she thought of it. She said, "I know a woman just like this," and she introduced him to Julia White, who was ninety-seven years old and had come to North Adams from Latvia with her Russian parents when she was ten months old.

"She was just such a wonderful, funny, lovely person. I asked the director, 'Can you get me any more people to interview?' And, of course, once word got out, everyone in St. Joseph's wanted to be interviewed."

By then, he had started to think about a book. The richness of the history of the town and the warmth of its people had won his heart.

"I didn't really know anything about North Adams, I didn't want to tell people anything. I just wanted these people to speak and tell their stories."

Steeples gives voice to some twenty-five of North Adams' older residents. Their oral histories recall the days when the empty place that Joe encountered in 1996 were "shoulder to shoulder with people and the streets were crowded with cars." Not all the voices are old: Audrey Witter is in her thirties and came to North Adams from Pittsfield to open a cafe. She found the right location, an old clothing store on Main Street, and she spent weeks sandblasting the walls and ceilings of the old building, to expose the bricks. When she was done, she tackled the rest and soon opened the Appalachian Bean Cafe, aka "the Bean," the place that inspired Joe to write about North Adams.

"North Adams is beautiful," she said to Joe for his book. "Since the mayor got the street done, it's really gorgeous. I ride my bike all over, and when you get up on the roads with the big hills, you can see everything. Who wouldn't want to live here?"

With testimonies such as these and the vivid descriptions of the city as it once was, as well as the black and white photographs of the demolition of the downtown, the book is a beautiful portrait of a place.

But, Joe Manning maintains, it's not about nostalgia. "I was not trying to write a history book. I was trying to capture a snapshot of the city in 1997, to recognize it as a city in transition."

Joe Manning's favorite place to walk in the city is on the railroad tracks, the very channel that brought the first vivacious wave of life to North Adams back in 1875. The Hoosac Tunnel has been called one of the greatest engineering feats of the 19th century. For twenty-four years the railroad tunnel was blasted through nearly five miles of granite. From drowning, fire and explosions, one hundred and ninety-five lives were lost but in the end, the opening of the Hoosac Tunnel brought the railroad and prosperity to the city and to the area west of it. It also brought the people — Italians, Irish, Scottish, Russian, Welsh, French — workers from all over the world poured into this mountain town, lured by the enticing prospect of earning two dollars a day.

Joe Manning loves knowing what the railroad brought to North Adams but what he loves most about the railroad tracks is the view. "You get to look at the way people would have seen the city from the train, when they came that first time, particularly the French Canadians. Moving here to work at the mill, their first glimpse of North Adams would have been from the train."

I follow Joe through a short tunnel which is pitch-black and drizzling cold water from its arch. The trains still run through North Adams, but Joe knows the schedules like his twin daughters' birth date. At the end of the tunnel, we reemerge into the sunlight. "Look up," he says, "look up!" Looming above us and virtually teetering at the edge of the tracks is the big façade of a tenement that rises five stories and appears to be all but abandoned. "This should be on the Historic Register," he says, flushed with enthusiasm. "I've read through the city directories and most of the people who lived here were laborers. Can you imagine what it would have been like, in the heyday of the trains, the *noise* inside that building?"

Joe Manning likes looking through other people's eyes. Through his interviews, he has looked through the eyes of Julia White and Tony Talerico, Hulda Jowett and Audrey Witter, Silvio Lamarre and dozens of others and there he has found something beautiful. He has also looked through the windows of the city's remaining structures, the flatiron building, the Newberry Block, 85 Main, and through all this, he has seen beauty.

He can't always explain what it was that drew him to North Adams nor what it is that holds his fascination. Perhaps it was the fact that he was about to retire from so many years of carrying heavy caseloads as a social worker. "In discovering North Adams, I kind of discovered who I am, at an important moment in my life. I'm sure there are other places but I came upon North Adams at that time in my life when I was looking."

Just before *Steeples* was published, Joe threw a party at the Bean for everyone who had been interviewed or otherwise involved in the book's development. He gave out free copies to all the people in the book and offered a tribute to each of them. "That was one of the happiest moments of my life," he says, without reservation.

When the book was officially published, four hundred people showed up at the North Adams library and Joe was there for five hours, talking and signing. This connection is what it was all about anyway.

"It was the people, they take so much pride in their heritage. There's so much love here, for what they have, for what they had. I'm hoping the people here will get over the grief for the city they lost and that the young people will learn from it. *Steeples* is not about North Adams, in many ways. It's about the country, it's about many other cities and towns. I don't want people to forget what happened here."

With his already substantial investment in time and money, the book was not destined to make Joe much money. Though he barely broke even, he donated a portion of the sales to benefit the city's public library.

When MassMOCA finally opened, Joe Manning was the first in line to enter, not by design, just by chance. He likes that small fact. The museum is a triumph and Joe Manning seems to feel as proud of it as if he had built it himself. A forty million dollar project fused into the ruins of the enormous thirteen-acre factory complex that was, in the 19th century, a textile mill and in the 20th an electronics factory, MassMOCA opened in May of 1999. "Exactly thirty years after the wrecking ball rammed into that first building on the main street of North Adams," Joe points out. "MassMOCA is a much more reasonable way of renewing a city than tearing it down."

Our walking route has taken us down the railroad tracks, through the cemetery, and onto River Street, and the entrance to the big new museum. Inside, in the cavernous industrial space, there is an installation by Robert Rauschenberg that takes up the space of a football field. It is titled *The 1/4 Mile or 2 Furlong Piece*, as if the space it takes is more important than the message it conveys. An adjoining gallery reveals what looks like huge, elephantine turds on a freshly varnished floor. In another yawning space, we walk past wrecked automobile parts, welded together as sculpture.

Some visitors find these displays shocking but Joe walks right past them and stands at the window. "The star to me is what you see out the window, the old tenements, the river running by. This is what the workers saw while they were working."

He also loves the walls, which have been left with the many layers of paint from the decades, indeed, centuries of work that gave this mill its story, that gave this city its story. To Joe, these streaks of gray and pink and green are like the best abstracts. "The first time I came, I told the curator that they have natural art on the walls and he said, 'We're afraid that people will come here only to look at the buildings and that they won't see the art.'"

No art in North Adams seems lost on Joe Manning. From Mass-MOCA, we walk down the hill. Even after a long day of walking, his steps quicken here. "At the end of this, you get the best view, the best view of all. You get to see the flatiron building. It's like a ship coming in. I can never get enough pictures of that. No. Never. It's so beautiful. Just so beautiful."

October 2001 Yankee magazine

SINCE THIS ARTICLE *was published, Joe Manning says, "I've continued to grow as a writer and as a historian." His fascination with North Adams has expanded into many projects. MassMOCA invited him to write an introduction to one of their books, which led, loosely to a project tracking the descendants of photographs Lewis Hine took of child laborers. He discovered many of them lived in North Adams.*

He lives in Northampton and travels to North Adams about one hundred times a year. "It takes me about an hour to get there," he says, "one very beautiful hour." He also does a lot of volunteer work in North Adams and in their schools. "I've been retired now for almost eleven years and they have been the eleven most exciting years of my life," he says. "I've done a lot of things I've never done before and a lot of things I never thought I would do."

Steeples *is in its third printing.* Disappearing into North Adams *has sold even more. "A lot of people ask why I have never moved to North Adams. For me, going to North Adams is still an adventure," he says. "If I lived there, I'd probably be complaining about why my road hasn't been paved. I like to remain objective. But North Adams has really become a very big part of my life. All my friends are there now."*

To find out more about Joe's diverse projects or to order one of his books, go to his website: www.morningsonmaple.com. He has all the articles ever written about North Adams on this site and much more.

An Affair to Remember

In southern California, the streets run in grids and palm trees grow up like points from the edges of houses, placed on perfect squares of the desert earth. On one of these streets, where the lawns are so exact, they look razor cut and hand colored, there's a bend in the road and in that curve, set back from the road, stands a little red-and-white bungalow, around which everything grows differently. In the ample front yard, no grass grows, only tangles of wild ivy. The trees that rise up and shelter the roof are not palms. They are olive and persimmon and, in the backyard, a big old gnarly elm tree has grown so wide it's joined into the corner of the house, as if it were part of the structure. A garden of roses and gardenias carries on in the midst of this ever-increasing summer refuge of shade. A small, frayed, typewritten card is fastened to the front door with thumbtacks:

POSITIVELY
NO Jehovah's Witnesses!
NO Mormons or proselytizers of any kind.
NO solicitors for good causes or charities.
NO pedlars of any kind.
ALL POETS WELCOME!

Inside, things grow differently too. This is the home of Jean Burden, who every week for the past forty-five years has received packages filled with poems, sent to her from the *Yankee* offices in New Hampshire, a place where she has never lived and only rarely visited. Jean, a small woman wearing a pink robe and leaning on a bamboo staff, welcomes me into the home where she has lived since the big elm behind her house was a young tree. The elm, she has told me, is a reminder of her own Midwestern roots. It is November. When I left New Hampshire the night before, I was wearing sweaters, a scarf, and mittens. Now I am sleeveless and intoxicated by the warm air coming down off the San Gabriel Mountains which are set like a painted backdrop to this desert backstreet. On the trees, I see lemons. In her garden, I see pink roses, blooming.

I am here to talk about poetry, a subject Jean can talk about without ever tiring. Indeed, poetry is so vital to her that she surrounds herself with its essence. Even her gardener is a poet. "We talk about literature more than we talk about the garden," she had once told me. For these many years, her work for *Yankee*, from this faraway place, has been the center of her varied and interesting life and her work has been *Yankee*'s voice of passion.

"I hear a great big *thud* on the porch, and I know the package of poems has arrived. It doesn't matter how many years have passed, I have never felt anything but excitement when that package from *Yankee* arrives," Jean says. Her bright, gem-like eyes shine as she speaks.

With all those years behind her, Jean is a glass through which we can look back at the rich decades of our 20th century American poetry heritage. Her years spent as *Yankee*'s poetry editor are only a small portion of the exotic life that she has led, which includes participation in an early clinical experiment with LSD and deep friendships with a kaleidoscope of poets, ranging from Alan Watts to Howard Nemerov to Mark Strand and, notwithstanding, with the founder of *Yankee* magazine, Robb Sagendorph. There is no poetry without love, she would say.

Inside the packages, three hundred, four hundred hopeful poems come to her and she sits down at the desk in her small study, the windows of which are shaded by a lemon tree, and she reads. From all these poems, she selects one, or maybe two, maybe none, carefully folding the verses and tucking them back into the return envelopes, sending them back, sometimes with a scribbled comment, often with nothing but the notice of its return. A sad task for one who has written poems since she was seven and who has had published poems in such diverse journals as *Poetry, The Hudson Review, Saturday Review*, and virtually every distinguished journal, and hence one who has received many of these same returned envelopes, returned hopes. It is the one poem she holds and prepares for publication that redeems all the rest.

A life-long free spirit, Jean is a woman whose beauty is at least as treasured as her poems. She no longer drives a car nor even goes out of her house very often, yet she keeps a closet bulging with colorful fashion statements, capes and scarves, sequins and satins. She wears her reddish blonde hair, which falls full and wavy and past her shoulder blades, pulled back in ribbons. If you come upon her from behind, you might think her a very young, very beautiful woman.

By the time she encountered *Yankee*, Jean was in her forties and she had been an editor and writer of published poems for a long while. It was with an article, not a poem, that she first approached the magazine. Like her poems, she folded her typewritten pages into an envelope, addressed it to *Yankee,* Dublin, New Hampshire, placed a stamp in the upper, right-hand corner, and sent it on its way. This was back in 1954 and the magazine, which had been founded almost twenty years earlier in a one-room shed behind the Sagendorph family home on a hill outside of Dublin, was doing well. In the beginning, Robb used to say that every single one of his one hundred subscribers were his friends and neighbors, coerced to subscribe, but now there were also readers he did not know and he had already hired a helper or two, a bold move for a dedicated penny pincher. At that time, he had one employee, a woman who took care of the books. His wife, the artist beaTrix Sagendorph, provided paintings for every cover. Robb took care of editorial matters. And so the article (whose subject Jean no longer recalls) came to him from Jean Burden, with the return address of southern California. "I had no idea what kind of a magazine *Yankee* was," Jean recalls now. "I didn't know that everything in it had to be about New England."

Robb wrote back to her, not a form rejection but a hand-written letter. Jean recalls that it was "so full of wry humor and folksy charm, it sounded as though it had been written by a craggy, aging New Englander, probably sitting at a rolltop desk with his feet on the fender of a Franklin stove, a knitted scarf draped around his stooping shoulders."

Sitting down at her typewriter in her kitchen, she wrote a reply, the first and last time she ever remembers answering a letter of rejection.

And so began a correspondence between the two, east to west, west to east. In the months that followed, they told each other the stories of their lives, revealed the hidden places of their spirits, and exchanged photographs. Jean studied the black and white image Robb sent to her. "There was the Lincolnesque face with crinkly eyes and sad mouth, the stooping, bony, six-foot-four-inch frame. He was in his fifties, but he looked a good ten years older." She further discovered that he really did have a Franklin stove and he even wore a wool shawl on bitter winter days.

It seemed unlikely they would ever meet. The letters sustained them. "I loved his letters — gossipy, droll, ardent, fatherly, bawdy, poetic, often almost exalted with the wonder he felt for life, especially now that I was at the center of it," she says now.

Then one day he called her on the telephone. (In those days, long distance calls were prohibitively expensive and rarely indulged in, especially by the thrifty.) It was the first time they had ever heard each other's voices. Soon afterwards, Robb was taken to San Francisco on business and asked her to meet him there.

"We took separate rooms in a small hotel," Jean says. When they met, she recalls that he was wearing a battered felt hat "that looked as though he had just been sitting on it," and, under a rumpled trench coat, he wore a tuxedo. He offered her a small corsage of roses.

Together, then, by car, they traveled the coast of California, stopping in the tourist villages — Carmel, Big Sur, and Laguna Beach. It was March, and so, at San Juan Capistrano Mission, she took him to see the swallows return. He was skeptical, right up until the first black wings appeared. Aiming his Rolleiflex at the swooping birds, Robb declared their entrance "the goddamnedest thing I ever saw!" and the next year, the photos appeared in *The Old Farmer's Almanac*, whose existence Jean took as proof of Robb's mettle as a shrewd businessman. "He bought it for a pittance when it was going broke and built it into a flourishing enterprise with two million circulation," she says.

But that wasn't what drew her to him. "He was a man somehow connected with the good in the world," Jean concludes.

There was no real end to the story, except that he returned to his family in New Hampshire and he and Jean resumed their correspondence. They rarely saw each other again. Though she can't recall the chronology, somewhere in the midst of this, Robb asked her to become *Yankee*'s first poetry editor. "I don't know a damn thing about poetry," he wrote to her when he made the proposal.

"He offered me twenty-five dollars a month," she recalls, "which I gladly accepted. He had a pile of poems he didn't know what to do with. So he sent them all to me. They were all pretty bad so I wrote to the poets that I knew and said, 'Send me some poems.' They did and pretty soon we were in business." Early poets in the pages of *Yankee* included Donald Hall, Hayden Carruth, Richard Eberhart and, surely the most unusual writer ever to appear in *Yankee,* the mystic Alan Watts.

Having studied under Thornton Wilder at the University of Chicago and published poems in the leading periodicals, Jean Burden was as well qualified as anyone Robb Sagendorph could have found to be the editor of his poetry page. But she did lack that one elusive quality: New Englander. Not all readers were as enthusiastic as Robb was.

Jean Burden quickly became the most controversial member of *Yankee*'s editorial staff. Although letters were mixed among expressions of approval, there was a great wave of protest from readers. "Some of them were sure I was making my selections in a dark room at midnight by jabbing at a pile of manuscripts with a pin," she has said.

Those who had sent submissions wrote indignantly to ask why the returned poems came to them postmarked Altadena, California, and she wrote back and said, "Because that's where I live." Others wrote in disgust with the "contemporary" poems that were appearing, some of which did not even rhyme! "Why do you pay money for all that modern, meaningless verse when you could reprint 'Hiawatha' for nothing?"

Jean concluded that these readers wanted the kind of verse they had memorized in grade school. "To criticize poetry because it is too 'modern' is simply no criticism at all," she wrote in conclusion to all the brouhaha. Who knew so much passion lay behind the printing of a few poems? Not long after she took over in 1955, someone wrote saying, "I wish you would quietly drop Jean Burden into Dublin Lake."

"Let 'em yell," Robb wrote to Jean when she expressed concern. "You're doing a wonderful job. Circulation has doubled between July and January."

Throughout the years, Jean has held firm in the face of what she calls "the poetry far right." More recent poets whose work has been published in *Yankee* include May Sarton, Ivan Doig, Jane Kenyon, Maxine Kumin and the Pulitzer prize-winning Mary Oliver, whose first poems Jean selected in 1967.

With Robb's unwavering support, Jean carried on, making her selections every month, ducking the brickbats from under cover of her warm California nights. Meanwhile, she was building an ever-stronger reputation for herself as a poet. Her two collections, *Naked As the Glass* and *Taking the Light from Each Other* were critical successes. Mark Strand praised her poems as "beautifully controlled, perfectly stated, musically and rhetorically just right." Other reviewers called her work "human, witty, passionate" and "silky, meditative, and purposeful." Jean

Burden continued to publish, everywhere but in *Yankee*, from which she exempted herself on principle.

In 1970 Robb Sagendorph was diagnosed with bone cancer. His outlook was not good. Once again breaking through an old-fashioned barrier, Jean Burden telephoned him from her Altadena bungalow. It had been years since they had seen each other but the letters had never stopped. The wires hummed. Jean asked Robb if he would like her to come to Dublin. "No," he said, "Don't come. I am doing all right and really feeling better."

Soon after, Robb Sagendorph died, on the Fourth of July. "So fitting for Mr. New England," Jean says. She misses him still.

That was thirty years ago, and Jean has continued to select poems for *Yankee*'s stony New England pages from her sheltered cottage in the shadow of the San Gabriel Mountains. In 1983, California State University at Los Angeles, where she has taught poetry classes for many years, established a poetry reading series in her honor and named it the Jean Burden Poetry Series. Recent honorees have included such luminaries as Richard Wilbur, Mark Strand, and Donald Hall.

This month of June in the year 2000 marks the forty-fifth year of Jean Burden's reign over *Yankee*'s poems. Robb Sagendorph brought *Yankee* many things but perhaps the most exotic legacy he left was Jean Burden, *Yankee*'s hothouse flower, a pink rose in November.

June 2000 Yankee magazine

YANKEE *stopped publishing poetry in 2002. Despite her many other honors, Jean Burden felt that her work as* Yankee*'s Poetry Editor defined her. The decision to discontinue poetry in the magazine broke her heart. Jean Burden died at her Altadena home in April of 2008 at the age of ninety-four.*

The Center of the Universe

IN THE RING, the six-foot seven-inch, four hundred forty-pound black bear named Pemi stands up like a man and tosses a basketball through the hoop. Pemi's mate, Echo, a three hundred thirty-pound female, has just finished her act, riding around the ring on a Segway, raising the flag and dancing. With them is a small, pixie-like blonde woman and a big, gruff, red-headed man wearing an Australian bush hat. Outside the ring, Victoria paces in her pen, rattling the gate. She can't wait for showtime.

One of thousands of acts that have taken place over the past sixty years in this roadside ring in Lincoln, New Hampshire, is underway at Clark's Trading Post, a place where generations of bears have worked alongside generations of Clarks. The blonde woman and the red-headed man are brother and sister, Maureen and Murray A. Clark, the third generation to train and perform with bears.

Founded in 1928, Ed Clark's Eskimo Sled Dog Ranch gradually morphed from souvenirs and sled dogs to bear acts. The Clarks, it could be said, are perhaps the most ingenious entrepreneurs ever to set down stakes in the White Mountains, substantially influencing the growth of the tourist industry in that region. And, further, it should be said that when you say "the Clarks," you are talking about not only the direct descendants of the founders, Edward P. and Florence M. Clark, and their two sons, Ed, Jr., and Murray, but their offshoots as well, in all a family the size of a small town, each of whom has shared in the growth of this family empire. But in recent years, only Murray the elder, his daughter, Maureen, and Murray the younger, his son, have performed with the bears.

One day last fall, after the Trading Post had closed for the season and the three bears were preparing to go into hibernation, the three showmen stopped to talk about their years with the bears. Talking with these three is like talking to one person. They finish each other's sentences, which run together as smoothly as the waters of the Pemigewasset River that tumbles behind their legendary Trading Post. Today, the roadside attraction has evolved into a full-service entertainment resort that features not only trained-bear shows but a facsimile 19th century village, an authentic wood-fired steam train that takes visitors chugging through the countryside, a museum that is an accumulation of the family's own treasures, even a Segway ride. This old-timey place has a history firmly rooted in the New Hampshire soil.

Murray the elder performed with the bears — Jasper, Ebony and Midnight, Ursula and Onyx, to name a few favorites — for fifty-seven years, beginning in 1949 when he was twenty-three years old and retiring from the ring in 2003 at the age of seventy-seven. He is eighty-four now — you can still see the bearman in him — and he rarely misses a show, sitting beside the ring, quietly watching Maureen, fifty, and Murray the younger, forty, do as he taught them and some that he didn't. Both Maureen and Murray the younger have worked with the bears in one way or another since they were children. Maureen toddled around with her baby bottle alongside the bear cubs, also drinking from their bottles, which made for good snapshots. Since the cubs are raised in the Clarks' homes, the family albums are full of such images. "You haven't lived until you've raised bear cubs in your kitchen," Murray the elder often says. "Down come the curtains, off comes the tablecloth, over goes the milk pitcher."

The cubs ambled around the house and occasionally went for rides in the car. Murray the younger describes a bear cub like this: "A bear cub has little rounded ears, small dark eyes, needle-sharp teeth and claws, and the shortest temper on record."

Maureen cares for bears of all ages and the training is nonstop: "When you work with bears, it's every day, every day, constant, constant, constant. People ask, 'When is it that you are training the bears?' The answer is all the time. Every show is a training as well."

Murray, his hoarse voice that of a sage elder, has this to say: "People ask, how do you do that? Practice! And you take advantage of each bear's talent. You find their inclinations and then develop those talents, reward them for everything they do. We use no clubs, leashes, whips, sticks, none of that! It's all animal handling. I've been an animal handler since I was yea tall. What will work with one animal won't work with another."

When he was sixteen years old, Murray was mauled by one of the bears. "I was cleaning the pen and I went to pick up something in the gravel, put it in the pail and I frightened the bear. He turned on me and butchered me up pretty bad. I ran directly home. My father saw my clothes torn off, my head bleeding, my scalp all asunder and he turned around, picked up a rifle, and went down and shot the bear. That was it."

It was 1943, and at that time there seemed to be no other choice in a desperate situation. Our understanding of animal behavior has evolved since then; today we have additional options and approaches and no doubt the outcome would have been different.

Like thoroughbred horses, bears best suited for training are bears descended from trained bears. This is the ideal but not always the case. It's illegal to take a bear from the wild but bears occasionally come to the Clarks through Fish and Wildlife. Both New Hampshire and Vermont keep the Clarks in their Rolodex, relying on them as they would a rehabilitation center. Moxie is one who came to them that way, a little cub who kept showing up at the home of a woman who lived in northern Vermont. She knew enough not to take the cub in but worried about the motherless child. The Clarks were called. They went to rescue the cub, a little tot so sickly the vet told them she would not live long and warned them not to become attached to her, a tall order for any member of the Clark family.

"She was about the size of a housecat when Dad and I went to get her," Maureen recalls. "She was very sick. We took her anyway. My brothers, my mother, my father, myself, we all took turns sleeping with her, even my sister's dog was brought into it. She feels more than your average bear, if something is going wrong, she gets upset. She always sides with the underdog. We love her. She's twenty-five now. But she was in the ring only three seasons."

That doesn't matter at the Clarks. Currently the three show bears, Pemi (short for Pemigewasset), Echo, and Victoria, perform regularly throughout the summer and fall. But the Clarks keep eight bears altogether; the three oldest live in a large habitat behind Maureen's home, and the others have moved into new, spacious, natural accommodations nearby. Some of the inactive bears are retired, and some just never enjoyed performing.

"They have to love it," Murray the younger says. "They have moods, they have emotions. In many ways, they are very humanlike." Physical attributes help as well. "Bears can manipulate the hands to do things, they can hold, grab, push, shove, stand. They can sit and run on two legs. So with that mechanism already in place, it's not like working with a cat or a bird or a species that is not inclined to pick things up or stand up and walk around. They enjoy going to the next level."

Not that training a bear is easy. Murray the younger explains: "You put in all this time and energy and it just doesn't seem to be paying off and then one day, like magic, they've got it! Repetition is the key. So, I don't know if it's a measure of intelligence so much as it is diligence but they are all different, you just can't compare. Just like people."

Complaints about trained-animal acts have been something of a constant over the years. "We have always had that to contend with in that they make their feelings known to us but once they witness a show, that is it, no problems," Murray the elder says and Maureen adds: "Occasionally someone will write a letter but if you look further, you find that they have never been here before."

Murray the younger says: "There is a whole group of people who object to any trained animals, Seeing Eye Dogs, bomb-sniffing dogs, search dogs. They don't want any animals to be trained in any way."

To the Clarks, their show is their statement about how intelligent bears are and how profound their relationship with people can be. Murray the younger says, "We try to educate people as well as entertain them. The first part of the show, before the bears even come out, I teach things about bears. It's always been that way.

"After a show, folks tell us that they didn't want to come because they don't believe in animal acts, but when it's over they have changed their minds. They see we are not only treating them well but that these bears are our friends."

Maureen adds, "A number of hunters have come up after the show and said that they had hunted bears but now that they've seen how smart they are and how close we are to them, they won't hunt again."

"Yes," Murray the elder concludes, "we've converted a lot of people."

Each Clark has his or her own favorite bear. Murray the elder's best bear was Jasper, a five hundred and thirty-five-pound male who towered above Murray when he stood up, which was often. Jasper and Murray had a wonderful relationship. In the show, Murray would sit on the big bear's belly, walk on his stomach, tickle his feet, all while Jasper was lying placidly on his back, drinking from his bottle.

And then Jasper would pick Murray up and carry him around, give him bear hugs. They'd dance together, cavort around the ring like best buddies on a lark. At the end of the show, Murray would say, 'Ladies and gentlemen, what do you think of my friend Jasper? It's been my pleasure working with him all these years!'"

It was a deep love. Jasper was special but so are all the family's bears. Murray the younger says, "They are very special, these bears. They are our co-workers. We talk to them as if we are talking to humans. After a while they pretty much understand what we want."

It could be said that Clark's is the only bear show of its kind in this country and the longest to run continuously in one place. But it isn't a claim that they make. In fact, when asked about that, they seem not to have thought about it. There are no other shows like theirs that they know of, maybe in the world. Murray the younger thinks about this for a moment before he says, "This is the center of the universe. That's what I've always been told and I believe it. There's nothing else outside of what we have here. This is what we know and where we want to be."

One of the saddest things that can happen in the Clark universe is the death of a bear. The life expectancy of a bear in the wild is only six to twelve years; they may be hit by a car or hunted, or, if they raid trashcans, may ingest plastics or food packaging. Most of the Clarks' bears, however, have lived two or three times longer than that. One bear, Rufus — Jasper's brother — lived an extraordinary thirty-eight years.

Inside the park, there's a small cemetery for the bears who have passed on, with ornately carved and decorated tombstones for each one. When one of their bears dies, the Clarks all grieve. When Onyx died of liver cancer a few years ago at the age of fifteen, Maureen wept and wept. "After a while, I just couldn't cry anymore," she told a reporter.

Just like the passing of the elders of the family, the legacy of the Clarks' bears lives with them, always. Right now, Maureen favors Victoria, a youthful nineteen years old. "She's my best friend," Maureen says. The bears generally work until they no longer want to and then they retire. "She doesn't even think about retiring. There are certain times when she doesn't want to work, especially during mating season," Maureen explains. "However, towards show time she'll sit and watch and wait for her turn, pacing back and forth. She's ready to go."

Maureen and Victoria share the special relationship that Murray the elder had with Jasper. "She thinks I am her mother. If another bear starts giving her a hard time, she hides behind me. She'd always think I would protect her. I know she'd do the same for me."

Once the bears make their nests in their pens and curl up for the long winter's nap, it's a long winter without the bears. Maureen, who does not have children of her own, misses Victoria, especially. "When I miss her, I just go down to her den and wake her up. And she'll sit up in the corner like a giant teddy bear. I snuggle in close to her. When I start to leave, she grabs onto my sleeve to get me to stay."

But Maureen does leave. She goes home to sleep. And dreams about the spring when she'll be with Pemi and Echo again. And Victoria.

May 2010 Yankee magazine

Over the years, *Murray Clark was interviewed countless times. This was his last interview. Thirteen weeks after I spoke with him the last time, he passed away. He always started his day, every day, by reading the* Union Leader. *When he was done, he'd fold it and say, "Well, I didn't see myself in the obituaries today so I guess I have to go to work." On January 7, 2010, for the first time in his life, Murray Clark didn't get up and go to work.*

The Gift

"THIS IS HEAVEN on earth, right here." Charles Borders, a big, raw-boned farmer, holds forth from the wing chair beside the window inside the house that is the heart of the one hundred and ninety-seven-acre Rhode Island farm that surrounds him. It is the house where he was born, the house where he has always lived and the house, where, with any luck, he will die. He tells the story of how he has managed to put his farm into preservation, ensuring that it will stay a working farm after he dies and long into the future. There are many diversions in his story.

"I was born in this room, by the big fireplace. My mother's cookstove used to set here, and the couch was there, and that's where my mother delivered me," he says as if clairvoyant in memory. "A midwife came, but I cannot remember her name."

The cookstove is now in the kitchen, and on this June morning, the big black iron stove is piled high with cartons of eggs, soon to be delivered to customers.

Borders Farm is one of the last two farms in Foster, once a town full of farms. When Charles' father came to this place in 1923, it was just a small farm with a rundown barn and lots of woods. "The barn was so bad that the floor collapsed and the cows hung by their necks all night. The place was not taken care of very well those last few years before my father bought it. So my father built a new barn. The first year, I know he had to buy hay," Charles says, referring to the fact that at that time, there were no fields to mow. Charles, still just a boy, helped his father clear the land by hand, using horse and stone boat. They rented pastures from the neighboring farms, pastures that they eventually bought, stitching the big farm together like a patchwork quilt. "Now I've got maybe fifty acres of hay fields," he guesses. Charles is eighty-one and he's run the farm since he was just twenty-three, taking over when his father died in 1948. This long time on the farm has given him many lessons on the ways of the land.

The farm, less than twenty miles from the city of Providence, is a feather in the cap of the littlest state in the union, hungry for farmland. Charles and his wife, Marjorie, had no children, and as they reached their seventies, they began to talk about what they should do with the farm, dear to their hearts and dear to the hearts of their neighbors. They invited their neighbors to form a committee to talk about their options. With a half a mile of frontage on North Road, Borders Farm could easily have been sold to developers for hundreds of thousands of dollars. Maybe more. But they had no interest in the money.

"Hi, Charles!" Jed Dixon, the neighbor from down the road and member of the Borders Farm Preservation Trust, lets himself in the front door. Charles introduces Jed as the vice chairman of the Borders Farm corporation.

Jed, a woodworker and self-described "hobby farmer," was involved in the efforts to preserve Charles' farm from the start. He sits down and adds his perspective to the story. "It was a long process. Charles' wife, Marjorie, opened the subject with me and my wife. The most important thing to them was that the farm remain a farm. They didn't want it to become a nature preserve or just open land. The farm was the only thing that meant anything to them. They wanted it to be farmed and stay the way that it always had been."

The world was changing and the town of Foster with it. The remnants of life in a small town seem to revolve around the rural nature of these farms and the way of life within them. "Foster is the only town in Rhode Island that does not have a traffic light," Jed points out.

"Yes, and I hope we never get one and I hope we never get one of those damn MacDonald's!" Charles adds, his blue eyes, clear as marbles, widening, his voice sharp with emotion.

Jed continues: "After a whole lot of discussion and talk with lawyers and so forth, the committee founded a 501(C)(3), a nonprofit corporation. Marjorie had passed away by this time — that was four or five years ago. We were kind of in the middle of all this when she died. I would say that she was one of the most respected people in this town. The way it ended up, Charles donated the farm to the corporation, which we call Borders Farm Preservation, Inc., and then on the same day, the state bought the development rights from the corporation. This gave Charles life tenancy here and he rents the agricultural rights for a dollar so he can still farm."

On the day the state announced it had given $550,000 to the Borders Farm Preservation group, a member of the group told a *Providence Journal* reporter: "Not many people give away a half-million dollars every day. People like Bill Gates do but Charles Borders is a man who worked with his hands all his life." The paper wrote in an editorial: *Modernity has placed most of the high cards in the hands of developers. Only by such creativity as displayed at the Borders Farm can Rhode Island's delicate balance of city and country survive.*

Though once he had a large herd of dairy cows, Charles has not milked cows in about twelve years. "I've got seven heifers and almost fifteen Herefords in the pasture. They keep the brush down. That is one thing that is so important to a farm," Charles says, "to keep the brush down, 'cause if you leave the door open, the brush is going to come right into the house." Charles lets this sink in, his rough hands folded over the rough denim of his coveralls. "That's not quite the truth but if you know anything about land, you will know that much."

Charles still has one hundred and fifty chickens and he collects the eggs each morning. "I donate to the food bank and to the church and to the Foster Center. The hens are laying like heck right now. Last week I donated forty-five dozen. I sell the rest to my neighbors. I've got about twenty, twenty-five customers. Some of them buy one dozen a week and some buy every other week. How anyone could live on just one dozen eggs a week, I'll never understand. Holy smokes, if you've got a family, that's just six eggs a week. That doesn't seem near enough to me!"

Outside, Narragansett turkeys wander in the yard, their gobbling coming through the screen as we talk. "They're just pets," he says. "I've got thirteen or so — three or four are setting right now. After Marjorie had her stroke, she was in a wheelchair and I used to push her out into the yard. There was one who used to come and sit right down next to her, just like a dog. Eventually a coyote got that one, but he didn't get her babies. I've still got 'em."

Borders Farm is something of an oddity, a farm on the edge of the metropolis. Once a week, Charles drives to Providence to pick up day-old bread for his turkeys. He loves the feeling of driving back into his own driveway, safe at anchor after the rough voyage.

The house, like the farm, is a treasure chest of memories, a vast collection of Charles Borders' time on this earth. He can take you upstairs and show you the wicker chair he bought at an auction when he was ten years old, and he can show you the branding iron he bought most recently. But most everything else falls somewhere in between those two objects: tiny oil lamps, arrowheads and an Indian axe, pieces of Plymouth Rock, a gadget that automatically turns the page for the minister. Something of everything but not much of anything, he likes to say. It's all around him as are his stories, like the one about the day during the '38 hurricane when the henhouse blew over with all the hens inside. The hens were never found again. These stories crowd in and likely there is not time left in his lifetime to tell them all.

Charles can take you on a tour of the town and show you where the boiling spring is and where the big oak, fourteen feet in circumference, was and the pond where he and his father used to cut ice. And, with great pride, Charles Borders can show you the Foster town meetinghouse, which was purchased in 1795 for fifteen dollars. And he can show you all the fields he used to mow where now there are houses. Big houses on small lots — a painful sight, an offense to his farmer's heart.

Forming the corporation and shepherding the farm into preservation took ten long years and much anguish. It wasn't easy for Charles to give away the farm he's been on his whole life. But he understands the beauty of the gift. "You see," he says, "I could have left it to my relatives but they'd just sell it — and then what? This way, I can stay as long as I want."

Just like heaven.

April 2006 Yankee magazine

AT AGE EIGHTY-FIVE, *Charles Borders continues to live, very happily, on his one hundred and ninety-seven-acre farm in Foster, Rhode Island. He still delivers eggs, though he no longer drives into the city, and he continues to work on the farm as he always has, tending to such matters as birthing calves and keeping the hens happy. He was thrilled when, after this article appeared in* Yankee, *a man from Amarillo, Texas, called him to say that he had read the article and recognized the house as having belonged to his grandmother. They now enjoy regular phone conversations, exchanging information about the history of the house and those who have occupied it over the generations. He is delighted with the way the corporation, Borders Farm Preservation, Inc., works, ensuring he can not only stay on his farm but also be able to take care of the house as it ought to be. Recently, the corporation received a grant to put a new wood cedar roof on the house. "What do you suppose that is going to cost?" he asks. "Forty-four thousand dollars!!" But, "it'll be done right," he says, "and it's beautiful. It does my heart good."*

So Charles Borders' gift has brought him many gifts in return.

The Oldest Newspaper Columnist on Earth

Ruby Hemenway is a writer who never was a writer before she was asked to tell what she knew. Then it all unfolded like poetry. Every Saturday Miss Hemenway sits down at the maple drop-leaf table beside the big window in her living room, sets a carbon between two sheets of writing paper, and writes in longhand another of her columns in which she brings back such things as bed sticks, snow rollers, the county poor farm, and water pipes made of wood. She also may tell stories like the one about when her father was doing chores and the bull got loose or about her father's horses, Polly and Peggy, who were as affectionate toward him as dogs. It takes her about an hour, and when she comes to the end of three handwritten pages, she slips the original into an envelope and mails it to the *Greenfield Recorder*, which she remembers more completely as the Greenfield *Courier and Gazette*, in Greenfield, Massachusetts. Her column, "I Remember When," has been a weekly feature of that paper for the past ten years, during which time she has never missed a deadline, never taken a vacation, and never repeated herself. "We occasionally fix run-on sentences," Irmarie Jones, a writer for the paper, said recently, "but other than that, we rarely edit Ruby's column. And we never have given her ideas or suggestions." Miss Hemenway began her writing career at the age of ninety, and on the twenty-ninth of this month she will turn one hundred. She is probably the oldest newspaper columnist in the United States, perhaps on earth.

In addition, she was one of the major sources of information for the much-heralded *Dictionary of American Regional English* (DARE), eighteen years in preparation, soon to be published by Harvard University Press. "She was my prize informant," Audrey Duckert, field researcher for the dictionary, said recently. In her research throughout New England, she interviewed many of what they call "informants," older residents with good memories for colloquial words and phrases. "A lot of people that I talked with would want to show me pictures of their grandchildren till the cows came home, but they'd avoid the questions. Ruby answered the entire questionnaire, which consisted of one thousand eight hundred questions, and then she wanted more. There was no one like her."

Miss Hemenway's column is about how things used to be for her in the Connecticut River Valley in the last part of the 19th century. Her topics, which run anywhere from the old-fashioned way to make cider applesauce (with oat straw at the bottom of the pot) to using skunk oil to cure a cold, are well-rounded and anchored in fact. Though her readers by now know the characters who occasionally appear in the column — Grandma Pierce (pronounced 'Purse' back then) and Grandpa Hemenway — it avoids the sentimentality that personal reminiscences can fall victim to. Most often her columns are evocative:

> *One thing I recall vividly from my early life on the farm is the wonderful smell of hay coming in my east bedroom window at night and the whippoorwills singing where they sat on the warm stones of the retaining wall. . . . My sister and I used to go just as it was dusk, out to the Mill Hill woods and sit on the stone wall around the mowing and listen to the wood thrushes sing. First just one, away off and faint, then another, nearer, then they began coming from all around, but never interrupting another's song, so we got the beautiful clear "u-o-lee, u-o-lee," over and over again in varying degrees of volume until it was almost dark.*

In spite of these idyllic recollections, there is no sense that Miss Hemenway is pining for the good old days. She often points out to her readers that the old days weren't necessarily the best. At the end of one column she wrote: "Times change and they do improve! How would you like to beat all your egg whites on a platter with a fork or maybe a whisk?"

In fact, she views almost all the changes that have marched through her lifetime — the telephone, electricity, the automobile, computers — as positive and, above all, interesting. "I like to make the contrast to today, to see how one single thing, such as electricity, has changed the whole business of living. There is no question that electricity was the one big change that really affected modern society. You see, we didn't know it was hard to read by oil lamps because nobody had anything better. The kerosene lamp seemed so much better than the candles that they could remember. I thought it was wonderful to be able to get a light just by pressing a button and not to have to bother with matches and a chimney. But I can remember a woman who told me that she preferred the kerosene lamps to electricity. She always was a queer specimen, anyway."

It was almost by accident that the column got started. Miss Hemenway used to read a column in the *Recorder* by Wayne Smith, who had lived near her when they were growing up. She enjoyed his column, which was about life in the Pioneer Valley, and she wrote to him some of her own recollections. She did this rather regularly, and he rather regularly excerpted her letters in his columns. At ninety she made her writing debut: "I never aspired to be a writer at all. There are still plenty of subjects that I can write about. Somebody generally says something in conversation and sets me off to thinking, and then I write about it. Sometimes I think my writing sounds rather labored, but sometimes it's not hard at all. I write just as if I were talking to somebody."

Her life has been by no means narrow, and the farm is not all she's known. Following her graduation from high school in 1903, Miss Hemenway worked all her life at a variety of jobs in a variety of places until she retired at the age of sixty. She worked in Boston, in Wellesley, in New

Haven, and she spent a summer in New York City. But she dismisses urban life in a sentence: "I don't like cities." It is the farm with its undying cast of characters that she writes about.

Surprisingly, from the volumes of practical information available in her column, Miss Hemenway was not a tomboy when she was growing up. But she watched everything that went on at the farm and listened carefully to the conversations that filled the house. She heard and remembered the words and the ways of her parents and grandparents.

For someone with such an encyclopedic mind, Miss Hemenway has never done many things: she never did chores on the farm; she never rode or drove a horse; she has never tasted alcohol; she never has been married; she has never driven a car; she has never been sick.

And yet she can tell in rich and vivid detail how loggers lived and worked and how shoes were made and how a horse was harnessed. She can also recite recipes for plum duff and farmer's pudding sauce, listing ingredients as "a pinch" and "a good chunk of." And she's told her readers how to "whack up a mess of biscuit." These snippets from the vast patchwork of her memory are what make up her column, which is read not only by residents of Franklin County, but clipped by many of them and sent to members of their families who have moved away.

As a girl, Ruby Hemenway was tall and slender and broad-shouldered, and she had hair that was red. Now her hair is the color of the December sun, and she wears it tied in a knot at the back of her head. She has sharp eyes behind rimless glasses and the long thin legs of a schoolgirl. In conversation she scowls a lot, not out of disapproval but rather in an effort to recall, in an effort to get it right. "I find that sometimes I come on a topic that's rather big and not specific enough so I'd dare to write about it. I'm afraid that I'll get it wrong. I'm so old now, there's no one left to ask." She speaks in a voice full of flat *as*'s and whistling *s*'s, and she is apt to use words unfamiliar to young ears. Miss Hemenway calls this her "twang," and it is a manner of speaking rarely heard anymore, even among the old-timers.

Though she hasn't lived there since the 1920s, the farm in North Leverett is the focal point of her column. "My father's was the then-common one-man farm. He had between four and seven cows — all one man could handle — one or two pigs for meat and salt port, a flock of chickens, and a pair of horses. It was a farm that my great-grandfather Elihu bought in 1820 and it stayed in the family for four generations. There at the farm my great-grandfather was a blacksmith, my grandfather was a shoemaker, and my father was a farmer." Miss Hemenway doesn't need to go back to remember it, but when she does go back, the stories and memories flow out like a freshet. She says she knows everyone in the North Leverett graveyard, who the people were and what they died of; she knows where the houses were that burned and what barns fell in. She can tell you who lived in the old houses along the roads that crisscross the town, who their children were and how they turned out. She doesn't know who owns the houses now, though, not many of them anyway.

On a blustery day last fall she took me on a tour of North Leverett, past the farm where she grew up. We started from her apartment in Turners Falls, not such a great distance from her birthplace. On the way we followed the road that runs alongside the Sawmill River which, she told me, once supported seemingly numberless mills and shops.

"To get to school in Montague Center, we walked ¾ of a mile, and then it was a four-mile ride in a bumpy old school team drawn by two horses. It used to be pretty coming down through here in the morning when it was frosty because every twig and every branch would be covered with hoarfrost from the river. Boy, it was cold. Bump, bump, bump, all the way down through. We would start at quarter past seven from the village, and we only got down there in time for school at nine. But they picked up children all the way down. There were probably twelve of us by the time we got to school."

We pass a center-chimney Cape set into a bank. "This house was an old cellar kitchen house, but the way they've changed it around, it can't be used that way any longer." We pass a house where she says a woman lived without a furnace. "She'd leave a door from the cellar open and all winter she'd have flowering geraniums." Another house, a big rambling Colonial with windows with many lights, she recalls has a "spring dance floor" on the second floor. "The (floor) boards were long and left free so they would spring up and down when people danced."

It is her recollection of such things that made her such an invaluable source to Audrey Duckert. "In the eighteen hundred questions we asked about the weather, time, buildings, foods, cookery, people — we asked about everything that people have words for, and Ruby knew them all. I first went to see her on a Monday evening, and she answered so many questions that I went back and went every Monday night after that for at least a year. It grew into a lifelong friendship." Miss Duckert conjectures that Miss Hemenway's retention of archaic dialect has a lot to do with her conservative nature. "She is extremely conservative. We had known each other for three years and saw each other sometimes more than once a week, but I called her Miss Hemenway and she called me Miss Duckert. Finally one day she said to me, 'We've known each other a long time. Why don't you call me Ruby and I'll call you Audrey.' She is offended when people she doesn't know well call her Ruby, as if she were the neighborhood cat." Miss Duckert and Miss Hemenway, who are some thirty years apart in age, shared many afternoons in the country, hunting for wildflowers, for which they both have a penchant, and searching through graveyards for interesting reads on the stones. Miss Hemenway told Miss Duckert about terms such as a lowery day, which is a kind of a day with blue-black clouds hanging over the hills, and about a skift of snow, which we now call snow flurries. "She told me about rowen hay, which is the last cut and which her father used to think was the best. She said he kept it in a special place in the mow and would give it to the cows on Sunday mornings. Something like that is so special to me. It gives me a window into the 19th century."

The next road is a dirt road, marked Hemenway Road. "Turn here," Miss Hemenway says, pointing. Her father once owned much of the frontage that passes along the side of a ridge that slopes down across meadows edging the river. On the other side of the river, wooded hills gently rise. A bridge made of wooden planks with no railings crosses over the river. "This is the meadow bridge. It was always wooden, and from the house, we could always hear the cars coming across, *clat-a-clat-a-clat-a.* I've heard my brother-in-law say he used to fish for eels off this bridge. Fresh-water eels. And that was all cleared over there. There was an old Frenchman that lived down here in this boggy place. When I was a child, there was just one old coal (charcoal) kiln down across the way. When they were burning the kilns, you could smell the smoke clear down to Montague Center. That old Frenchman used to run the kilns. He was puckered up, looked as if he'd been dried in smoke. His name was spelled M-e-r-c-i-e-r but they always called him 'Mercy.'"

Moving up out of the boggy area toward the ridge, I notice some newer houses set in the woods. "This is the beginning of father's farm. The people who bought it have sold off a lot of this pastureland for house lots. I'll bet one of these building lots brought as much as mother got for the whole farm and all of the buildings on it."

When we reach it, the farmhouse, a long one-story Cape with two chimneys and a single dormer in the roof, is recognizable from an old photograph she showed me before we left her apartment. No additions have been built, but the burly maples out front were only saplings in the photo. She points to the window in front and tells me it was her grandmother's parlor. She once wrote this about that room:

One winter I slept downstairs in the front room that used to be my Grandmother Hemenway's parlor. There was no fire that side of the house so I had Grandmother Pierce's goosefeather bed. People who say these beds aren't healthy don't know much about them. They can be lifted, punched, and poked until all the feathers are separated with air in between so the whole bed is soft to sleep on. . . . With a soapstone inserted between the outing flannel sheets, wool bed socks, and lots of warm wool blankets, I slept better than any other winter in my life. . . . No matter how cold it was, I had my window open a few inches. One morning when I'd put on a coat and wool gloves to go in and make my bed, it seemed unusually cold so I put a thermometer on the bureau and it registered zero.

I strain to see in through the windows, which are shut up with curtains. I want to imagine the scenes she has described to me, cooking supper — maybe plum duff — on winter nights by the light of a hand lamp. I see the cellar sash is propped open which makes me think of a story in her column about her mother:

One winter some rats, the barn variety . . . got into the cellar and had gnawed potatoes in an open bin. . . . One day my mother went down to get some potato yeast and had a large heavy iron mixing spoon to stir it. Just as she got to the bottom of the stairs, she heard a little noise and looked up and there on a beam almost over her head was the patriarch of all rats. Quick as scat, she raised that spoon and banged him and down he fell, stunned. Then she dispatched him for good.

I ask Miss Hemenway what she misses most from the old days. Nothing, really, she says. "I'm glad to see all the changes." Then she says, "I do miss, though, an apple pie made the way my mother used to."

Further past the house is a huge and stout red barn. Leading from a stone embankment is a sagging wooden ramp that passes steeply up into the mow. Lightning rods poke from the ridge of the roof. "My father built this barn. He had great fun planning it. I was out of high school when he built it. The summer he built it, we had a series of terrible thunderstorms. They found a place in the meadow where a rock had been split open by lightning. Another time, at night, my father was milking and there was a fearful thundershower. He said he could smell sulfur, and he thought the barn was afire. The pigs were squealing down below. He expected to find one of them dead. So he went down and then upstairs to the mow and checked all around and found nothing. The next morning, in the daylight, when he looked he found long splinters, a foot and more long, splintered off from below the nail heads. Lightning had struck on the nail heads but had not set the new barn afire."

She thinks back to those times and says that the young people today pursue things too intensely, to the sacrifice of a good life. "The more successful ones entirely give up their lives to their pursuits. They don't take enough time to have a happy life. Their marriages oftentimes aren't pleasant. I don't believe they take enough time for themselves." She counsels young people to take an interest in everything that's around them — "Don't go through life with your eyes shut!" No part of her long life has ever seemed boring nor time a burden. Being one hundred, she says, comes as a surprise to her. "I really have to stop and think that I am as old as I am. But I don't want to live any longer than I can enjoy my life."

After we leave the farm, we drive to the end of its boundaries. "My father owned to where the woods came. There is a stone wall where the farm ended." But the fields have gone back to woods and it's hard for us to spot the wall. Miss Hemenway is struck with the changes in the landscape. "Places grow up so. All over, this way, down through here used to be farmland. Nothing remains the same." She pauses and then adds, "Except the rocks."

January 1984 Yankee magazine

RUBY HEMENWAY *died in 1987 at the age of one hundred and three. This article was reprinted in* Reader's Digest *and spurred interest from television's Charles Kuralt who visited with her for his program and Willard Scott who came to film her for her one hundred and first birthday. A lengthy and scholarly study of Miss Hemenway's writings and of her contribution to* DARE, *published in 2004 by the University of Nebraska Press, concluded, among many other things, that Ruby Hemenway was an early feminist.*

Into the Mystery

IT IS THE AFTERNOON of February 20, 1977. From behind the curtain at the Cabot Street Theater in Beverly, Massachusetts, a booming voice enters the darkness, filled now with an expectant audience of men, women, and children. The voice draws out the syllables and rolls the r's. *Ladies and Gentleman! Welcome to the world of magic! It's a wonderful world of marvels and mysteries, of fantasy and illusion, a world filled with a sense of enchantment, a world where anything can happen!*

As the curtain lifts, there comes a rebel yell, the lights dawn, music swells, and the lithe figure of Marco the Magi prances down the steps, robes floating, parasol twirling. Around him are fourteen of his closest friends, dancing, twirling, bowing, leaping. They have fashioned their costumes from fabrics found at yard sales. Their shoes are sneakers painted gold and frosted with glitter. It is their great adventure. *Let the magic begin*!

Flinging off his robes, Marco slides into the casket-like box, playfully waving goodbye to the audience as Le Grand David seals him in. Flourishing a saw, the white-turbaned David makes the cut, halving the box. Gesturing here and there, he demonstrates how it could not possibly be a trick. Clowns and princesses dance on the sidelines. Lights swivel. At last the box is put back together again and, improbably, the hatches are opened and out leaps Marco. The Magi. Marco, the wise one, the sorcerer.

It has not always been on stage that Marco has escaped the sealed box and leapt to safety. Under the robes and behind the makeup, Marco the Magi is Cesareo Pelaez, and for the past forty years, he has been on a kind of magical mystery tour which began in Cuba, balanced briefly in New Hampshire, wound its way around the world, and then in 1975 came to rest on the North Shore of Boston, where the tour is ongoing. Though he spent nearly his entire career teaching psychology to college students, his fame has come not so much from this august pursuit as from his life as a magician, two worlds which conjoin far more harmoniously than might at first seem possible. Both are his own spectacular creations but if you ask him which is more important, Marco or Cesareo, he will reply, simply, "Don Quixote or Cervantes — which is the real one?"

At that moment, on that evening in 1977, it would have been almost impossible to imagine where that adventure would lead. Marco the Magi's production of Le Grand David and His Own Spectacular Magic Company is now the longest running magic show in the world and the largest magic troupe in the world. Cesareo Pelaez has been ranked among the greatest magicians in the world — inducted into London's famed Magic Circle on par with Devant and Houdini. Each show now features hundreds of costumes stitched from fabrics acquired around the world. There are dozens of intricately constructed backdrops. Their shoes and hats are bejeweled, sparkling with silks, sequins, and stones. There is nothing in this show or about this show, not even the smallest detail, which the members of the company have not created themselves, under the guiding hand of Cesareo. Their accolades would fill pages.

Cesareo and his friends have performed seven times at the White House, for presidents and heads of state, and they have been called the only show like it on earth. For Cesareo, magic has many meanings but one of the most fundamental is the relationship. "More than anything, magic is about *people*. Magic is about *relationships,*" he says, a statement that does not make much sense until and unless you know who Cesareo is and where he has come from.

This story does not begin on that cold February afternoon but instead in Cuba, in the 1930s, in the little seaside town of Santa Clara, where Cesareo's father owned a hotel. "In those days, Cuba was a center for all sorts of traveling theatrical adventures," Cesareo explains. His voice is a stage whisper, the tones of his homeland still present in the syllables of each word. "The great magic caravans of the old days used to stop on the island and perform. The first memory that I recall was Fu Manchu — the David Bamberg show."

He was four years old and Bamberg called little Cesareo onto the stage, an experience that helped Cesareo understand the essence of a great magic show. Cesareo was asked to hold a handkerchief, a simple task that did not seem to have anything to do with the spectacular trick Bamberg enacted while Cesareo stood spellbound. But the experience caused Cesareo to understand that it is not the one thing that is happening onstage but the many. After that, he often staged impromptu magic shows in his father's backyard.

By the time he was fifteen, Cesareo, whose nickname then was Mirre, had his own magic troupe, Mirre's Follies, which included as many as two dozen of his friends. A bright boy, Cesareo went on to study at the university in Santa Clara, earning his doctorate. He was eventually certified to teach psychology, his other passion, or perhaps the same passion. If you ask Cesareo what magic has to do with psychology, he will say, "Everything."

After those early happy years came the revolution. Communism spread throughout Cuba and forced Cesareo into the box and locked the doors. One minute, it seems, Cesareo was teaching at the university and the next he was sleeping on the streets of New York City. The work he was able to find was menial. He had escaped but he felt almost as trapped as he had in Cuba. At that time, he was twenty-nine years old, an educated man with dreams and ambitions. But he could not speak or write English. In New York, he was dismissed as illiterate. In despair, he wrote a letter to the great American psychologist, Abraham Maslow, explaining his predicament. Almost incredibly, Maslow wrote back to the young Cesareo, inviting him to come to Brandeis University, where he was teaching. Hungry and without money, Cesareo hitchhiked to the Waltham, Massachusetts, campus, almost falling upon the carpets of the professor's office. It was a day Cesareo will never forget and a day that sent him on the long mysterious journey that seems only to get richer with each passing year.

Through Maslow, Cesareo was able to resume his teaching and also his dreams. Of his relationship with Maslow and his wife, Cesareo says, "It was like an adoption."

The adoption led to the founding, in 1968, of a "center for personal growth" in the hilltop village of Dublin, New Hampshire. Cesareo named it "Cumbres," which translates roughly to "where the sky meets the earth," or, the joining of the two worlds. With his penetrating jade green eyes and flashing matinee idol smile, the long-haired Cesareo cut a charismatic figure in the small New England town. It could have been predicted he was destined for the stage. The center, based largely on Maslow's teachings, drew students from all over the Northeast. Webster Bull was among those who hitchhiked to Cumbres to experience this Cesareo, about whom he had heard so much. He was then a sophomore at Amherst College and his roommate, Tom Brenneke, came with him. Of the experience, Webster has said, "Cesareo represented a whole new world of possibilities." Avrom Surath came from Brandeis. Rick Heath. Ellen Sheehan. Leslie Bartlett. To say that they came under Cesareo's spell would shortchange the relationships that have flowered since. But, there is some substance to what that means — if dropping everything in one's life and following someone is to "come under their spell" then that is what happened. When Cumbres folded, Cesareo suggested a trip to Europe to study all kinds of theater. Webster and Tom and Ellen and others — upwards of fifty — bought tickets and climbed aboard Cesareo's wagon. Traveling by boat, by plane, by train, by thumb, however it happened, the merry band of someday-to-be wizards followed their man, to mime shows, puppet theaters, street theaters, opera, and stage events of all kinds. They did not know that they were studying for a lifetime of magical theater, a lifetime of relationships.

After they returned, Cesareo settled in Rockport in 1972 and began teaching psychology at Salem State College. Webster and Tom and Ellen followed him there. They had absorbed so much in Europe, it had left them hungry for a stage. When the rundown movie theater on Beverly's main street came up for sale, Cesareo was the first to know. He called the others. "It was our opportunity!" he says. The asking price was $110,000. He wanted at least seventeen of his friends to come up with $10,000 a piece so that they could buy it together for cash and restore it with the remaining money. He found eighteen willing to invest in it as a cooperative venture.

The theater was in disrepair. They first cleaned it, thoroughly, and opened it as soon as possible to show foreign and art films. This could provide operating revenue while they fashioned their dream. While movie reels clicked in the projection booth, the troupe worked feverishly to meet Cesareo's deadline: the first magic show on February 20, 1977. Late nights were often spent building props and sewing enormous backdrops onstage. By that date, they had restored the theater to its former grandeur, choreographed the show, and perfected the illusions — a two-hour extravaganza which would include a new trick every four minutes. Included in the show were appearances and disappearances, levitations and penetrations, dancing handkerchiefs, white doves, muscovie ducks and a rabbit that turns into a guinea hen — all of this choreographed to the stirring music of the likes of Rimsky-Korsakov and Debussy. The amazing ride of Le Grand David and His Own Spectacular Magic Company had begun. Cesareo stepped on stage as Marco the Magi and Webster's younger brother, David, who had joined the irresistible group, took the starring role as Le Grand David. After that first spectacular show, it did not take long for word to spread. Magazine and television reporters turned up week after week.

Seven years later, when Beverly's other old vaudeville theater came up for sale, the magicians got out their wands. In spite of the fact, or perhaps because of the fact that it was only three blocks away, they decided to repeat their Cabot St. Miracle and make the Larcom rise from its ashes as well. Also once one of the grand theaters of the early part of the twentieth century, the Larcom, at the time of its purchase by the magic company, was showing pornographic movies. If they were not already there, this second purchase drove Le Grand David deep into the hearts of the grateful citizens of Beverly. No other city in the United Sates, indeed in the world, can boast a magic theater with weekly performances. Certainly no other city in the stratosphere can boast two.

During those early years in Rockport, Webster had introduced Cesareo to his younger brother, David, the quiet, long-legged, dark-eyed dreamer who looked like Errol Flynn and moved like Nureyev. David, who was then a high school senior intent on studying psychology in college, would eventually become the principle magician in the troupe — a magician celebrated internationally — but at the time, he had no particular interest in magic. David, now forty-seven, says, "Cesareo was, in my mind, a psychologist. The magic came later. In fact, if you had told me twenty-five years ago that this is what I would be doing, I would have suggested a weekend of periodic rest and feeding at a quiet facility somewhere in the country."

That is perhaps what most of the other members might say. Most, if not all, developed other, rather distinguished careers outside of magic. During the week, one is an architect, others are bankers and lawyers, psychologists and teachers. Webster Bull, who is currently the company's president, owns a publishing company that specializes in family memoirs and town histories. It was their fascination with psychology and their love of theater that drew all of them together to begin with, and they see no reason why that core should ever leave them. Financially, the company is a completely shared enterprise.

With their careers, their families have evolved as well. Eventually Tom married Pam. Their children Heidi and Will began performing onstage almost as soon as they could walk. Leslie Bartlett's son, Seth, became "Seth the Sensational," coming onstage in the arms of Cesareo at the age of three and growing up almost before the eyes of devoted followers. Webster married Katie and their two daughters, Martha and Marian, were the main attractions for almost all of their growing up years. Many of the company's posters bear their cherubic faces. They are distinguished in the world of magic as being the only girls who have ever performed at that age. All of them, husbands and wives, daughters and sons, brothers and sisters, share the stage with each other. Of all the children, Marian remains onstage while others have gone off to college. Seth is now married, the father of two. He has a lucrative career as an investment banker, his memories of his life onstage safe in scrapbooks for the time being.

No matter what they are doing during the week, on weekends they come together, paint their faces, pull on their wigs and headdresses, robe themselves in the splendor of Cesareo's magic and perform the illusions. They have now performed the show they previewed on that afternoon in February in 1977 more than 2100 times. The doors to the company are not closed to new members. One of the troupe's youngest and newest members is TJ Shimeld, whose grandmother brought him to the show when he was seven and who has been fascinated by magic ever after. As a teenager, he started a magic magazine and wrote to Cesareo in hopes of an interview. He not only got the interview, before he knew it, both he and his girlfriend had joined the magic show. "It's an adventure and it continues!" TJ, now twenty-four, says. "I've amazed myself."

Cesareo listens, smiling, to TJ's story. "Yes, and did he tell you the story of how he came with stars in his eyes and how I took him into the bathroom and gave him a broom and told him to clean the bathroom? It was the first time in his life he ever cleaned a toilet! Imagine at that age, he had never cleaned a toilet!"

It is a hallmark of Cesareo's teachings, this reminder to be practical in life, that inside the magic always dwells the mundane. Several, including Tom and Webster, acquired business degrees at Cesareo's insistence. "Dreams without practicality? Forget it!" he loves to say.

It is this rub with reality that Cesareo has urged on American students ever since he came here from Cuba. "When I first came to America, at Brandeis, the first question I asked my students was how many of you have ever seen a birth and how many of you have ever seen a death — None of them! These are the two fundamental principles of life!"

That Cesareo has never married and has no children of his own might enhance his own sense of mystery. It was his father who took him to the magic shows when he was little. "He used it as an excuse to see the magic company," he says. "I find now that many men — we have more men than women who come to the shows — come with their children. The children are the excuse for these men to come to see the magic. There is this mystery of why men love magic more than women. It's got to be that way. The greatest magic of all is the production of a child. Women are naturals at it. One of the greatest moments of life is childbirth — what magic! Men have simply to watch!"

In fact, it was the birth of the children of his friends that in Cesareo's mind mark the defining moments of Le Grand David. If you ask him when he felt that his struggles were over, he will reply that it was on the day that Webster and Katie's daughter, Martha, was born.

Cesareo is nearing seventy. For him, life has indeed been a world of magic, where anything can happen. He has retired from his teaching position at Salem State but continues his weekly performances in Beverly. Eight years ago, he collapsed on stage. David revived him and Cesareo continued his performance, checking into the hospital only after the final curtain. He sometimes feels frustrated by his physical limitations. But for a man whose mind stretches so far, these constraints are small. "Death," he says, "is the first note of an unfinished symphony." It is the spirit, he maintains, not the body which drives us. Of that he is certain. And at the core of everything is magic. "It does not matter how much we have done with science, how much technology encroaches, no matter how much we know, the need for magic in the world will never die. We don't need much magic, just a very little, but without it, we wither. Magic is an emotional state — the fascination and the wonder of the mysteries of life will prevail. Perhaps I cannot understand how the man is sawed in half. I can study it and make some assumptions *but*! Let's enjoy it. Let's just have a good time!"

March 2002 Yankee magazine

LE GRAND DAVID *and His Own Spectacular Magic Company recently celebrated their 33rd anniversary. Though Cesareo has retired from the stage, the company continues to perform every Sunday at three and on selected Saturday afternoons. Their Believe-It-Or-Not record of continuous performances remains unbroken. David Bull continues in his role as Le Grand David while his brother, Webster, left the company in 2000 to give more attention to his publishing company, Commonwealth Editions. Katie continues in starring roles but their daughters have graduated college and gone on to other pursuits. Eighteen of the original members of Le Grand David Magic Company, all of whom enjoy careers outside of the company, remain in the cast, still in love with magic. Call or write the Cabot Street Cinema Theater, 286 Cabot Street, Beverly MA 01915, 978-927-3677, for a complete schedule of their ongoing performances.*

The Mysterious Life of Little Audrey Santo

SOMETIME AFTER NOON on a hot August day in 1999, the ambulance stops in front of Christ the King Church. Police barricades have stopped the noon-hour traffic on the busy main road that cuts through the heart of Worcester, Massachusetts. The road is already congested. Huge tour buses muscle the shoulders of either side of the street and satellite trucks from various Boston news organizations monopolize the corners. A crowd stands in a long line behind barriers. Many of them arrived five hours ago, folding chairs in hand. Photographers, who have been sitting beside the church shrubbery for what seems like hours, leap to their feet and elbow into position.

"*She's here*," runs through the crowd. Though they number in the thousands, they have formed an orderly line, two and three abreast, that snakes well out of sight. A rope and two guards is all it takes to hold them back. Those who are able rise and stand on tiptoes to see if they can glimpse her. Love is in the air.

The ambulance backs up the wide slate path that leads to the big double doors of the catholic church. The backup lights beep in rhythm, a shrill prelude to the arrival of sixteen-year-old Audrey Marie Santo, or Little Audrey as her admirers love to call her, the most famous "victim soul" in this country in this century. Little Audrey Santo is what the Catholic Church refers to as an intercessor — through the suffering of this innocent child, they believe, their prayers reach their God.

Audrey! they call. *Audrey, darling!* They wave as if to a teen idol or an adored political icon. They have come in hopes of being healed, mind, body, or spirit.

A group of men and women close ranks around the back of the ambulance. They wear name tags and sunglasses. "*Stand back, please,*" they say to the jostling crowd of photographers and reporters.

The doors to the ambulance open and the men and women wearing sunglasses and name tags join hands in a circle and, as the gurney is lifted from the vehicle, they stand close around their Audrey, whose mouth hangs open, tongue exposed, and whose eyes gaze skyward. The gurney is edged in lace. Audrey's famous four-foot length of thick shining brown hair is gathered with lace. The pillow on which her head is laid shimmers with pink ribbons.

Thus surrounded, the burly ambulance drivers wheel their charge into "the crying room," a small, glass-enclosed room at the rear of the sanctuary which is traditionally used during mass by mothers and their crying children. Today, on the twelfth anniversary of the accident that struck Little Audrey dumb and motionless, the crying room will be Audrey's tiny sanctuary. For the next five hours, she will be available to her followers from behind the glass wall.

Inside the sanctuary, the music begins. Accompanied by his electronic keyboard, Bernie Choiniere wails out *Little Audrey's Song*, which he has written and recorded and which is available on tape by mail order. A nun who has traveled here all the way from Illinois in order to read for Audrey begins the litany. *Hail Mary, Mother of Grace . . .*

The rope is untied and the people begin to file into the church. Silently, apprehensively, they approach the glass behind which Audrey lies, like a fallen leader or a slain head of state. A tracheal tube provides her with air. A tube in her stomach provides her with food. But these obstructions are covered with the blinding whiteness of the sheets. They have waited all year for this. A heavy-set woman with a huge sunflower painted on her t-shirt clutches her rosaries and walks, eyes nearly shut.

A black woman with a turban made of colorful fabric makes her way toward Audrey, her hands folded as if in prayer. Some are in wheelchairs, some lean on crutches or walkers. The sick, and those who are apparently healthy but who may bear illnesses in their hearts, stand and wait. Many of them believe that Audrey, surely more gravely afflicted than any who have come today, can bring them peace and perhaps even heal them of their suffering. Some have come every year "to see Audrey." While standing outside, a woman in black told me, "I think it's about time something like this happened. Yes, I believe in miracles!"

Last year, Audrey celebrated her anniversary outdoors, at the football stadium at Holy Cross College. It was a blistering hot day. She wore sunglasses and a tiara. Her sheets were lace. A small house had been constructed for the viewing. Air conditioning was provided through one side and on the other side, a big glass window was installed. Bulletproof glass was used because of the fear, oh, very slight, but still, the fear that there might be a nut out there, the fear that someone might take Audrey's life.

Ten thousand people came. They wiped tears and knelt in prayer. They swooned in front of the little house, sought shade beneath the big scoreboard and beneath the huge blown up photographs of the four communion wafers that reportedly bled during a Mass for Audrey two years ago. The bleeding communion wafers are only one of the many miracles that followers and priests believe have occurred in the presence of Audrey.

Into the microphone, the nun continues: *Blessed are the fruits of Thy womb . . .*

AUDREY MARIE SANTO, the daughter of Linda and Steve Santo, a housewife and an automobile mechanic, was born on December 19, 1983. This much we know is true about Audrey's life. The rest is apocryphal and perhaps can never be verified. Around Little Audrey, there exists a membrane of belief and disbelief. Around Little Audrey, there exists a mystery.

Such is the life of a legend. Is Audrey's life a miracle? If you assume that Audrey's parents might be the source of "the truth" about Audrey, you are leaving much to faith. Reporters who are seeking the truth are quizzed on their religious affiliation and whether or not their publication is "spiritual." I was told by the family spokesperson that Linda Santo "would not be available" for an interview. But while I was there, she was busy with reporters from television's *48 Hours*, which does not, that I know of, have a spiritual inclination. However, these are private decisions that the family can make, managing Audrey's spiritual career, exposing her when they wish, withdrawing her at their own discretion.

The elements that comprise Audrey's story have been told many, many times in newspapers and on television shows, and in a book that Audrey's parents sell from a back room of their house. *In God's Hands*, by religious writer Thomas W. Petrisko, is Steve and Linda Santo's authorized version of the events that comprise what they call "the miraculous story" of Audrey Santo. But their version is heavily corroborated by outside sources, albeit faithful followers of Catholic doctrine. Priests such as Monsignor Donato Conte, a priest from Rome, Italy, who provided the lengthy forward to this book, concur that Audrey very well might be "the finger of God." Whether or not she is a miracle is currently under investigation by the Roman Catholic Church.

If she is a miracle, it's been a long time coming.

As a toddler, Audrey was well known to the priests at their neighborhood church, Christ the King. John Riley was a priest in training the year that Audrey turned two. "A live wire" is how he remembers the pretty little girl with the long hair and penetrating brown eyes. Audrey was the youngest of four children and, by all accounts, a normal little girl. Except that she suffered from apnea, a breathing disorder that required her to wear a heart monitor. Since her three older siblings all suffered from various forms of heart disease, perhaps this did not seem out of the ordinary to Audrey's parents.

In spite of frequent hospital stays and doctor visits, Audrey was, according to her parents, "lively," "fun," "precocious." Linda Santo was fond of calling Audrey "the Energizer bunny." The little girl enjoyed telling stories and singing songs while accompanying herself on a toy piano. That was before "that day."

That was the ninth day of August, 1987, when Audrey was playing with her older brother Stephen in the driveway of their Worcester home. Everyone else was inside. Linda was doing laundry. The older sister, Jennifer, was upstairs, on the phone. At some point, they all converged inside. Except for Audrey. *Where was Audrey?*

Minutes later they discovered Audrey floating face down in the family's above-ground swimming pool. She was blue by the time they pulled her from the water. Certified in CPR, Jennifer tried to revive her lifeless little sister while Linda called 911.

The aftermath of these horrible moments in the otherwise tranquil summertime backyard becomes heavy with recrimination — Linda continues to maintain that, after Audrey was revived, the doctors gave her an overdose of Phenobarbital. Linda also maintains that several months later, physical therapists broke both of Audrey's legs and dislocated her shoulder. In their official version of these events, the family does not mention Audrey's existing breathing disability or how that might have factored into this tragedy. A subsequent lawsuit was dismissed but Linda's bitterness toward the doctors remains apparent.

In the midst of all this, Linda's burden was compounded manyfold: Steve walked out on Linda and the family, leaving her to make the decisions that followed.

Whatever it was that happened in the hospital following Audrey's accident might never be known but what is known is that Audrey lapsed first into a coma, which lasted several days, and then she progressed to a netherworld known medically as akinetic mutism, which can only be loosely translated as a persistent vegetative state. In the opinion of most doctors, Audrey was a vegetable. In the opinion of most doctors, Linda should find a suitable institution for Audrey where she could be cared for until her inevitable death.

Linda, however, a devout Catholic who believed in the sanctity of life, all life, no matter how compromised, would not, could not hear what the doctors were saying. Audrey was her daughter and she would care for her at home, whatever it would take to accomplish.

Linda's religion provided her with the hope that the medical establishment could not. She read about a place called Medjugorge, in the former Yugoslavia. There, in 1981, miraculous apparitions of the Virgin Mary had appeared to three teenagers. Since then, in spite of an escalating civil war, millions of Catholics had come from all over the world to this rustic Bosnian village in hopes of seeing Mary. The Marian apparitions had come again, and again, to certain visitors. According to Petrisko's book, "Linda began increasingly to believe that on the one-year anniversary of her accident, Audrey would be healed." Where best to be on that date but in Medjugorge?

And so, in July of 1988, nearly a year after the accident, Linda set forth on her pilgrimage. Having secured a loan of $8,000, which she estimated would be the cost of transporting Audrey to Bosnia and back, Linda Santo, accompanied by a registered nurse, loaded the immobile child and all the necessary medical equipment into the back six seats of a jet bound for Dubrovnik. To some people, taking a nearly comatose patient on this journey, which required passage over rough roads in substandard vehicles, might seem like the wish of a crazy person. Even her mother said to her at the time, "That's impossible!" But to Linda, this was the only logical step to be made toward the healing of Audrey.

They not only survived the flight and the three-hour journey from Dubrovnik to Medjugorge, but, by special permission of the church, they wheeled Audrey into the church and shouldered her upstairs into the "apparition room." Along with the rest of the paraphernalia, Linda carried Audrey's sandals, "So that she could put them on and run up the mountain afterwards."

After two visits to the church, Audrey did appear to come to life, however, not quite enough to don her sandals and cavort across the countryside. Back in their hotel room, Audrey moved her head and her hands. Her eyes seemed to come alive. Linda went into a swoon of joy, which turned abruptly to horror as Audrey fell back on her bed and had a heart attack.

Medical care in Bosnia was less than what we expect here in the United States. Far less. Antiquated equipment and no oxygen greeted them at the first hospital they could reach. For long hours, they zig-zagged across the region, looking for something better, somehow keeping Audrey alive. Finally, Audrey was Med-Evaced to Frankfurt and then home, still alive, still Audrey. A $25,000 mortgage had to be taken out on their house, to pay for these unexpected expenses, and Audrey did not receive a healing, as they had hoped. Utter despair might have followed such a devastating experience but instead of despair, Linda felt joy. Now the miracle was that Audrey had *lived* through this grueling experience. Not healed. But alive. God works in mysterious ways.

It was after the journey to Medjugorge that things began to happen. Inside the house, statues in Audrey's room began to weep oil. And then blood. The odor of roses permeated the house, even though there were no roses present. Communion wafers bled.

Of course, in accordance with such seemingly miraculous events, people began to make their way to see Audrey. A few at first. They had heard of strange occurrences, "a beautiful presence." Visitors would go into Audrey's bedroom and kneel beside the motionless child and pray, put their hands on her forehead, kiss her luxuriant auburn hair, which flowed across her stillness like a flag of life. Some reported healings. A man claimed to have been cured of throat cancer. Another said that the pain of her cancer had decreased after seeing Audrey. None of these "healings" have ever been verified, but in response to these rumors, the number of visitors grew.

Linda claims that Mary spoke directly to Audrey at Medjugorge and asked her to become a "victim soul." This is a special term given sparingly to those who take on the suffering of others. The church does not concur with Linda's claim but that does not prevent Linda from calling Audrey a victim soul at every opportunity. Though Linda has never provided photographic evidence, Linda and her nurses claim that Audrey developed the stigmata — marks on the hands and feet that represent the wounds Christ received on the cross. Linda even reports that her daughter has shown the marks of the crown of thorns on her forehead. Twice.

Eight years passed before the church slowly turned its massive head toward Little Audrey. It's such a fine line between faith and insanity, between religion and the paranormal. The Roman Catholic Church does not want to risk sanctifying an event that might turn out to be a hoax. Or a supernatural event, unexplained by faith or science. So for many years, they let the spectacle of Audrey pass without their notice. Bishop Daniel Reilly of the Worcester Diocese is supervising the ongoing investigation, the next phase of which will include analysis of the blood, tears and oil that has invaded the Santo household over the past twelve years. The first phase of the investigation was completed in 1998 and the investigative panel (which consisted of two psychologists and one theologian) concluded that there was no apparent evidence of fraud. Lab tests on the blood and the tears remain to be done by the diocese, however, tests already done by independent sources have revealed that the blood was human blood, the tears were human tears and the oil was eighty percent olive oil and the rest, "an unknown substance."

Word spread. The visitors increased. They came from all over the world. Seeking Audrey. Neighbors complained about the extra traffic. Problems escalated, inside the house. A pilgrim tried to cut a piece of the rug from Audrey's room. Someone else yanked a hair from her head. Restrictions had to be enforced.

The Santos turned their one-car garage into a chapel. They put carpeting on the floor, covered the walls with wallboard and painted them white. They built an altar and moved an old pew into the space which used to house the family car. On the walls, they hung shelves and placed statues of Jesus and Mary on every available space. This is the manifestation now of Audrey's soul, they said, as the statues oozed oil and the legs of Jesus ran blood.

Even as recently as a year ago, visitors could step from the chapel into a space where a glass window would let them see their Audrey. No more. A little bureaucracy has grown up around Audrey. A group of volunteers who call themselves the Apostulate of the Silent Soul, Inc., now man the phones and schedule time to "see Audrey." Three days a week, for four hours at a time, volunteers open the chapel, hand out information on Audrey, and patrol parking violations on the street near the Santos' home. Once a year, they "guard" Audrey at her public appearance. John Riley, the priest who knew Audrey as a toddler, is one of the Apostulate. He agrees that Audrey leads people to Jesus. "It's really biblical. You see people coming to her mass and it could be two thousand years ago. The religious authorities are threatened but they were back then, too."

Those who want a *real* visit with Audrey, at her bedside, just like they could in years past, are told in dulcet tones that this cannot happen for at least a year, as Audrey's schedule is booked. Through the Apostulate, followers or the curious can buy videos about Audrey's life, the book that tells the family's version of Audrey's story, or subscribe to their monthly newsletter. Seekers can also request the oil, but only by mail. It will come to them absorbed into a cotton ball and safe inside a Zip-loc bag. For the oil, there is no charge. "A gift from God," they say.

The oil can supplant the need for a visit. A man from Long Island claimed that, using the oil-soaked cotton ball provided him, his sister-in-law recovered not only from lymphoma but also from a stroke-induced coma. Her coma lasted five months until he applied the cotton ball to her arm, while praying. "I believe she has made a miraculous recovery," he wrote to the Santos. Apparently, healing can be achieved without a visit, without the oil — just through the miracle of television. One person from Quebec, identified only as "S.K" in the family's newsletter, wrote the family after watching a story about Audrey on television and reported "my extreme pain from cancer of the bones was relieved."

Mary Cormier, a neatly dressed woman in her sixties, first visited Audrey two years ago. "Just coming into the house was an experience I couldn't explain," she said recently. "I found that I just kept coming back. I spent more and more time here." At that time, Mary was living in Salem, New Hampshire. "Pretty soon, I was just here all the time." Mary left her family in Salem and moved to Worcester. "I've devoted my life to this now. I'm here seven days a week. I miss my kids, I miss the beach," she says, somewhat wistfully. "But we formed the Apostulate to help the pilgrims and to help the family. This is an honor. I felt that God called me down here. Audrey has changed my life, most definitely."

Mary is now the spokesperson for the Santo family, who are as difficult to talk to as Audrey.

But the chapel is open to all comers. No reservations are necessary. Priests arrive spontaneously from all over the country and say mass. "You never know what is going to happen," Mary Cormier says, delighted. "Every day is different."

On a late summer day, inside the little room, a couple of dozen men, women, and children gather. The air is close, in spite of the efforts of a fan that turns back and forth, back and forth. The faint scent of roses hangs in the air. Beneath our feet, the carpeting is stained with oil and the surface of the altar is pooled in oil. Certain surfaces are covered in plastic, a halfhearted attempt to protect what apparently cannot be protected. Even the big red bible on its stand runs oil out of its cover and the picture on the wall of the Last Supper is stained with oil in the shape of a chalice. Mary Cormier points this out to us, in case we miss the shadowy likeness of the Holy Cup. "It's a mystery," she says.

The question of what, exactly, is miraculous, hangs in the balance and the Bishop's commission continues to probe. "The presence of oil is not proof, direct or indirect, of the miraculous," the Bishop's statement reads. "Paranormal activities in and of themselves . . . do not provide a basis for proving the miraculous. . . . One cannot presume that the inability to explain something automatically makes it miraculous."

Mary often introduces the story of Audrey to visitors to the chapel. Her talk goes on for ten or fifteen minutes, as she explains the various strange phenomenon familiar to Audrey's followers. Toward the end she says, "We believe that Audrey does two things: We believe she is a statement of life in a culture of death and we believe that she brings you to Jesus." The visitors listen in silence, occasionally shaking their heads, sighing or muttering exclamations. "Audrey hasn't said a word to you but she has brought you here and it seems as though God speaks volumes around her."

A small boy places a quarter on the oil-stained table and then steps back next to his mother. Donations come, large and small.

The Bishop's investigation has stated that there does not appear to be any financial gain for the family through the events that surround Audrey. According to the family, contributions and donations collected for Audrey are used to help with her medical bills, which includes round-the-clock nursing care. The Bishop's lengthy report came to one conclusion: "The most striking evidence of the presence of God in the Santo home is seen in the dedication of the family to Audrey."

Tied to the feet of the crucifix that hangs over the altar, a small plastic cup captures the dripping oil. A large statue of Jesus stands in front of the altar. His feet are cloaked in red plastic and from the tip of his pointed beard, a large drop hangs, about to fall into another small plastic cup, tied around his neck. Statues on every shelf are wet with oil. A woman in a wheelchair clutches the hand of the woman who has brought her. Tears run from her old eyes.

From inside the crying room, Audrey Marie Santo looks out. Her glistening eyes appear to watch as each hopeful visitor reaches the window and gazes in, hands on the glass. Some leave roses. One leaves a small stuffed teddy bear. Others turn away and weep. A police woman stands beside the window. The ecstatic pilgrims want so much to linger but they must not. They have been told: *keep moving, please.* There are thousands more outside, waiting in the hot sun, many of them too sick to stand. But they inch forward in line.

For long moments, Audrey's eyes seem to focus on the faces that file past her. With her wide eyes and open mouth, she seems to wear a look of surprise, to see her admirers. A white-haired woman in a tailored suit stops and puts her hand on the glass: "Hi, Audrey," she says. "Darling Audrey!" A young Asian man carries his brain-damaged daughter in his arms. They stop, gaze raptly and then wave to Little Audrey. Touching the window with their fingertips and signing the cross, the pilgrims shuffle past obediently, with their secret needs, their silent prayers. Photographers balance on the tops of the pews, for better perspective, and their lenses wheeze.

The nun continues her litany.

For the sake of His sorrowful passion. For the sake of His sorrowful passion. For the sake of His sorrowful passion.

"An innocent, bed-ridden girl," is how Bishop Reilly characterizes Little Audrey. But, a miracle? He is not ready to verify that claim. "This will take significant time and resources." A victim soul? "One would have to determine that Audrey, at the age of three was, and presently is, capable of making a free choice to accept the suffering of others," his statement reads.

Healing Audrey seems to have been lost in all that has occurred since her trip to Medjugorge. There is a peculiar logic that pervades all who surround Audrey, so that whatever it is that will happen bends back toward Audrey, as the source. The idea of Audrey's recovery is not mentioned in their literature or in their video but, when asked, Mary Cormier told me, "We pray every day that she will get up and walk. There is always hope. You just look at her and you feel hope." But the reality of Audrey's celestial celebrity seems to have completely sunken in. When asked recently whether or not she wished that the terrible drowning accident had never happened to her daughter, Linda Santo was hesitant to reply. "I'm not sure," she told the reporter.

A pink, lace-edged vision, Audrey's lifeless body communicates nothing to the unaffected observer. To the faithful, she communicates everything that they can possibly imagine. Lying inside her unexpressed, unknown life, she is the very embodiment of faith, a mustard seed, a grain of sand. What is a miracle? "An extraordinary event manifesting divine intervention in human affairs," explains Webster's. Perhaps a miracle is simply what we are willing to believe. Apparently thousands of people are willing to believe in Audrey, without the official sanctification of the Roman Catholic Church. Perhaps that is all that faith is.

The nun has intoned the rosaries for hours, with hardly a break. She has sung, a capella, the soothing *Oh, Maria* and the pilgrims have joined with her in song, the verses going round and round.

Outside, on the green lawn beside the big church, Linda and Steve Santo hold a press conference. Last year, Steve returned to Linda and the family. They have called this "one of Audrey's biggest miracles." Today, they are upbeat and appear to shine from all the attention given to their Audrey. Audrey, they say, "knows everything," and people are "constantly" being healed through Audrey's intercession. All life is precious, Linda Santo says.

In the crying room, a nurse vacuums the inside of Audrey's mouth and from the pulpit the nun starts the wheel again:

O My Jesus, save us from the fires of hell. Lead all souls to heaven, especially those most in need of Thy mercy.

February 2000 Yankee magazine

LITTLE AUDREY SANTO *died from cardio-respiratory failure on April 14, 2007 at home with family, friends and members of the clergy by her side. At her funeral mass, hundreds of mourners wept as her gleaming, off-white coffin was slowly wheeled down the aisle of St. Paul's Cathedral in Worcester, Massachusetts. The year before her death, the Diocese of Worcester had conducted an investigation and concluded that there was no evidence of trickery and that the happenings surrounding Audrey were "deep mysteries" but not definitive miracles. Still, many testified to the contrary after her funeral mass. "I've seen the miracles, I've witnessed them," Pat Coyne, one of the many volunteers who had worked at the Santo home during her life, was quoted as saying.*

In September of 2007, Dr. Andrea Ambrosi, postulator from the Congregation of the Causes of Saints, which oversees the complicated process for the canonization of saints, came from Rome to stay with the Santo family for four days. He began the Cause for Audrey by making her a Servant of God, a title given by the Vatican to deceased individuals who are being investigated for official recognition as a saint. The Little Audrey Santo Foundation, which is operated out of the Santo's home, maintains an extensive website that features, among other things, an offering of the oil they claim continues to weep from the images in Audrey's room. The oil that they offer is free. But there is also a catalog for Little Audrey gift items that can be ordered off the site. Included among the list of dozens of items available for sale is a Little Audrey magnet, a Little Audrey t-shirt, and a DVD of Audrey's funeral.

Thelma's Dream Quilts

THELMA HANSON's first quilt came to her in a dream. "I was blowing kisses for my granddaughter, that's what I remembered, and I wondered how I could make that into a quilt," she says.

With one hand under the hoop and one on top, Thelma pushes the needle up from beneath the quilted scene and back down into it again. Seated in a cushioned garden chair, leaning over the double bed, Thelma is in her "cubbyhole," which is what she calls the guest bedroom in her Lincoln, New Hampshire, home. Thelma is seventy-four and retired from a lifetime as a seamstress in Newport, Rhode Island. This is her seventh quilt, made up out of her head and without any instruction.

"It just hit me one day," she says. "I saw the picture in my head and wondered if I could do it."

To find out, Thelma brought out an old quilt top that her Aunt Mabel had made many years ago. It was the only quilt Thelma had, and it was unfinished, but she studied the octagonal configurations that Aunt Mabel had stitched together from old cloth. This was the traditional design known as "Grandma's Flower Garden." Thelma did not know anything about quilts and didn't know anyone who did but after years of making slipcovers, she certainly knew how to sew. In a closet, Thelma had a stash of aprons Aunt Mabel had left her. "I cut up all her aprons to make it. Mainly, I wanted to see: Could I do it?"

Thelma was a fast learner. Once she had done the "practice" quilt, she went on to make the kisses quilt for her youngest granddaughter, Samantha, who was three at the time. In the quilt, hearts in all shades of red rise up from the mouth of an old woman in the bottom corner. The quilt is a constellation of hearts on a cloth sky. Just like Thelma's dream.

After that, she made a baby quilt for a friend and a quilt for her other granddaughter that showed a pot of gold at the end of a rainbow. But instead of gold, Thelma put hearts in the pot. "I wanted her to know that it's not all about money."

Then she thought of a quilt for W. Murray Clark who owns Clark's Trading Post. It was to be the fiftieth anniversary of his landmark tourist attraction and she envisioned a quilt with scenes of his enterprise and in the center, she saw Murray with his famous dancing bear. Murray was an old friend to her and to her husband, Fred, and so she wanted to do the quilt as a surprise but it took her a year, two thousand hours of stitching. Word spread through the town. "I don't know how we kept it secret. Everyone knew that I was making it but somehow, Murray never found out. When they unveiled it at the party, he cried, oh, yes, he cried."

Since she started that first quilt eight years ago, Thelma has spent almost every day bent over her creations. She works from nine to five, most days. Each quilt takes her about a year to complete and Thelma's quilts are always made as gifts. She has never sold any and she doesn't think of her quilt-making in that way. "I do it for love," she says.

The quilt through which she is moving her needle today is for her sister. "This is my first pond," she says, "first water. I'm going to put what I *hope* will look like water moving. Not everything I do comes out looking the way it's supposed to be!"

All around Thelma are stacks of folded cloth in reds, yellows, browns, blues, greens. The table beside her is crowded with baskets holding pincushions, scissors, spools of thread, and small boxes of needles and pins. The bookcases at the end of the bed are lined with bolts of fabric, material saved from other jobs. From all this, she renders what is "supposed to be." Several fishbowls are stuffed with colorful but tiny scraps. "I never throw anything away," she says. Any of these snippets could become a shoe, a hand, a bow tie. She rarely buys fabric. "But that's what quilts were. They needed something warm and they made them out of old cloth — an old dress or an old pair of pants."

For the pond, multicolored gray fabric represent rocks. Around these patches, she has fashioned fish, frogs, and turtles and over the water, dragonflies hover. At the center, a big white swan glides. "I knew it had to be a swan. That's what I started with, because I know how much my sister loves swans." The quilting stitches that Thelma is making now are becoming waves and ripples to make the water move. The process of quilting the three layers of fabric together is Thelma's favorite part. "I hate to see it end. The quilting is the fun part. It brings it all to life."

Her last quilt, which she considers to be her best effort, she called "Country Fair," a busy scene that started with a carousel in the center and evolved into a buzzing summer day in the 1930s, a time that Thelma seems to prefer to the present. Working on the quilt took her back, and she liked the journey. "It reminded me of when we were children. We didn't have what the kids have today. The carousel was all we had at the fair, plus the animals. And the band. We never had money to go out to eat, so Mom always brought a picnic lunch. The fair was a big deal back then. We kids did simpler things and still had fun."

Thelma grew up in Gloucester and her father played in the American Legion Band. "Every time there was a carnival or something going on, we were there because he was playing. We had an awful lot of fun and we weren't afraid. Today there's a lot of fear and a lot of cruelty in the world. We didn't have that then."

In the bottom corner of the Country Fair quilt, Thelma created a bandstand with a ten-member band playing their little cloth instruments. On the grass outside the bandstand, little gingham girls dance.

Thelma counts one hundred and fifty-eight people in this quilt with various scenes all over its immense 118" x 116" landscape. "I have ladies showing their quilts, kids eating candy apples, displays of jams and jellies, kids climbing the tree, men playing horseshoes, people spreading their blanket for their picnics. I had to end it. I had so many people, I just had to end it."

The swan quilt is a pastoral scene. "I didn't want to have any people in this quilt. I thought this time, I'd like to have just a quiet time."

Thelma works a long, seamless day while her husband, Fred, works in town at the local ski area. The room in which she works is silent. "I don't like music or TV on or anything." The only sounds are the ticking of the hallway clock; the rhythmic snores of her little dog, Ebony, who sleeps at her feet while she works; and the sound of thread puncturing and passing through cloth. The hours fly.

Thelma learned to sew from her mother. "Mom sewed everything cause she had to. She made all our clothes. I just came by it naturally."

Her fingers, bent somewhat from arthritis, move deftly across the colorful scene. "I've got a lot of holes in my fingers," she says. The holes come when she pushes the backs of the needles up through the cloth. She could use a thimble to protect her finger but "it gets in the way," she says. A millinery needle suits her purpose better than a quilting needle. "They're short and fat, and I don't like the way they feel. This millinery needle is thin and easier to handle." Thelma snips the finished thread, pulls a new length through the eye, and begins again. Each quilt absorbs something like two thousand yards of thread.

She doesn't sketch her pattern or plan it in any concrete way before she begins. Her scenes come out of her head, out of her dreams. "That's one of the things that's fun, making it come out so it looks like it should but I'm not trying to be perfect. It's by hand, it's from out of my head. I guess it shouldn't be perfect."

While she's working on one, in her head, she's designing the next one. "I can see it finished, I know what I want," she says. "My next one is going to be a winter scene. I've never done winter before. I want to make an ice pond with kids skating and a hill for sledding."

Although she has had plenty of invitations, Thelma has never shown her quilts. She's afraid something might happen to them while they are out of her hands. "Well, you have to leave them at the show. I'm seventy-four and I figure if I leave them and the place burns down, I probably wouldn't live long enough to replace it." But she's had some endorsements that personally warm her. "I had a lady come when I was working on the fair quilt. She belonged to a quilt guild in Texas, and she said 'I've been in it for twenty-five years and I've never seen a quilt like this one. That belongs in a museum!' That made me feel pretty good, from someone who knows quilting, because I don't know quilting."

It may not be the textbook method, but it's Thelma's way. "I don't quilt like you're supposed to," she says, and she laughs.

She is a bit mystified how it all came to be. Although she spent thirty years making slipcovers, she made them by machine. "I did nothing of this sort before," she says. "I don't know why I got into this. It just hit me one day. Something to leave behind, I guess."

July/August 2000 Yankee magazine

THELMA IS STILL *making quilts at her home in Lincoln, New Hampshire. Her masterpiece, the quilt in honor of Murray Clark, is on display at Clark's Trading Post in Lincoln. About a year after this article was published, she and Fred surprised me one day, driving down to Dublin with a large bundle which the two of them ceremoniously unfolded to reveal a queen-size quilt she had created for me. She told me that she had spent more than six months making this complicated quilt, working each day, nine to five. This was the most amazing gift I have ever received. In the center of the quilt was one of my columns, transferred onto the cloth by some magical process I don't understand. The column was about how many of us have front doors that we rarely use. Beside it, she quilted a big front door. The rest of the quilt was a rendering of my house, in all four seasons, one season for each side of the quilt. She had never seen my house but had imagined it from what she had read in my column. It was unbelievably similar to my house. Thelma dreams in real-life.*

The Queen Bee of the North Woods

In the early summer of 1975, twenty-four-year-old Roxanne Quimby arrived in northern Maine, having driven across the country with her boyfriend, looking for a place to homestead. Between them, they had $3,000. Their journey had taken them to Northern California (too expensive), Oregon and Washington (they didn't like it and no one liked them, bearing as they did those nasty California license plates), and Vermont (too expensive). Northern Maine, they were told, was the last place to find cheap land. In Guilford, a mill town fifty miles northwest of Bangor, they found thirty acres of woods on a back road for that sum. Like thousands of other young people at that time, they planned to build a cabin and live off the land, there at the edge of the fabled North Woods. On the day of their arrival, as Roxanne stepped out of that road-weary Volkswagen bus onto the carpet of pine needles that was to be her home for the next twenty years, you might, if you were paying keen attention, have felt the earth tremble just slightly beneath her feet, for the state of Maine would never be quite the same again after that moment.

Just a short while later, in 1976, the last logs of the North Woods tumbled down the Kennebec River and brought to an end the legendary world of the river drivers, which for generations had been alive with teams of oxen, timber cruisers, camp bosses and loggers, a place that resounded with the ring of the axe, the stomp and snort of the horse or ox, and the smell of fresh sap. When those last logs drifted into the boom, it is possible that no one quite knew the changes that lay ahead for the ten-million-acre kingdom called the North Woods. Rather than seeming like an end, this may have been perceived as progress. Logs would move on railcars and on trucks, as they had been increasingly for many years. It seemed as if nothing much else would change. That chapter of the Maine woods might have been over but the framework that had supported it all those years — the paper companies that owned all that land — would remain. The woods, everyone assumed, would continue to regenerate and the need for wood and paper would never end.

The purpose of owning this vast timberland was to harvest the trees. Whatever else went on on that land didn't much matter to the paper companies. Thousands of hunting camps rest among the pine and spruce and at the edges of those ponds, there by virtue of the hundred-year lease, given out by the paper companies to whoever staked a claim. Hunters and their families built camps, often of logs cut from the property, and knowingly at risk of someday losing the land beneath their efforts. But nothing ever happened. Hundreds of miles of snowmobile trails were cut through the forest. Recreation became the North Woods' secondary use. For generations, paper companies allowed a special kind of privilege: public use of private land.

Roxanne knew little about any of this when she arrived. She was not a woodswoman but an aspiring artist. Having just graduated from art school in San Francisco, she envisioned a life in the woods where costs would be low enough so that she could paint canvases and sell her work. But first, there had to be shelter. She and her soon-to-be husband, George St. Clair, used a bow saw to clear enough of the trees to build a 20x30-foot cabin. There would be no running water, no electricity, no phone, which they did not regard as a hardship so much as a challenge to their spirit. They opened a space in the woods for a garden, which would feed them. And life began for them in a place unlike anything they had ever known. "We were very idealistic. We did a lot of wood splitting, a lot of bow saw work, a lot of hauling of things. It was very different from the way I had been raised," Roxanne says now. "It was really important for me to be able to prove to myself that I didn't have to live the way my parents lived."

Roxanne, who had grown up in Lexington, Massachusetts, and had gone from there to San Francisco, had much to learn about the place and the culture of northern Maine. Roxanne found work as a waitress and George worked occasionally as a disc jockey at a local radio station. The old VW bus died and so they walked where they needed to go. At the end of each year, they had enough money to pay their taxes and buy the small things they needed. Four years later, Roxanne gave birth to twins, a boy and a girl. After a few years, George found a life elsewhere.

So it was Roxanne and the twins, in the cabin. Roxanne needed more money than what she was making. One day, she stopped to buy honey from a pickup truck parked by the side of the road. She became friendly with the man selling the honey, a gruff, bearded beekeeper named Burt Shavitz. He was older than she by fifteen years and was having trouble with his back. She offered to help him, lifting supers and moving hives, and he gladly accepted as he could use a woman with a good strong back. So, for that summer, she worked for Burt, learning how to keep bees, learning how to render honey. "I was really inspired by the bees, the way they all worked together, I thought, oh, what good little communists they are. Well, except for that queen in there," she says.

She and Burt became partners, partners in life and partners in business. She put the honey into prettier jars, pouring the golden sweetness into little bears and hive-shaped containers. Packaged in this way, their honey business picked up.

In his barn, Burt had a lot of wax. Burt saw it as waste from the hives; Roxanne saw it as candles. "What are you going to do with that wax?" Roxanne asked him one day. "You can have it if you want it," was Burt's reply. So she started making candles and decided to take these two products, honey and candles, on the road to craft fairs.

The honey sold steadily and the candles sold well in the fall and through the Christmas season but people didn't seem to want to buy candles in the summer. They melt. They have no allure. So Roxanne looked around for something else to do with the wax and found an old book with some recipes that called for beeswax. On her woodstove, she made up cauldrons of boot polish and furniture polish and poured the substances into little tins. She liked the tins. They looked old-fashioned and homey. And then she discovered a recipe for lip balm.

She labeled the products Burt's Bees. Burt had all his hives stenciled, Burt's Bees, and when Roxanne was out there working the hives, "I used to think that was so funny, as if anyone could actually own a bee!" So she put it on the tins. She found that when people came by her table, even if they didn't buy anything, they liked the name. "People would go, 'Look, honey, Burt's Bees!' and they would laugh and keep walking, saying things like, 'Burt's Bees, Burt's Bees! Mind you own beeswax!' They seemed to love to say it," she recalls. "It was so simple, down to earth, two syllables, nothing fancy, sort of like Burt, sort of like the product, sort of like the lifestyle I was trying to paint. So I thought, OK, yeah, that's a good name."

Some may have chuckled over the name but most of them bought it. Once she put the lip balm out onto the table, it flew. She couldn't make enough of it. She moved all her wax and the cauldrons to the abandoned schoolhouse in Guilford. It didn't have running water or electricity either but she barely noticed, setting the cauldron onto the gas range and working sometimes till midnight by the light of kerosene lamps. She added a drawing of Burt onto the label, his bearded face representing anything but beauty. Buyers embraced the product even more, enjoying the straightforward approach.

That was the beginning of Burt's Bees, which today is the best-selling natural personal care brand of cosmetics in the country, a brand market researchers call "lightning in a bottle."

But this little handcrafted product was hardly so back then. Roxanne followed the destiny of her creation one step at a time, a road without a map that led her, after twenty years living and doing business from this remote Maine town, to North Carolina where she felt the business climate was more favorable than it had been in Maine. Maine was high on taxes and low on accessibility. Shipping her products now all over the country and beyond, she discovered Raleigh, North Carolina, was exactly halfway between New York and Miami. It was 1994. Her twins were in boarding school. As much as she hated to leave, Roxanne left Maine for the south, where she had never been. She had seen *Easy Rider* back in those days and she had clung ever since to the idea that the south was a scary place. Now she was not only going there but she was moving there, not with a backpack but with a three million dollar business of her own creation in tow.

THE SAME YEAR Roxanne left Maine, Scott Paper, one of the two largest landowners in Maine, sold everything they owned to SAPPI — South African Pulp and Paper Inc., which represented, if anyone was watching, a shift in the global market and a shift in the life of the Maine woods at least as significant as the end of the river drives. Apparently no one foresaw that opening the world to free trade would one day steal away the North Woods. Markets in China and South America became easier places to find wood and paper. And much cheaper. As if by the work of a thief in the night, the North Woods went up on the block. Tracts of thousands of acres of land came up for sale. A Seattle-based firm called Plum Creek — which turned out to be as much a real estate developer as a timber company — was buying. a timber company from Seattle.

Four years later, in 1998, SAPPI sold the land to Plum Creek. In all, it was nearly a million acres surrounding Moosehead Lake, New England's largest lake. Shrine to many, Moosehead Lake is a place almost as stoked in memory and legend as Katahdin. If the arrival of Roxanne Quimby caused a tremor, Plum Creek's arrival caused an earthquake throughout this, the largest expanse of wilderness east of the Mississippi.

"Plum Creek is now the largest landowner in the United States," Jym St. Pierre says. Jym is the Maine Director of an organization called RESTORE: The North Woods. In 1994, RESTORE put forward the idea of creating a 3.2 million acre park: Maine Woods National Park (MWNP). "I saw the signs on the horizon, even back in the 1980s, that things were going to change," St. Pierre says. "What I didn't predict was the speed of it. I didn't think it was going to happen this fast. This is not evolution. This is *revolution.*"

By 2005, Plum Creek had proposed a plan to develop four hundred thousand acres surrounding Moosehead. The plan included the development of two large resorts and nearly a thousand residential lots. "This is the largest, most controversial project ever proposed in the history of Maine," St. Pierre says.

Unable to gain approval from the state's LURC (Land Use Regulatory Commission, which acts as a zoning board for Maine's unorganized townships), Plum Creek has revised the plan three times. The current proposal is under review. Plum Creek has emphasized that much of the land will be placed under conservation easement, a move to calm the fears of environmentalists. St. Pierre explains that the easements, which will continue to allow forestry activity, road construction, sawmills, cell towers, herbicide spraying, mining, even subdivision, are not for conservation but for continuous forestry. "You can shape these easements any way you want. Some of them are very good. These Plum Creek easements have no value."

Plum Creek, however, has forced the hand of many in these perilous times in a state where employment is way down and poverty is on the rise. St.Pierre quotes statistics: five thousand people once worked in the mills of Millinocket and E. Millinocket. Today, only five hundred are employed there. "I don't blame people for clinging to the hope that some of those days will come back," St. Pierre says. "The forestry industry will survive but it won't be the driver anymore. The biggest industry in the state of Maine is tourism and Plum Creek is trying to tap into that in a way that will give them maximum profit. They buy land cheap and sell it high. They still make money by cutting trees but they make most of their money cutting up land."

The debate in Maine over what should happen to this abandoned kingdom gets louder with each passing year. RESTORE has been vocal in their efforts to create the Maine Woods National Park (MWNP) but their proposal has been rebuffed by many an independent Mainer. One bumper sticker reads: RESTORE BOSTON: Leave the Maine Woods Alone.

"For a long time, we had this big place, over ten million acres, as big as the whole rest of New England, that people just forgot about," St. Pierre says. "It was a big blank spot on the map and now everybody's scrapping for it. Everything about this is big. It's the last big place. Look around the country. I don't know of any other place that's in play like this. Even Alaska. We're all trying to figure out what the brave new world will be up there."

St. Pierre cites the paper companies' indulgence in allowing the public to use their private lands. "The biggest reason we don't have a national park in Maine today is because we've had a defacto park for generations. People feel entitled to that land, just because it's always been there."

St. Pierre's father and grandfather worked in the mills and in the woods. "People thought this land was like a permanent institution, like the US government," he says. "They thought it was going to be there forever and always be the same. Well, no matter what happens, that is not the case."

ROXANNE, WHO has never worn a wristwatch and never will, was by then surely the most unorthodox CEO in America. In her corporate headquarters in North Carolina, she conducted herself in the spirit of who she had been, back in those hippie days. Dogs and children were welcome in the workplace. She didn't have a private office, but instead kept her desk in the art department, making herself available to any of her three hundred employees. She shunned focus groups: "They only confirm what you already know. A consumer cannot vocalize what is missing in their lives. You have to give them something they don't know they want."

She never advertised Burt's Bees. "I always felt it was much more important what people said about us than what we said about ourselves," she says of the product that sold mostly by word of mouth. Roxanne found that a key to the success of her products was the process of discovery. "Once (the consumer) found Burt's Bees, they felt like it was theirs, it became personal. They put their flag in, as if to say, *This is mine, I discovered it!* And they became really loyal."

Burt accompanied Roxanne to North Carolina but lasted only two months. According to Roxanne, he kept losing his car in the parking lot, which is a way of saying life was too crowded down there, too overwhelming. And so Roxanne bought out his share of the business and he returned to his converted chicken coop in Maine, where he still lives, an abandoned bee hive in the front yard, goldenrod growing high all around it.

In 2003, having grown the business to a phenomenal $60 million a year, Roxanne Quimby sold Burt's Bees to AEA, a New York investment company, for nearly $141 million, but she retained twenty percent ownership. Not exactly overnight but in the comfort of time, Roxanne Quimby, she of the long skirts and wood-heated spaces, had become a vastly wealthy woman. "At that point, I said to myself, 'Now what, Roxanne? You are only fifty-six and you've got another twenty years of life on this earth, what do you want to do?'"

She went to Hawaii and to Antarctica and all the places she had always wanted to go. She shopped for a home in Palm Beach. She bought six. "I was questing," she says now.

And then she returned to Maine where the fight for the North Woods was on. She came to realize that "money itself is totally worthless. You can't eat it. You can't cover yourself up with it at night and stay warm. Money is only what it does and so I was trying to find the most meaningful thing I could do with the money I can."

And so she began to buy up the North Woods.

MAPS SPREAD before her on the long table, Roxanne Quimby draws red outlines onto a map of northern Maine. Roxanne is formidable, tall and imposing, dressed in black, her long dark hair hanging loose. It's as easy to see her swinging an axe as it is to imagine her in command of a large platoon. "Everything in red is mine," she says.

On the map, Baxter State Park cuts a clean, elongated block right in the center of the big ragged cranial head of the state of Maine. Baxter State Park is the creation of Governor Percival P. Baxter, who served as Maine's governor for only four years (1921-1925), during which time he tried and failed to make Mt. Katahdin, which he regarded as the state's crowning glory, a state park. In spite of that failure, "Mr. Maine," as he was sometimes known, never lost sight of that goal. Not a particularly vigorous outdoorsman, Baxter once climbed Katahdin and became feverish and ill. Through his fever that day, he vowed to himself that, if he lived, he would ensure that one day, the mountain, which then belonged to the Great Northern Paper Company and to one other private owner, would belong to the state of Maine forever.

Starting in 1930 and ending in 1962, Baxter quietly purchased twenty-eight separate pieces of land, a crazy quilt of mountains and streams, ponds and waterfalls that he put together to form what is now known as Baxter State Park, 202,064 acres, more than three hundred and fifteen square miles of stark wilderness, a place Baxter willed to be "forever wild," and which will remain so through the deeds of his trust. These were not simple purchases, given over for the asking price. As he bought more and more parcels and closed most of them to hunting, angry citizens raised their voices. A park, Baxter discovered, was not something everyone embraced. At the end, he conceded a section of the park to hunters and forestry. He realized the passion of these people and made these concessions.

Most of Roxanne's red rectangles are to the east of the park. She is stitching her own crazy quilt. These are plots of land she has bought. There are others she hopes to buy. Some are scattered and separate. By bargaining and swapping, she is trying to put together a whole. In concert with RESTORE what she has in mind is a national park. "I feel like my reason for being put on this earth will have been fulfilled because this will live on after me. A park is a demonstration that there is something in America that I can love," she says, her counterculture philosophy reemerging. "It's very democratic, a Mexican immigrant or a millionaire, for ten bucks, they both get the same experience."

She is sitting in the front room of one of her many homes, far from the cabin in Guilford. This particular house is in Portland and it so happens to have once belonged to Governor Percival P. Baxter, whom she admires a great deal and from whom she has learned a few things. "He is very inspiring to me," she adds, "but there is a difference between the two of us. Governor Baxter inherited his money. He didn't earn it. That makes for a whole different outlook. The way Percival Baxter went about acquiring his land must have been different, spending someone else's money. I fight tooth and nail for every dollar. I'm a business person. I don't want to be taken advantage of."

That Roxanne Quimby and Percival Baxter live and lived at the opposite ends of the American spectrum is true. The North Woods are Roxanne's passion now, as the bees once were. "It was part of the culture of our family, to be out in the woods," she recalls. "Both my kids hiked the entire Appalachian Trail. The fact that the paper companies were downsizing came at the right time for me. There were all these opportunities. They used the woods and owned the mills and that did, in some ways, preserve the wilderness because they never cut it up into pieces, so it's still fairly intact. Chesuncook, Northeast Carry, Kakadjo, people carry those places in their minds and even if they don't get there, it's important that it's there, that they could be there if they wanted to."

By the summer of 2007, Roxanne Quimby had spent $39 million of her fortune to purchase some eighty thousand acres of wilderness. Nearly sixty-five thousand acres of this surrounds the East Branch of the Penobscot River and substantially abuts Baxter State Park. To her mind, a park is the only reasonable destiny for this land. "If we leave this to chance, we will not have the opportunity to make decisions about what happens next."

In the process of making these purchases, Roxanne gobbled up hunting grounds, snowmobile trails, a significant portion of the East Branch of the Penobscot River and some beloved primitive camps families and hunters have passed down through generations. "I own it now," Roxanne proclaimed. "Buying the land also means I am buying the right to call the shots. I can do what I want with it."

Roxanne, now the undisputed queen bee of the North Woods, returns to the map. Her strategy is ironclad. "These two pieces of land here effectively stop all east-west traffic. This bridge, the Whetstone Bridge, here. It's one of the very significant nails in the coffin because it's the only way to get across the river for something like thirty miles. OK, you can go over the bridge but you can't go across my land with a car. So you can have your bridge but it ain't doin' you any good. I'm closing in and I'm doing this to demonstrate that you *can not* leave this to chance."

She is speaking broadly to those who oppose a park, those who ironically also claim they believe in property rights. "Yes, it's a private road but it's been in such permissive use for so many years, people forget that the state does not own that road."

Up there, where she is pointing, people slapped bumper stickers onto their cars and wore t-shirts emblazened with the slogan, "Ban Roxanne." Letters to the editor condemned her.

This reaction shocked her. "I couldn't believe it," she says. "I was really blown away. I could not believe people would come after me like that, so personally and with such venom. I thought I would be appreciated. I mean, doesn't everybody love a park?"

At the time, Roxanne was on the board of RESTORE. "People up there *hate* RESTORE so I put some distance between us at that point. I didn't need that."

But Roxanne and RESTORE work in supportive ways. "We are not a land trust," Jym St. Pierre clarifies. "RESTORE does not buy land. Rather, we are an advocacy group. We promote ideas. The idea of this park is still being hotly debated more than thirteen years after it was first proposed. MWNP remains robust, in part, because Roxanne Quimby has made it tangible. There is nothing more real than real estate and Roxanne has repeatedly said she would like to see the lands she has acquired become the seeds of a new national park. What she owns now would be a very credible beginning."

When Roxanne was growing up, she often played Monopoly. "I *loved* that game. I had two sisters and a brother, all younger, and they were always available to play. I hated to lose, so I always made sure, one way or the other, that I won."

This is how Governor Baxter got his park — one piece at a time with many setbacks and disappointments. But, in the end, he won.

Roxanne's plan is somewhat counterintuitive. She returns to the bees of her past. "To me, ownership and private property were the beginning of the end in this country. Once the Europeans came in, drawing lines and dividing things up, things started getting exploited and overconsumed. But a park takes away the whole issue of ownership, it's off the table, we all own it and we all share it. It's so democratic."

But first, she has to own it.

"It's becoming increasingly clear that I can chase them all over the place. I think they see now that I am not going to be stopped."

THE MUSCLY Piscataquis River runs through Guilford, a town of rugged people, about fifteen hundred of them, most of them working at the local mills, mills that have made for years such hardwood products as golf tees, toothpicks, Popsicle sticks and wooden nickels. Guilford's town manager Tom Goulette leans on the counter and talks about the time when surprised townspeople watched the long-haired Roxanne and her company outgrow his town. Everyone has a story about her, like that Burt used to borrow the town shovel and take it over to Burt's Bees and clear their walks, as if they couldn't afford to buy a ten dollar shovel for themselves. Same with the town broom, even the town fly swatter was borrowed. Burt's Bees stood out for their long-haired ways and for their unorthodox ways of doing things. "For all the make-up she made, I don't think she's ever worn any," he notes dryly.

"She made so much money in Maine, she had to leave the state to make more money," he adds, somewhat sour that she took her business to the south to take advantage of a superior business climate. But he corrects himself. "She was different. Hard-nosed, successful. She's made it and she deserves it, just like Bill Gates. I don't agree with her but I do respect her."

He stops. He's a tall man, bearded and probably the same age as Roxanne. For some years, they shared this town. "Now she's one of those kingdom holders. She's kicked out all the leaseholders. This doesn't go over very well."

With her purchase, Roxanne closed these lands to snowmobiles and hunting and gave notice to the camp owners. The land was hers now. She made statements in the press that fueled their fire but then she realized this was not the right path. "I needed to meet with them and hear what their needs were. I feel like we are both at the table as equals, I've never felt I'm entitled to anything more or less than anyone else so I think that puts me in a unique position to work with these folks. And they really like me, I don't feel any antagonism from them. They keep shaking their heads and thinking, 'You're just like a regular person, aren't you?'"

Terry Hill and her husband, Craig, have run the wilderness resort known as Shin Pond Village Campground in Patten, Maine, for some thirty years and were among those who felt steaming outrage — not only at the fact of Roxanne's acquisitions but also at her, this woman who came charging into the woods like a strike force, money on her belt like repeating ammunition.

"When this started, we were ready to fight," says Terry. Their one hundred acre resort includes campgrounds, cottages and miles of snowmobiling trails that cut right through Roxanne's land. Meetings were called. But Roxanne came to listen. A year of meetings has made a huge difference. "In the past year, I've done a one hundred and eighty degree turn in this process," Terry says. "She's listening. She's extended our rights for the snowmobile trails for another year. She's working hard to be a better neighbor. We don't know what the future of the Maine woods will be, none of us do. But we do know that we all love the woods, we love our land and maybe, in the long run, we all want the same thing."

THE OLD NORTH WOODS opens up like a trunk full of memories, smelling of camphor and pine needles, wood smoke and melting snow. When a river driver died, riding a log or busting up a jam, they would find his spiked boots downstream and hang them on a tree near the river. The shoes would hang there for years as a memorial until they disintegrated. We have nothing to hang on the tree now, no vestige of that life gone by.

The Lumbermen's Museum in Patten, Maine, is as close as we will likely get. Exhibits of the way things were in these woods fill nine buildings at this quaint and homey roadside attraction. Bud Blumenstock has been a docent there for several years, having retired from his work as a forester, managing wood lots from Fort Kent to Kittery. He sees these changes in the woods more optimistically than most, retaining the hope of a forest that will always support the people of that area. "Logging and lumbering have always been a big part of our economy. It's changed in that Maine is now a village woodlot in the global economy. We're up against Brazil and China. To be competitive, we have to be efficient. It's a very complex situation."

And the players have to bring themselves into that competitive mix: "A logger is no longer a man with an axe on his shoulder," says Blumenstock. "It's not unusual for a logger to have a million dollars invested in his work. When people like Roxanne Quimby come along, they have a lot of money and they want to buy land. I once told Roxanne that I'm a tree hugger *and* a logger and she said, 'How do you do that?' 'Well,' I told her, I hug the tree and then I cut it down.' Parks are nice but they don't produce any lumber."

THE GREAT TREES of these woods are long gone and much of the newer growth, thinner and less substantial, are not good enough for lumber. These trees are chewed up for wood chips or used in pulp mills to make paper. The country of the pointed fir is no longer — most of the pointed firs are lying on the beds of the logging trucks, zooming south to the mills. Most of the land Roxanne and Plum Creek have bought has been damaged by extensive logging. Plum Creek is proposing trophy homes and resorts. Roxanne wants her land to heal and return to wilderness.

Like many people around here, Blumenstock keeps his opinion of Roxanne to himself. "I don't want to say anything negative about Roxanne Quimby. She has her plan. It's her choice and her prerogative but logging is an important industry to the state of Maine. Trees grow. That is my one-liner. As long as we harvest them wisely, we'll always have a strong working forest in the state of Maine."

"OH, ROXANNE QUIMBY? She is my *hero*!" Wallis Drew is the ranger on duty at the check-in station at the Matagamon gate of Baxter State Park. Inside the log-built ranger station, Wallis, in her earth-brown uniform, makes out the ticket. Free for a Maine resident, twelve dollars for the out-of-stater. "We compare her to Governor Baxter. When Baxter was buying up the land for this park, people were mad about that too. He has it in the deeds: *forever wild.* That means no paved roads, primitive campsites. Most of us understand that these lands need to be preserved. Otherwise, they would be cut and cut forever."

From the station, you return to your car and leave this earthly world. It is almost impossible to describe the feeling. With grass growing between the dirt tracks, the narrow park road wanders, twists and turns, mile after mile, edged tightly by trees and canopied with their branches. At openings, there are waterfalls, marshes or streams, and eventually, the majestic Katahdin. The silence is prayerful, the treetops like spires, the park nothing less than an open-air cathedral, worship to nature, to the way things were.

Baxter's struggle to climb to the Katahdin summit remained his single experience on the big mountain, which rises nearly a mile high from the bogs of the lowlands. Instead of returning to the park in climbing boots, Baxter often visited the mountain in his chauffeur-driven Cadillac — surely a strange sight, the old man viewing his most important legacy from the backseat of a black limousine. He thought about that park every day, his chauffeur reported.

That is true for Roxanne as well. But her struggle is in sharp contrast.

Once, years ago, Roxanne came home from selling candles and lip balm at a craft show. It was three in the morning and twenty below zero and she was tired and discouraged. She had not sold enough to even pay for her gas home. When she got home, the wind had blown the windows of her cabin open and there was snow all over inside. "Sometimes you feel like giving up. I did that night," she recalls. "But then you pick yourself up again. I believe that success is getting up one more time than you fall. It's not one brilliant idea but a bunch of small decisions that accumulate. Never underestimate the amount of work involved, the amount of fear involved."

In November of last year, Burt's Bees was sold for nearly a billion dollars to Clorox, which stated that it was eager to "grab market share in so-called green products."

"It feels like closure," Roxanne said shortly after the sale. The little company that grew is now completely out of her hands. But twenty percent of the sale went to Roxanne. "That has put a lot more green energy into what I'm planning to do," she added.

In December, after a year of closed-door negotiations, Roxanne struck a new kind of deal with state officials and local civic leaders. From the Gardner timber company, she purchased eight thousand nine hundred acres east of Baxter State Park, which she will return to wilderness, and in turn granted the state a two-year option to buy five thousand acres of her Millinocket-area property plus a working forest easement on another six thousand six hundred acres, guaranteed to be open to motorized recreation and logging. She also agreed to keep open two important snowmobile trails that cross portions of her land, perhaps heralding a thaw in her relations with area sportsmen and residents.

Today, she is working on acquiring still more contiguous parcels on the east side of Baxter State Park. "This feels good," she says. "Yes it does."

April 2008 Yankee magazine

ROXANNE QUIMBY *continues to buy land that she intends to preserve. In January of 2010, she purchased another thirty thousand acres, close to or abutting her holdings. She has a great deal of support from Maine residents but there was another great outcry from skeptics and, mainly, snowmobilers at the time of this most recent purchase. She told me that she is continuing her advocacy work with the local stakeholders, as well as with the Department of the*

Interior and the National Park Service in DC. She said, "The new administration has put excellent people in charge of these matters and I am hopeful that we can get some federal protection on these lands before they leave office. Hopefully they will still be there in 2016, which is the hundredth anniversary of the National Park Service."

In addition to her continuing efforts to preserve the land of northern Maine, she has recently established an artist's colony, The Quimby Colony, based in Portland. As of this writing she has just sent out the first call for artists. "We are starting with Fashion/Textile/Costume and will proceed with other artistic disciplines as time goes on," she said. "It seems that Maine has a healthy (though underfed) population of creative, artistic people who value the independence that this rural state offers. It's very rewarding and I'm meeting with more support than I (had anticipated)."

It bears reminding that, in spite of all that Roxanne Quimby has accomplished to date, she started out in art school, with aspirations to become an artist.

The Man Who Loves Turtles

IN THE APRIL AFTERNOON, the sun sinks low, coloring the wide oval expanse of the marsh. David Carroll tugs his waders to the tops of his thighs and strides into the place he calls the Route of a Thousand Spotted Turtles. He moves silently through the tea-tinted water. The bog is numbingly cold and grows deeper as he pushes further into this vast sweep of nature near his home in Warner, New Hampshire.

It is the beginning of his year with the turtles. Carroll is here, as he is every day once the ice is off the marsh, in search of the dozens of different turtles he has acquainted himself with over the past eight years, including "13 April," "Male Beautiful," and "Ariadne," a spotted turtle he favors shamelessly and who is the star of his first book, *The Year of the Turtle.*

He has observed these turtles — painted turtles, box turtles, Blanding's turtles, snapping turtles, wood turtles, musk turtles — emerging from their winter slumbers; he has measured them and marked them and brought them into his home when they have needed care. He has sketched them and painted them and lain awake at night wondering about them when they have evaded him. He has stood for hours in the cold and in heat and in the silvery luminescence of midnight watching them mate. And he has crouched, stock-still, watching the wary females testily plant their eggs in the sand. And then he has done what the mother cannot: He has fastened screening over these nests that no predator can undo. In his walks, throughout the season, he passes by each nest, making sure.

The Route of a Thousand Spotted Turtles is only a part of a whole that Carroll calls "The Digs," land he does not own. He has no clue how large it might be — perhaps two thousand acres — but it is land he knows better, has spent more time in, than perhaps any human being since the beginning of time. He has made his own map, dividing it into little paradises, names of his own invention: Buttonbush Swamp, Blanding's Marsh, Moss Flats, Cranberry Hollows, Leatherleaf Islands, the Swale, the Great Swale. "This is simply an amazing place. There really is nothing else like it that I know of," he says.

A tall man, hunched as if by the weight of all these turtles at once, David Carroll is distinguished by his head of wild, honey-colored hair, which he wears in a swath across his head, the mass of it held down by a single elastic headband. Even so, it still demands his attention as he pushes it out of his face with the back of his hand now and again. His skin is browned from his long time in the Digs. Now, he walks cautiously. In some places, one foot can ooze down twelve inches or more without reaching solid bottom. He has waded through water waist high, chest high, at all times of day and night. To save himself, he carries a walking stick and, at the urging of his wife, Laurette, a whistle, in case he should ever sink down so far he can't get out.

He's been out here covered with blackflies while he sketches. He's been out here in violent thunderstorms. "Sometimes it's wonderful to get rained on," he says. "You feel as if you're part of something great. That's what I love about this turtle business. When you're with the turtles, you really enter their world. That's one of the things I've always loved about finding them. I've always loved the places where I've found them."

He has been out here in the Digs since morning. Early, he found a turtle concealed under a tangle of fallen pine and wild cherry. The turtle struggled as David gripped its shell and brought it up out of its hiding place. David flipped it and studied the underside, counting the rings.

"Sometimes I recognize the turtle right away," he says, squinting at the shell through a jeweler's glass to look for distinguishing marks. This turtle has one little toenail that curls under. "Not much to go on," David says. But this one he knows, a twenty-three-year-old male wood turtle.

David kneels down on one knee, and from the back pocket of his swamp vest — swamp vest to him, fly fisherman's vest to the catalogs — he draws out a spiral notebook and pen and begins to record. A bright bead of blood rises up on his wrist where the turtle's claw raked him. He talks softly to the old creature and calms him, holding the turtle upright in front of him with one hand, balancing the notebook on his knee and sketching with the other.

When he finishes the sketch, a black, cross-hatched rendition, he pulls calipers from another pocket and measures the length of the top shell and of the bottom shell. Holding the turtle up in his left hand and bracing a small camera against his cheek, he photographs the turtle's head. With a small thermometer, he takes the temperature of the brook that runs close (58° F) and of the air (50°F) and jots the figures in his notebook. He paces off how far the turtle was from the water's edge when he found him and records that as well. When he sets it down, the turtle squirts from his hands, his orange legs flashing beneath the dark water.

David surges back up out of the marsh onto the hard, sure path of the logging road and peels his boots back down. No sign of Ariadne, no sign, in fact, of any of the thousand spotted turtles he has known to take that route. In the failing light he heads back to his car, a faded blue Malibu, one of two cars that have been given him by friends who believe in him and who believe in his turtle mission. This one came to him from the family of a friend who died. Inside, the seats are torn.

"They wanted us to have this for our swamp car," he explains, "but this turned out to be our best car!" The engine starts without hesitation. David pulls it into gear and heads out of the sand pit towards home.

On that April day, David made notes on four wood turtles, a painted turtle, and a snapping turtle. One, a young wood turtle, he zipped into his backpack and carried home for further study. But he didn't see a spotted turtle, the kind that began it all for this fifty-one-year-old artist and naturalist. He marks it back to when he was eight years old, living in Groton, Connecticut. He and his brother used to explore the patches of woods that connected the housing developments near where they lived.

"It was late afternoon. The light was at that angle. Everything about that afternoon was magical," he says. He looked down into the grass and saw the shining black shell, as bright as lacquer, and the yellow spots, like drops from his paint box. "I still get that feeling. I hope I never lose it, that jolt, that start, when I find a turtle."

He says he cannot remember a time when he did not have turtles living with him. He thinks back to when he lived under a pet store, with a blanket for a door and his only heat coming from the big pipes that passed through the space. "Just a little shy of homeless," he says. Still, he had room for turtles.

David's house is three miles from the Digs. "Dumb luck," he says. "There's a guy in Michigan who has to go two hundred miles to get to his study area."

The house is old, shutters askew and paint peeling. Inside, sloping plaster ceilings are held together with tape, and the floors sag and creak as David enters and sets his pack on the chair beside the door. "Look here," he says to Laurette, pulling the wood turtle from the pack. "Isn't she beautiful?" The turtle's legs stroke the air. This may be the zillionth turtle David has brought home. Laurette, a tiny, dark-haired woman, touches the shell lightly, saying, "Oh, yes."

The house smells of wood smoke and asparagus. Laurette is making this "cheesy asparagus thing" that David loves, and in a black skillet, fish spatters and pops.

It was while he was living under the pet store that he met Laurette, also an art student. They have been married thirty years, and together they have raised three children. They have put together a life — selling paintings, writing stories, and studying turtles. But life has been lean, to be tactful.

"I tell Laurette not to worry until we're out of money. And she says, 'We *are* out of money!' and I say, 'No, we're not, I've still got three bucks.' You can't always laugh about it," David says. "There are nights when my hair almost falls out."

Laurette spreads a cloth across one end of the long wooden table for supper. At the other end of the table is a yellow plastic wash basin with four silver-dollar-sized hatchlings that David brought home yesterday. In a cardboard box beside the stove he nestles the new wood turtle into dried grasses and sticks. In the next room, within six aquariums, turtles of various ages and types creep about on small logs, swim in green water, sit completely still. They are here because they have been injured, or because they have been threatened, or because he needs to study them more closely. When they are ready, he returns them to the Digs. Some, such as the Chinese box turtle, David "rescued" from pet shops. One he has had for twenty-two years.

Laurette lights a tall candle. The plates are steaming. The last shafts of sun angle in flat against the big old house next door: Sibley's house. "Sibley," a woman from Washington, D.C., who spent all her summers in Warner, has been their landlady. For fifteen years she rented them their house, and every year, as things got tougher for them, she went down a little on the rent. Last year, at the age of one hundred and one, Sibley died and left this house and five acres to David and Laurette. Her kindness overwhelmed them. To them, this house is a palace, the most beautiful place in the world. And it is theirs. These gestures, the cars and the house, represent the kind of grace David needs and has somehow received. "In the absence of success, I'll take charity and luck anytime," he says.

Thirteen years ago, David put together a book about the turtles he had studied and painted. His watercolors were bright and infused with soft light. His sketches showed the turtles migrating, the turtles lined up on logs, the turtles sleeping, the turtles mating. An agent in New York was excited about the book. But it languished in her office for twelve years. At last, in the spring of 1991, *The Year of the Turtle* was published by Camden House, a small Vermont publisher. It was well reviewed, and a film crew from the "Today" show trekked out into the Digs with him. Annie Dillard wrote him a fan letter. This spring his book about trout, for which he made more than one hundred illustrations, will be published by St. Martin's, a New York publisher with nationwide distribution. His hope is renewed.

David considers himself an artist first and a naturalist second. Virtually all of his scientific expertise has been gained in the field. Because of this, he has been instrumental in fighting various developments that threaten turtle habitats. Last year his testimony delayed a small development south of his home in New Hampshire. Spotted turtles, once so common but now on the threatened species list, lived near the proposed site. And with the help of a state grant, he is writing an exhaustive report of his observations in the Digs for the New Hampshire Nongame and Endangered Wildlife Program. These reports are valuable. And rare. For reasons unknown, very little turtle data exist.

Perhaps because growing up he watched the places where turtles could live disappear, David is very concerned about the diminishing habitat for turtles all over the world. Nothing he can think of is more depressing. "There have always been wars, personal loss, heartbreak, death, and they are tough. But those things are part of life. What depresses me so deeply that I don't know a cure for is what is happening to these natural places. It makes me sadder than all the wars on earth."

The Digs are owned by several generations of the same family. They are farmers, and there doesn't seem to be any inclination among them toward development. "I have hopes that that will be my own place to roam for the rest of my life," David says.

By September the sumac is tinted red. The year of the turtle is almost over. In mid-October, he'll say good-bye to the Digs and go inside. It's been a pretty good year. Among other things, he's encountered Ariadne four times. Today David is looking for hatchlings. Since mid-August, he's been out here checking the nests that he has covered, probably 20 in all. But for every one he knows about, there are many that he has not discovered.

In a clearing, he moves toward a screened nest above a small sand pit. "That's just as she left it, at 2:07 a.m., June 29," he says, kneeling and lifting the protective covering of dried ferns. "This is the first-ever Blanding's turtle nest in this area," he explains.

Blanding's turtles, whose shells are marked with delicate yellow flecks, are increasingly rare. That June evening, David spotted one around 6:30. "She stuck her long neck out and threw a great arc of sand over her shell. I knew she was about to lay her eggs." David moved behind a screen of pine trees and stood still to watch. "There was something bothering her. I couldn't tell what it was."

Dusk spread. There was still enough light, however, for him to recognize the gray fox stalking the birthing mother. In the shadows he watched their delicate dance. After it was completely dark, he couldn't see, but he could hear her digging. He stood for hours. When he was satisfied she'd successfully laid her eggs, he moved out from behind the pines and marked the nest. It was two o'clock in the morning. "My back has never been quite the same," he says now, studying the nest for signs of life. There are none.

David moves on slowly, taking two steps and then stopping to look around him. He is looking for what he calls "tail drag," light, whispery lines in the sand. There are tracks everywhere — rabbit, coon, deer, black bear — but not that. What else is there, everywhere in the Digs, is the whorly pattern of the soles of David's sneakers. He points to a hole in the sand. Eggshells, dried and curled like thin white rubber, spill out. "Snapper," he says.

Farther on there are deep, wide circles in the sand. Kids have been there with their dirt bikes. David sighs. "This is just within the past two days," he says. Pain marks his face. "I get so tense out here sometimes." Over the summer he encountered his first evidence of a spotted turtle killed by humans in the Digs.

"Early one morning, I found an adult female who had been killed by haying equipment. There is no way, of course, anyone could have seen the turtle in the deep, dense grass." He didn't say anything. "I would hate to make such a discovery of Ariadne or of 13 April, turtles I've had a long association with."

It's a long day, and it is hot for September. He comes to the last nest, covered and flagged in the hayfield. There is no sign of life. This doesn't discourage him. There will be tomorrow. "One of the things I like about turtles is their sense of time. They're not all hopped up about things. They live a long time if things work out for them. They're the longest-lived species. They seem to have a sense of patience about them. Maybe that's just something I read into them. But they are just so at home in the world. We're always rushing around. We need food, we need water, we need air. Turtles can go six months without food, six months without air. It's OK with them."

The next day, just beyond the Route of a Thousand Spotted Turtles, David came across a hatchling spotted turtle, only the third hatchling he's found. "It was in about a quarter of an inch of water, jet black, tiny yellow spots, a little living jewel," he reports with obvious relish. It could be — it just could be — Ariadne's daughter. A little farther along, he found one of his covered nests full of half a dozen hatchlings. Wood turtles. He brought them home and measured and recorded them and then took them back out and released them. "They're out there somewhere," he says.

In the spring, with the kind of charity and luck that follows David Carroll, he may encounter them in Buttonbush Swamp or Cranberry Hollows or Leatherleaf Islands, somewhere within the enduring grip of life in the Digs.

June 1993 Yankee magazine

THE YEAR OF THE TURTLE, *which was critically acclaimed,was followed by* Trout Reflections, The Swampwalker's Journal, Self-portrait with Turtles, *and, last year,* Following the Water, *which together constitute what he calls "the wet-sneaker series." In 2006, David was awarded a MacArthur Grant, a $500,000 award, also known as the "genius grant." In their comments about David Carroll, the MacArthur Foundation had this to say, "David Carroll has the eye of an artist, the mind of a scientist, the voice of a great storyteller, and the soul of a conservationist. . . . Through his artwork, writing, fieldwork, and speaking, Carroll helps people of all ages see the beauty, history, and value in swamps, marshes, bogs, kettle ponds, and rivers."*

David and Laurette Carroll still live in Warner, in the house that Sibley left to them. After the MacArthur money came through, they renovated the kitchen — Laurette is thrilled to report that she now has countertops and cupboards, neither of which she ever had before. They also insulated the space and replaced the floor joists, which eliminated the creak and bounce of the floor. "When it was really cold, I used to have to put on boots and a jacket to go into the kitchen to cook. I'm so totally grateful to have this new space," Laurette says. They also bought a new car, an all-wheel-drive Subaru, another exciting improvement to their lifestyle. Of the MacArthur, David says, "It's the only thing that's ever come my way that's ever given me any support. After all, there was never any Plan B, so, well, it's helped tremendously."

The status of many of the key turtle habitats David has observed and written about for over thirty years still hangs in balance. Some conservation measures have been put in place. In the eyes of many, this equates to their having been preserved. But, as is nearly always the case, conservation has come with a heavy mandate for human access, a compromising human presence that is incompatible with true protection of unique, and increasingly rare, ecologies and biodiversity: conservation, not preservation. David elaborates: "Putting up signs, making maps and trails, listing such places in guidebooks, these things are like paving the way for the world to come in. They are being saved by being sacrificed to human service, and become not sanctuaries for natural processes but human playgrounds, theme parks." This subject is a major theme in his newest book, Following the Water, *which was a finalist for a National Book Award in 2009.*

David has not seen Ariadne in five or six years. "She could be still out there, but that becomes less and less likely as I return to her familiar places without seeing her. She could have been taken by a predator, or wandered out onto a paved road or followed a logging road and been run over or picked up and carried off. She became a big part of my history in this area over those first twenty or so years. But I recently found a spotted turtle I first saw when it was five years old, who is now over twenty years old; and there are spotted and wood turtles I still come across who go back a quarter of a century or more in my notebooks. These turtles can live for a century or more if the integrity and complexity of their habitats is preserved, or simply left alone."

In a renovated shed beside their driveway David and Laurette operate the Carroll Studio Gallery (www.carrollartgallery.com) where they sell prints and paintings by David and Laurette as well as work by their son, Sean Carroll, and their daughter, Rianna Frost.

A Rich Slave's Daughter

A COLD WIND BLOWS across the island. Many houses that front the harbor are boarded up for the winter. Traffic along the main road is light, almost nonexistent. An old dented gray Valiant with a front license plate that says "I ♥ Martha's Vineyard" pulls into the parking lot of Our Market. The driver arches her neck to see above the steering wheel, brings the car to a stop, and gets out. "Hello, dahlin' chil'," she says to me. Her eyes sparkle like small black suns.

This is Dorothy West, the daughter of a slave, the last surviving member of the Harlem Renaissance, a novelist who has lived on Martha's Vineyard since 1943 and who had vacationed there with her family since her first birthday in 1908.

To the close-knit community of this island, she is simply Dottie, the Oak Bluffs correspondent to the local newspaper, the *Vineyard Gazette.* She is wearing a red hat pulled down over her ears and a red plaid dress. She hurries into the market for a loaf of bread. At eighty-three she is bent, but still, in her bright red running shoes, her walk is almost a dance. Though child-sized, she is vibrant and alive, a firecracker of a woman.

Here beside the market was where her parents' first cottage stood, a big Victorian, summer home to an extended family that included many cousins and aunts. Her father, a wealthy black businessman, rarely visited. He found the island "too boring" and remained in Boston, tending his fruit and vegetable business. But the summer was like one long carnival for Dottie. Oak Bluffs was full of exciting people, many of them writers and artists and musicians. She could sit on the porch and watch the boats in the harbor. When she was four, the house burned down. They did not rebuild, but instead moved away from the water, eventually to a smaller cottage on a quiet sand road.

When she comes out of the market, small brown bag in hand, that is where we go, to the cottage on Myrtle Avenue. We cross the brief front lawn, ducking under and around the panoply of bird feeders, and go inside. It is dollhouse-small, a haven of a home. The kitchen has the big iron stove, still shining, that once cooked meals for her mother and her cousins. In the living room Dottie's chair faces the front door where the welcome face of a visitor might appear. Under the chair is her old dictionary, a foot high, and in front of it is her small writing table. She writes a regular column, and she is working on a novel, *The Wedding.* She sits now in this chair, at this table, and does what she enjoys almost as much as, perhaps more than, writing. She begins to talk.

"My father was born a slave, and he was freed at the age of seven, and my grandfather was born a slave. I never thought to ask them how was slavery. I think it's because I know what a slave was," she says.

After his emancipation Dottie's father, Isaac Christopher West, ran errands and saved his money. At ten he opened a restaurant with his mother in Richmond, Virginia. A few years later he hopped a train to Springfield, Massachusetts, where he opened a fruit stand. In his early twenties he already had a successful produce business in Haymarket Square. He was known as Boston's "black banana king" — it was said he could ripen bananas better than anyone. He bought a four-story brick house on Brookline Avenue and a summer home on Martha's Vineyard. He provided his wife and only child, Dorothy, with comforts to match any of the neighboring whites. Their only hardship, it seemed, was their color.

Most of Dottie's stories are about colored people. She has taught herself to use the word *black* in reference to her race, but when she is relaxed, talking away, she slips back into using *colored.* "I get so sick of the word *black,*" she says. Her voice is high-pitched, *fast*, the powers of speech apparently not quick enough for her mind. "When I was a young girl, we decided we were going to call ourselves Afro-Americans. Of course, I was never a part of the silly decision, I was only one of 'us.' In my family, we come in every color. My mother used to say, 'Come on, little colored children; let's go out and drive the white folks crazy.'"

Her mother, she says, was light-skinned — her body was cream-colored, and she had pink cheeks that Dottie dreams about to this day. Her father was a very dark man with blue eyes. Her mother's sister Helen had olive skin. Dottie's skin is the color of gingersnaps, but by her account she was the darkest child in her family. "What my mother meant when she said that, I think, was she liked to confuse people. There was a little boy in my family who was blonde as he could be, and my mother used to like to dress us up alike and take us out, the darkest and the lightest, just to see what people would say."

She tells a chilling story about her grandmother, who was the cook on a plantation in South Carolina, in the same way that she tells all her stories — detailed, circuitous, compelling. And always with a point. Her grandmother had eleven children by her master. Many of these children were fair, so the blacks did not particularly care about them and neither did the whites. One of the girls, Ann, was told to fan the family. The dog was circling the table and everyone was giving him something, and all of a sudden the dog yelped. The master said to her, "You stepped on that dog's tail on purpose." She argued with him until finally he took her out to the barn.

"My grandmother was sitting on the back porch, sewing. And the master came out with the little girl and took her into the barn to beat her, to whip her until she said yes she did, but she wouldn't say it, and so finally he came out and he said to my grandmother 'You better go see about your daughter,' and of course he had beaten her to death. All right. My grandmother went out to her. She picked her up. Ann was fifteen years old, so she must have been heavy, but no black slave said to my grandmother, 'I will help you carry your child," and no white person came forward to help either. I'm a writer and I guess my thing has always been, well, we'll go it alone."

And so she has. In a very distinctive manner Dorothy West has lived her life apart from her race, but intimately caught up in it.

She has been all over the world. But until recently she had never been to the South. A few years ago the University of Georgia invited her to speak. She politely declined. In truth, she was afraid. When she was growing up, her mother had always warned her: "Dorothy, the way you talk back, you'd be strung up on the first tree. She literally made us promise never to go to the South," Dottie says.

But the Georgia professor was persistent. "She was stubborn like my mother," Dottie says. She called four times, and each time the answer was no. But at last Dottie went. The trip was uneventful. A college campus in the 1980s is not the South of her mother's bitter memory.

Her cottage has been the scene for some of Dottie's more memorable short stories, just as the childhood home on Brookline Avenue became the home she portrayed in her 1948 novel, *The Living is Easy.* Reissued in 1981, the book brought the literary world to her doorstep. Suddenly the world remembered Dorothy West, discovering that Langston Hughes, Zora Neale Hurston, and Wallace Thurman — the literary circle that flourished with her in Harlem during the 1920s — were all gone. Except Dottie. To her it was surprising, even amusing. She laughs, a gentle melodic laugh, as she tells this.

"You see, I'm Dorothy. I don't know what's going on. Radcliffe was the one who said, 'She is the last surviving member of the Harlem Renaissance,' and then everybody wanted to come and see the last one. I live quietly here, and then I go to the big city and here come the cameras! Some young person once asked me, 'What was it like to be part of the Harlem Renaissance?' We didn't know it was the 'Harlem Renaissance'! It was called that *afterward*. We were all just struggling, trying to eat, and some of us were dying of TB. But the important thing was we were all young."

It was Oak Bluffs that led her to New York. Oak Bluffs is thought to be the first black resort in America. It attracted artists who told their friends and more came. One of the most beloved was Harry Burleigh, an arranger of Negro spirituals. On the island he was better known as the "children's friend," and that is how Dottie remembers him. He told her about New York City, and when she was seventeen, she packed up and went there. Her mother, whose own mother had sent her north on a train when she was fourteen, never to see her again, did not object.

"I had won this little prize [for her story "The Typewriter"] and I said that I wanted to go to New York, and she could have refused me, but she didn't feel she had a right. She identified, you see."

She had grown up used to having whatever she wanted. In New York she lived on frankfurters and pineapple juice. She wrote stories for the *New York Daily News* and for the *Saturday Evening Quill*. When she was twenty, she heard about a new play, *Porgy and Bess*, and went to audition. She was from Boston — she said *demahnd* and *commahnd, cahn't* and *shahn't* — and she didn't sound like the Southerners they were trying to portray. She didn't win a speaking part, but traveled as an extra with the cast to London where the play closed after only three weeks because, ironically, no one in the English audience could understand those Southern accents.

Soon after, she was invited (along with several other black actors, Langston Hughes among them) to Russia to act in a film the Russians were producing about the unfortunate lives of black Americans. At the Russian border the neighbors came from miles around to see the black actors. "They were lovely and friendly and sang and danced for us," she wrote. In Leningrad they were met with a brass band and several thousand applauding Russians. "I have quite got used to having my hand kissed," she wrote in a letter.

And this woman, for whom the difference between black and white has posed a lifelong conundrum, was transfixed by their white nights. On a ship crossing the Baltic Sea she stood on deck and watched the dimming sky that held no darkness grow bright again. On an overnight train, crossing into Russia, she stood by the window all night long, "watching the tall trees whiz by."

"YOU WANT to go out, Cat? Cat!" Dottie follows the dog-sized orange cat across the linoleum floor. The warm little house on the blustery island is far from those white nights. She opens the door and lets Cat out into the cold, cloudy morning. "Listen, I've had animals for forty years, and I never ordered one, you know what I mean? They come to me." She returns to her chair, sitting almost on the edge of the seat, alert. "Now what was it I was saying?" she asks.

In 1933 Dottie's father died, and she returned from Russia. At one time he hoped to leave her a million dollars. But business had run out on him, and there was no such grand legacy for Dottie. No matter. She had her work. In 1935 she founded a magazine called *Challenge*, publishing writers known as the "new Negroes" — Claude McKay, Countee Cullen, Zora Neale Hurston, James Weldon Johnson. And she wrote, using the name Mary Christopher. *Challenge* survived four years. Dottie was wooed by the Communists, but her answer was no. Her father, after all, had been a slave who worked his way up through the capitalist system into wealth. Her resistance to the Communists was firm, and because of their pressure she ceased publication.

She wrote, then, for the Works Progress Administration, the New Deal agency. The good times in New York continued. There was drinking, way too much drinking. The death of her friend Wallace Thurman from complications triggered by alcohol sobered her, sobered them all.

Once again it was time to go it alone. She came home to Oak Bluffs in 1943 to write, she says, "Because as a child, I thought it was always summer here, and no one ever called me nigger."

She worked on *The Living Is Easy*, and it was published by Houghton Mifflin in 1948. It was one of only a very few novels published by a black woman in the 1940s. Largely autobiographical, the book gives a vivid picture of Boston's black middle class in the early part of this century. It is a work full of the irony of this black urban existence, where a man could make enough money to hire a maid and yet still be looked down upon and called nigger. And it looks forthrightly at the trap upwardly mobile blacks set for themselves by pursuing false values.

In Oak Bluffs she watched what she calls the "black revolution" on TV, and she had and still has mixed feelings about its leaders. "It took me a long time to like Martin Luther King. He had that Southern Baptist preacher style. To me it seemed insincere. And Malcolm X — I thought he was crazy. Just crazy. And I cannot stand Jesse Jackson. I absolutely cannot stand him."

The business about what to call her race came up again, and Afro-American was replaced by black. "My mother used to call this 'color foolishness.' Because you are the color that God made you. A friend of mine had just come from New York, and the young people had suddenly decided to call themselves black. She asked me to lunch up island, so I went and we were sitting there and she said, 'Dorothy, as a colored person, how do you want to be called?' And I said, 'I want to be called to dinner.'"

"WOULD YOU like some tea, dahlin' chil'?"

Another cold day. Dottie is in the kitchen, fixing a meal for Cat. On a dinner plate she arranges a portion of Ocean Buffet from one can, a portion of Chicken Chunks from another can, so that when she is done, it looks like a full meal for a hungry man.

Dottie never married and had no children, though she says perhaps her one and only ambition was to have six children. At one time she wrote a letter to Langston Hughes, asking him to marry her so that she could have a child. If she has any, these are her regrets. "What is the point of having regrets? The only thing I ever wanted was children, and I couldn't have children."

She puts Cat's banquet on the floor, and we move back into the living room, settling into the chairs that had held us so well the day before.

Once back on the island, she needed to pay the bills. She went to the venerable *Vineyard Gazette,* then edited by Henry Beetle Hough. In the early sixties she worked in the office, filing and so forth, and while she was there she would tell her stories and people said, "Oh, Dottie, you ought to write that story." Her first appearance in the *Gazette*, however, came under a pseudonym. She calls this her "dark secret."

"I knew a beautiful woman who had a column in the paper all about the birds. We had a little writers' club, and when she went away, she asked me if I would write the column for her. I write pretty well, but not about birds. It never occurred to me to give myself a byline. I knew this woman's background — she was an expert. I wrote about what I saw at my feeder. So I called myself 'The Highlands Waterboy.' It amused me because the waterboy, as you know, was the one who carried the water. He was a slave. I did it for fun." One reader wrote the *Gazette,* "I hope you keep that boy, that boy writes beautifully." Her laugh rings out. Dottie loves this, her own joke on the world.

Even at the *Gazette* there was friction, tension between herself and another writer. Dottie was fired. She told almost no one. "Because I am black, I did not want any of the black people to know that I'd got fired. I didn't want to hurt them."

She came back, though, as a columnist, writing about the people of Oak Bluffs. In her stories she never said who was black. "They didn't tell me not to, I just knew better." She wanted to, though. To her there were some rich stories to be told about the black residents of Oak Bluffs, many of them professional and some of them, like Adam Clayton Powell and Edward Brooke, known far beyond the island. "Mr. Hough, he was a Yankee, an older man. I would not have asked him. He would have said, 'Oh, Dorothy, are you sure the colored people' — the word was not *black* then — 'would want this?' He would have been timid about it, and then he would not have been sure that the white people would want it."

She turned instead to her ally at the paper, Colbert Smith, a young editor from the South. "I said, 'Colbert, there are many black professional people on the island, and I know that Mr. Hough sees them and assumes that they are Edgartown servants. I don't want to ask him, but I would like to do a column about these people."

Colbert said yes, so she wrote the column the first week about a doctor who was the first black college president, and the next week she wrote about another successful black resident. "On the third week I was sitting at my desk, and Mr. Hough came by. You know what they say about black people being invisible. Well, he passed right by me and went over to Colbert, and he said, 'There were all of those wonderful people here, and I never knew they were there!'"

The column, called "The Cottager's Corner," continued into the late sixties."When integration began, I thought I should not do it anymore, and I think I was right. I mean, do we want to be exclusive or do we want to be integrated? I still write about blacks, but not exclusively."

Her column, from then until this day, is headed simply, "Oak Bluffs," and sometimes it contains only news of the goings-on of the townspeople. When a young lady of ten came from West Palm Beach, Florida, to visit her grandparents for the summer, Dottie wrote, "There is no other place she loves so much, because of its permanency . . . the woods and sea are unchanged, and the Flying Horses, her chief delight, still seem to have whirled down from heaven. This year the Dixons have air-conditioning and Donna is very disapproving. She has air-conditioning in Florida and closed windows. Here she wants the windows open in the old way, and the curtains gently moving."

Many people ask her to write obituaries for their loved ones. She writes them beautifully. Once she wrote the obituary for a neighbor, and when she went to the funeral, she found that the minister, instead of delivering a eulogy, read what she had written for the *Gazette*.

Sometimes, in the winter especially, when the population dwindles, there is nothing much to write about, so she writes out of her own experiences, out of her memory. All the same, she takes it down to the offices in Edgartown. "I always say, 'It may not be any good,' and he always says, 'Dorothy, you always say that.' But I mean it. How do I know if it's any good? With a painter, you know. You can *see* if it's good. But these are just words. How do I know that they are the right words?"

What has happened to her in the past few years has been unexpected. For years she never left the island. Never. And then the invitations started. She is quite used to it now — making appearances, that is. But she will never get used to getting there, for leaving the island and returning to it is never a quick and simple procedure. She doesn't like the boat. She usually flies. Sometimes these experiences become material for her column.

A couple of years ago, in March, after a weekend appearance in Boston, she woke up in her hotel room and raised the shade to see what kind of day it was. It was snowing lightly, but by the time she got to Logan Airport, the snowstorm had intensified. She got her boarding pass and took a seat. "But the waiting began to extend itself," she wrote. "The snow was now falling steadily, and the view outside the window was beginning to be eerie, as if seen through a descending fog." She was the only passenger. It was a terrifying flight through the blind sky of a blizzard. To make it worse, there was mechanical difficulty. They flew full circle back to Boston. "I was certain I was going to die," she says.

At last, with a clearing sky, she was airborne again. "I touched the Vineyard soil. I have lived various places, but the island is my yearning place. All my life, wherever I have been, whenever I yearned for home, I yearned for the island. Long before I lived here year-round, in my childhood, in the years of my exuberant youth, I knew the island was the home of my heart."

It is time to go. The ferry leaves soon. As Dottie knows all too well, you cannot just leave this island impulsively. You have to wait until they are ready to take you. Dottie gets up and walks outside with me. Our breath spills out in clouds. Birds of every color flutter in and out of her feeders. Cat sits on the porch rail. "Will you come back to the island?" she asks. "Please do come back. It's you young people who keep me *alive.*" She goes inside, into her yearning place, and turns, and from behind the storm door she watches me leave and waves.

March 1991 Yankee magazine

IN 1995, *at the age of eighty-five, Dottie published her second novel,* The Wedding, *which became a best-seller. Oprah Winfrey turned the novel into a television mini-series by the same name. This success spurred the publication of a collection of her short stories and reminiscences, entitled* The Richer, The Poorer. *The last remaining member of the Harlem Renaissance, Dottie died on August 16, 1998, at the age of ninety-one. In 2001, the* Vineyard Gazette *published a collection of her writings from the* Gazette. *Dottie's papers are now in the collection of the Schlesinger Library at Harvard University.*

Hartford's Hidden Historian

THE WIND BLEW the snow across the intersection in sheets. It was February 8, 1945. Tony DeBonee was at the corner of Main and Pearl streets, the windiest place in all of Hartford. He wanted a picture of the snow, one that would show the feeling of people struggling against the wind. He had his camera in his pocket. He was the only person out. He waited. He was just a kid, barely into his twenties. He wore no gloves; he wore no hat. He rubbed his hands together and blew into them. He needed someone in the picture. Come on, someone! Ten minutes passed. A half hour passed. No one came. Forty-five minutes. He hopped up and down. After an hour, he spotted a woman coming down Pearl Street, her umbrella filled with wind, the snow swirling around her like a veil. Bless you, lady, bless you! Tony took his camera out of his pocket and squinted into the viewfinder. The umbrella moved into the center of his scene. Click.

Tony got his shot in the blizzard, as he has continued to do ever since. Tony DeBonee is a historian, a Hartford historian, though he doesn't have a lot of degrees. In fact, he never went to college, but his high school diploma is hanging on the walls of a busy cafeteria in downtown Hartford among a sampling — that is to say, dozens, including the one taken in the 1945 blizzard — of his photographs. His kind of history.

Tony DeBonee was always crazy about Hartford. He started out collecting postcards — only Hartford scenes — when he was ten. After a while he decided he could do it better himself. So when he was nineteen he bought a Brownie box camera and starting snapping. That makes 1942 the beginning of recorded history for Tony and for the Hartford Historical Files Society, of which he is founder, president and sole supporting member.

Even at that age, it was for the record. His mother had given him a few old family photographs. "But she never had enough," he explains. "All they did was pose and pose and pose. They didn't show a trolley car or an aeroplane or the old nickelodeons. You never knew what it was really like." That was his mission, to show what it was really like. His photos, especially the early ones, are alive with street scenes and horse drawn milk wagons and workers on strike and celebrations at the end of the war — anything, so long as it is Hartford.

Tony is a small, wiry man, a coil of energy, with brown eyes and thinning brown hair that is usually covered by a fedora worn at an angle. There is something faintly musical about him, as if, walking down the street, he might suddenly do a Navy kick or quick tap dance, break into song. He speaks quickly and sincerely in a tough, gravelly voice, a little like James Cagney. On his fingers he wears rings, gem-studded rings, that glint as he smokes his cigar. "My only fault," he says. In his life, he has worked as a diamond tool-maker, a cabinetmaker, a typewriter assembler, not to mention the thirty-six years he spent as a sheet-metal worker at Pratt & Whitney. He is the father of eight, so there had to be some income coming in. The photos were not work — they were his passion.

He lives now in East Hartford, over the line, out of bounds, in a pink house down a narrow side street. It is the first time he has lived outside Hartford, where he has spent nearly all of his life. "I've lived all over Hartford — the North End, up in the Mark Twain area, in three different places on Park Street, I lived on Main Street, yeah, all over." He went over into East Hartford because it was cheaper, but also because he says it gives him some rest. When I'm in Hartford, all I want to do is take pictures."

His youngest daughter Samantha, who is nineteen, moved out a few months ago, and he is alone now for the first time. "Sam thinks I'll be lonely. Lonely? With all this?" he says, flinging his arms out. Tony is a man of such order and organization that the casual visitor might not notice that the house is jammed with negatives and photographs and collections of Hartford memorabilia. No clue, except for the camera on the kitchen table.

"Here's my famous little camera," he says, picking it up and holding it in his palm. It is a Kodak Instamatic, the most recent in a lengthy lineage of cheap cameras. "I got it for fifty cents at a flea market about twenty-one years ago." Tony only takes the pictures. He doesn't have a darkroom and doesn't know the first thing about that part. "I leave that to the experts," he says. Neither has he ever had any instruction. He learned as he went along. "I never had any money in those days. I just had money for film, so I'd buy a cheap camera, and when it broke I'd go get another one. But this is my favorite," he says of the battered little box. "It's the one I carry with me all the time. Now, why do I need an expensive camera? It would just be stolen."

The negatives made by the cheap cameras are in the file drawers, cross-referenced with the prints and the contact sheets that are in other file drawers, and the slides are in another cabinet altogether, numbered, dated, categorized. The slides are newcomers to the historical record. "What happened was a woman sold me a roll of film for slides, and I didn't know it. So I went around taking pictures, I got them developed, and they came back slides. I liked them! So I said, what the heck, I'll take slides, too."

Some of the files are in his bedroom, which he calls his office or, sometimes, the arcade. There he has pinups and pictures of all his old girlfriends and his first wife, his second wife, and his favorite singer Deanna Durbin. In the kitchen, bottles and mugs and jugs, anything that was made in Hartford, line the walls and the cupboards and the windowsills. He displays some of his favorite photographs in the dining room, which serves as his gallery. It is an exhibit that he will often completely change, depending on who is coming over. The tops of the two sideboards, on either side of the table, are loaded with frames propped side to side, no room for another. The walls are so tightly hung with pictures that there's hardly a line in between that shows the plaster. The dining room table is covered with plate glass, under which he slides his newest favorites. "There would never be space to show them all," he says, which rather goes without saying.

The living room, however, shows astonishing restraint. The pink wallpapered walls are bare. "I try to keep Hartford out of here," he says. There is one exception. In the corner, next to the divan, a big framed collage displays the faces of eight tender newborns, with the dates of births marked next to each, 1959 to 1967. "These are all my kids. This is why I call this my family room." He thinks a minute. He can't help it, "They're all born in Hartford hospitals! All Hartford products!"

In the basement, though, the theme picks up again — more files, more scrapbooks. And the shelves of what was once a root cellar are packed solid with his collection of the different editions of *Huck Finn* and *Tom Sawyer.* Tony doesn't see the need to point out that Mark Twain lived in Hartford. Everybody knows that. And, in the corner, he has his brick collection. Bricks from dozens of buildings that have been demolished in Hartford during his lifetime. And a cobblestone from the rail yard before they tore it up. This is also history to Tony. "The history that took place on top of this cobblestone, you know, you just couldn't record it," he says, hefting it like a gold bar.

But these other collections are momentary fascinations, most likely taken up when the light was too dim to take pictures. More than anything else, his pictures have been his records. And it is only recently that he has shown his pictures to anyone but his family. "I did it for my kids. I wanted them to have this after I'm gone." In spite of himself, his pictures were discovered, and people started to call and write to ask for copies. For 43 years I was well hidden," he says, still surprised. "Somebody discovered me, and it's been crazy every since." He doesn't charge people who write asking for prints. "If they send me a few extra bucks, it's nice; I can use it for film. But I'm not a professional. I'm the common man's amateur photographer."

It was kind of a snowball. Two brothers, Bob and Dave McKay, were looking for pictures of "old Hartford" to put up in their Main Street restaurant, the Municipal Cafeteria. They heard about Tony from a friend of a friend and went all over to find him. They finally did, and he was so pleased to think that someone else would enjoy the pictures that he gave Bob and Dave armloads of pictures and memorabilia, including his diploma — why not? The old pictures drew a lot of attention; people wanted to know where they came from, and the Hartford *Courant* found out and did a piece on Tony. "That's me! In the paper!" he says, showing a clipping which he has preserved in a plastic casing. The library found out, too, and put up an exhibit that stayed in their lobby for several months. That's when the phone calls started — because what his pictures show are what it was like.

They are not art; they are not perfect. Tony is the first to admit it. "I don't use any lighting. I don't use any props. Everything is handheld and trust to God that he gives me the light that I want." But Tony thinks he's figured out what's so special about his pictures. "In my day, there weren't too many people walking around with a camera! Today, everybody's got a camera. And yet very few people carry the camera *around* with them. The only shots in their scrapbooks are in the backyard or at the beach or at a graduation."

Tony has spent a lifetime recording the city as it changed. He showed up at dedications for buildings, groundbreakings, demolitions. He used to go up on roofs of buildings — go up fire escapes to get to the top. A lot of those buildings are gone now, and there's not a fire escape in sight. "But I've got a record of all of them! I had some lean years, you know. I had two marriages and eight kids, and there were some rough times — when the kids started coming along it got a lot harder to go out and take pictures. But every once in a while, I'd sneak into town. But then I was single again, and I'd take snowstorms, and when St. Joseph's caught on fire, the smoke was still there when I got there; then there was the strike at Pratt & Whitney, and I took pictures of the ambulances when people got hurt, and I went up in an airplane and took pictures up there. I was on my way again." There was another marriage and another round of kids. "That slowed me down again." But here's what I did. I started the Hartford Historical Files Society. It's newspaper clippings, things about things I couldn't go out and take pictures of. Even when I was tied down, I made sure I never missed a thing." He still goes out, any day that he can, and takes pictures.

One day not long ago dawned sunny and bright, and Tony invited me to go along with him on one of his jaunts. There is always plenty he can show someone from out of town, since even people who live in town don't know the city the way Tony does. The night before he made up a list of the places the tour would include. He had the list on a clipboard under his arm as he locked the back door. And he had his camera. "I'm armed!" he said, patting the pocket of his trench coat. "And plenty of ammunition," he said, flipping a yellow film packet from out of his vest pocket.

Tony drives a gold Lincoln Continental Mark V, a car whose front seat is so big and so plush that when he gets into it, pulling the armrest out from its concealment, it's like he's settling down into an easy chair. "This is a vintage car. That's why I love it. It's ten years old and built like a tank." He put the clipboard on the dash, for reference.

Tony loves the chance to go over into Hartford. "My kids want to go out for a hamburger, and I say let's go to McDonald's in Hartford; that way I get a chance to take pictures, and on the way back I can take pictures."

He maneuvered the car out into the narrow street. The big, wide fenders moved ahead of us like guardian angels, all but grazing the sides of cars parked on either side. Tony didn't notice; he was talking about how much the city has grown in recent years. "Hartford, Hartford. When

I was growing up, it was always the same, nothing changed — nothing doing for years! Then, all of a sudden, *boom*! It's almost more than one man can keep up with. I try to cover everything — I read the paper, word of mouth, everybody is always telling me about something that's going on, so I write it down on my schedule and try to get there."

Tony figured that at that moment there were eight projects going up and four in the planning stages. "I've got all these sites photographed from the ground up, every step, so that if I was to flip the pictures fast in front of you, you'd see the building go right up."

To get into Hartford now he has to go out onto the interstate, and as he came off the exit ramp into the city limits, the cluster of Hartford's high buildings popped into view. "You're coming into the skyline. When I was a little boy, there were only three buildings that stuck up — the Travelers, Hartford Bank and Trust, and G. Fox. Look at this now!" The tall, glassy new buildings reflected the sun, a dazzling sight. On the edges, giant cranes hoisted steel girders and buckets of cement up onto new frames. "Sixteen square miles, I don't know how much more they can do; they'll have to move out."

He turned into downtown Hartford, busy with rush-hour traffic. The sun rested on his face. His eyes were turned upward. He pointed. "See this white building over there — looks like paper clips or hairpins. Isn't that beautiful? That's the Hartford Square North, going up."

He turned a few more corners. "There's the boat building — the only two-sided building in the world! They call it a boat because it's set into a pond, like a moat or something." It looked like a boat, with glass from the top of its tall height all the way down to the street.

Many of his early photographs were taken on the street. He doesn't take random snapshots on the street so much anymore. He has found it has its dangers, more so in recent years. He was once chased for four blocks by someone who wanted to know why he was taking his picture, and his car has been stoned going through different neighborhoods. "And I don't like to see my car banged up, you know? So I have to pick days that are crowded. When you go in on a weekend, when it's quiet, all of a sudden, boom! rocks and whatnot. But! It's the hazard of the trade."

He cruised through a red light, majestically, as if making a conquest. A horn sounded. "No problem," he said. He was concentrating on the buildings. "Every building has a history, believe me. And every street has a history."

He pointed to a side street. "There's Park Street — my favorite street! That's where I grew up."

He showed me where the floodwaters came up to the steps of the meeting house, and he pointed out the cross on top of the steeple on St. Joseph's Church, which he says he rubbed for good luck before they hoisted it up. We crept slowly past the Colt factory, with its distinctive Russian-inspired onion dome, painted blue and speckled with gold stars; and the stilt building, which Tony had to circle before we could see its spidery supports; and past the gold building, which Tony particularly likes to photograph when the sun hits it and makes the buildings around it shimmer with watery sunlight; and the home of one of Tony's heroes: the man who invented the Gatling gun. We passed an old boarded-up factory near the railroad tracks. "See that window right there? My mother waved to me from that window when I went to war."

At the Comet Diner he made a note on the clipboard to come back and take a picture. He never takes a picture haphazardly. He studies each site, noticing when the light will be right. "It's pretty hard to find something that I haven't got pictures of," he said. The Comet is one. It used to be the Aetna Diner. "I asked my first wife's father if I could marry her in there. It's pretty hard to photograph because the sun doesn't hit it till late July. But it's on the agenda. Yes, I want that one."

He made a left, past the Mark Twain House. "We're heading into Katharine Hepburn territory," he continued. She is another of his collectibles. A picture of her is under glass of the sideboard in his dining room. "This is the end of the Nook Farm, where all those literary characters lived." He motioned to a parking lot, girded with a chain-link fence.

"Right where these cars are parked is where Katharine Hepburn's house was."

He took me past the Royal Typewriter factory, where he spent over eight years putting together typewriters; past the Kane's brick factory and the Heublein factory, where they make vodka; past the Fuller Brush building, where brushes are no longer made. He has pictures of all of these.

He swung onto Prospect Street, which is the city line. The other side of the street, which is East Hartford, is no man's land. "I only look at this side of the street," he said, pointing to the Hartford side. "I have to limit myself, believe me, otherwise it would be endless."

He drifted through another light that had turned red. An oncoming car swerved.

Tony said he was starting to feel hungry and headed back over to the center of town to the Muni, where he is as regular as the guy behind the counter.

The Municipal was starting to crowd up, and the dishes clanking and the rising conversations made it hard to hear Frank Sinatra singing in the background. There were old pictures everywhere. Many of them I recognized as Tony's. He loves the way people enjoy the pictures at the restaurant. "I don't ask for anything. I want the people to enjoy them. I'm happy just to have them know I took the picture. They say, 'Hey, you took that picture?' and I say, 'Yeah!'"

From up front, Tony got a roast beef on a hard roll and a coffee and took a table in line with the door so he could see who was coming and going. A man with snow white hair and a bright red scarf around his neck came in. "Hey, Bob!" Tony called out.

Tony introduced me to Bob Echelson who took off his scarf and sat down next to Tony. He had spent the morning in the legislature, and he and Tony talked for a minute about Hartford politics. I asked Bob how long he'd lived in Hartford, and he said, "Forever, all my life." He looked at me, like he was about to give away a secret. "It's a boring town, you know I'm not like Tony. To me, Hartford is dull. What's so great about Hartford, Tony?"

Tony's brown eyes went from me to Bob, Bob to me.

Finally he said, "I don't know. If I had been born in Boston, I would have been crazy about Boston because this is my nature. It's my heritage, that's what I love — where I was born, where I went to school, where I was married, where all my kids were born. For me it's always been Hartford, Hartford. But if I moved to Boston or some other place now, no, it wouldn't have that attraction. I haven't got that long to live! I'd still continue on with Hartford. I'd still get the Hartford *Courant*. This is a lifetime."

Bob said, "You've always been a romantic, huh, Tony?"

Tony thought a minute. "I might get married again, you never know."

Bob laughed and jabbed him in the ribs. "Oh, jeez, I didn't mean *that* kind of romance, Tony."

Tony got up. From the pocket of his trenchcoat, he drew out the camera and walked backward, eyeing me and Bob sitting at the booth. He bent his knees a little bit, brought the camera up to his face, his elbows out like wings, and said, "Ok, nice smile, botha you! Atsa way!" and the flash popped, a brilliant light in the midst of the lunchtime crowd, ca. 1987. Tony's kind of history.

November 1987 Yankee magazine

TONY'S HARTFORD *renown only grew, his photographs appearing here and there throughout the city and becoming increasingly prized for the history they illuminated. Hartford mayor, Michael P. Peters, declared May 7, 1998, "Tony DeBonee Day," at which time Tony told the* Hartford Courant *that he was proud to have spent more than half a century "behind a cheap camera." Tony died in April of 2001 at the age of seventy-seven. His extensive collection of photographs, known as the DeBonee Collection and which consists of more than 40,000 images, is on file at the Hartford Public Library.*

Another Rose for Provincetown

THIS IS THE STORY of a man in love with a boat, a boat he has never seen. It was a boat he dreamed of as a boy, a boat that brought pride to his family and to his town and to his people, the Portuguese. Eleven years ago he set about building a model of that beautiful racing schooner. When he finished, it was the largest scale model in the world. At sixty-two feet, it could go to sea, but it never will. It wasn't meant to. It was meant to be a reminder of what Provincetown used to be — a town filled with Portuguese fishermen and their families, their whaling schooners tied to the docks or silently skimming the waters on the Grand Banks, bringing in fish like no other fishermen on earth.

It started with the church. About thirty years ago the congregation of the Methodist church wanted to sell their building, a huge English baroque building that stands out like a monolith among the low crowd of shops (all of which were once fishermen's homes) along Commercial Street, where gay bars now proliferate and churches continue to die. It was too much for their dwindling numbers to keep up. There was resistance, but the church was sold to a wealthy man who turned it into an art museum for a while, but it was not a success; and in 1974 it came back onto the market. Three options arose: one man wanted to turn it into a pornographic movie theater; another wanted to gut it and turn it into an indoor bazaar; and yet another wanted to tear it down and make a parking lot. Though pornographic movies are popular in Provincetown and parking spaces are dear, there was an outcry from a certain sector of the population. Most of the Portuguese are Catholic, but they are also proud, and these buildings are the finest in the town. The intricate woodwork inside shows the work of their forefathers.

Josephine Del Deo envisioned the old Methodist church as another kind of museum, one that would show off all that they were most proud of in their ancestry, one that would show the town's heritage. This church, after all, is the first building that the fishermen see when they return from sea, and that makes it, in her mind, a statement of their community pride, of the old Provincetown.

And so, after all this, in 1975 the town voted to buy the building and turn it into a museum. The old Methodist church was to become the Provincetown Heritage Museum, to commemorate the town's significant Portuguese heritage. Josephine had visited the museum down in New Bedford, and she had seen the kinds of things they had on display, including a scale model of the *Lagoda*, and certainly in Provincetown there was no greater ship than the *Rose Dorothea.* To the eternal pride of the Portuguese, she had overtaken Gloucester and Boston to win the Lipton Cup in 1907. What Josephine Del Deo thought would bring the greatest pride to this town would be to have a half-scale model (the original *Rose Dorothea* was 108.7 feet long) of this great ship. She wanted the model to be sixty-two feet. That would make it the world's largest scale model, a superlative that could mean a lot to Provincetown, and certainly there was no one else but Flyer to build the *Rose.*

Flyer Santos lives on Commercial Street, right near where he was born seventy-four years ago. Flyer lived there long before the cabarets and the male revues, even before the parking lots. I visited him there one summer day. The house is sturdy, a comfortable house that tells a story better than any book, as good a place as any for Flyer to settle down and tell me his story.

At birth, Flyer was given the name Francis, but, he says, "As a boy I never walked anywhere, I always ran, so they called me The Flying

Machine. Later on that came down to Flyer, and it's stuck with me all my life." Age has not diminished this — he is still a bit of a spinning top. When he tells a story, he will occasionally get up out of his chair and act out the part of the person he is describing, waving his arms and jumping up and down with spry grace. With thick gray hair and dark eyebrows, Flyer has an intelligent face, lined with the wisdom of his years and light green eyes that seem always to be looking at the horizon.

Flyer spent his life building and repairing boats, and for most of his life, since he was a small boy, he's been fascinated by the *Rose Dorothea*. His grandfather, John Pavon Santos, was a crew member aboard the *Rose* when she won the Cup. When he was a boy, the name of the *Rose* had already assumed legendary status. "All the time growing up, all I heard about was the *Rose Dorothea*," Flyer told me on another day, this time in his shop, a little room beside what then was the nearly completed model of the *Rose*. All around him were his tools, including a Portuguese hand adze with a handle Flyer carved of ash. "In the old days, you had your meals right on time. Supper came at five and then right around six — there wasn't any TV then — all the men would get up and go on back down to the boatshop, and they'd tell stories, all about how the *Rose Dorothea* was the fastest boat in the world."

When Flyer was twenty-one, back in 1935, he built a model of the *Rose Dorothea* for a Knights of Columbus parade. It was thirty-eight or forty feet long, and the masts were so high they didn't clear the wires when they rolled her down Commercial Street in the parade. Back then the man who had stitched the sails for the original *Rose Dorothea*, James Maguire, was still alive and living in Provincetown, and Flyer asked him to make the sails for the model. The model for the float is long gone, but he's still got those sails up in his attic.

A year after that, Flyer met a pretty French girl from Providence named Irene. She had blond hair and she loved to laugh, and not long after that they were married. They bought a house on Commercial Street near where Flyer had been born. There was a beach out front where Flyer could work on boats, but more than that, the house, he knew very well, had belonged to Captain Marion Perry, who had built the *Rose Dorothea* and who had captained her to victory in the race for the Lipton Cup. It was also the home of Rose Dorothea, known as the prettiest girl in Boston, who came down to Provincetown to marry Captain Perry. "Her father ran a bar room in Boston," Flyer said. "Her name was Rose Dorothea McGowan, and she was supposed to be the prettiest girl that they ever saw. She was the only one who ever came down to Provincetown in a bridal train — there was a whole car just for her. Everyone in Provincetown came down to the square, just to see what Rose McGowan looked like. Later on she became Rose Dorothea Perry. He was Portuguese and he married an Irish girl."

After he and Irene moved in, he searched upstairs in the attic and found a big framed picture of the *Rose,* charging along through the open ocean, her sails filled with wind. He dusted it off and brought it downstairs and hung it in the living room.

When tourists began to come to Provincetown, Flyer and Irene rented out rooms, and they called the place the Rose Dorothea. And when Irene gave birth to a baby girl, the fifth of their six children, Flyer wanted to name her Rose Dorothea, but Irene said, "No, I'm not naming my baby after a boat!" They compromised and called her Dorothea. (That's Dora who knows well how much her father wanted to name her after that great racing schooner. She smiles to tell of her younger brother, Arthur Joe, who recently came home to tell his parents he was going to marry. The girl's name is Rose. What Flyer said when he heard was, "I've finally got my Rose!")

There are innumerable stories of Flyer's attachment to the *Rose.* Those are just a few. And so when Josephine Del Deo asked him if he thought he could build a half-scale model of the *Rose Dorothea,* the question wasn't *if,* it was *when.*

He first needed blueprints. The first year, 1976, was spent in search of them. The *Rose Dorothea* was a spoon-bowed schooner designed by

Tom McManus. Flyer, of course, first looked upstairs in his attic, but he figures that those early Portuguese fishermen couldn't read or write, so there were no papers there. They looked also in the town archives, but there had been a fire, and models and drawings had been destroyed. They finally went to a man in Quincy who had drawn the blueprints for the restoration of the *Mayflower*. They didn't have enough money for a good set of blueprints, but he made them a set of rough drawings, without a lot of detail, but it was enough to work by.

Scaling it down, making it fit into the museum was hard, especially without blueprints. The boat, they had agreed, would be built on the second floor, a big open space where the congregation once worshipped. Flyer traveled to Mystic Seaport in Connecticut. He knew they had the *L. C. Dunton*, similar to the *Rose*, and looking at her helped him. "I took quite a lot of photographs. A picture is worth a thousand words. You could look at the blueprint for six hours, but there's a lot of the things you don't get. Boatbuilders don't use blueprints as a rule. They go down to the shore and they look."

Flyer has been building boats since he was fifteen — all kinds of boats: trapboats, scows, draggers, even a twenty-six-foot racing sailboat that he's captained to victory in the Provincetown regatta five years in a row. But he had never built a boat like this before, not a schooner. "I mean, the main boom on the *Rose Dorothea* was ninety feet long — the boats I work on are small compared with that."

The boats Flyer built at his boatyard, "Flyer's Boatshop," down a narrow lane off Commercial Street, were commercial fishing boats, up to thirty or forty feet. He's worked on most of the boats in Provincetown fleet, the ones that are made of wood. The fleet is down to about thirty-five boats now, and all of them are draggers, a method of fishing that Flyer assumes would be disdained by his grandfather and by his father, who was also a Provincetown fisherman. "These boats (Grand Banks schooners) had twenty-six men on them and twelve dories. They didn't drag nets — no, they would be very ashamed of anyone who did that because when they do that they kill more than they catch, and they ruin the bottom. But in 1915 they started putting engines in the boats and that was the end of an era." It bears remarking that Flyer was born in 1914.

That model Flyer made for the Knights of Columbus parade was like a dry run for this one he's created, which, that first time we talked, had a plaque on her side that declared it "completed" in 1986. But it was still quite a ways from being finished, as far as Flyer was concerned. Just the same, the enormous model filled the sanctuary of that church that once boasted two thousand two hundred members. The hull, which stops just below the red waterline, was set flush with the floor where the pews once were; the great masts rose up through the ceiling into the steeple; and the bowsprit thrust forward to, nearly touching, what once was the altar. The original *Rose* weighed one hundred and eight tons, and the model, as it grew, came to thirty-five tons, weight enough to worry whether or not that great church could bear it. Flyer put marks in the beams in the cellar, and he'd check them every once in a while. Her hull had been painted a shining black, her decks and mastheads and booms a shining white, the colors of the Portuguese fleet. "This boat is my heritage," Flyer said.

As much or more a part of his heritage than the boat is his grandfather, who came to Provincetown from Portugal on a whaling ship. But his grandfather was a silent man and imparted few of the stories that Flyer yearned to hear. He prizes the one story he was able to pry from him. "My grandfather couldn't read and write, and I used to go visit him at night. I was about twelve years old at the time. He didn't smoke or drink, and he wasn't a conversationalist. He'd sit there by the hour and stitch liners for his boots. He'd do that while the others would be playing cards or playing instruments. I was teaching him how to read and write out of the Sears Roebuck catalog. One day we were on the page with overalls. He was interested in them. They cost 89 cents. I kept money, silver, on the table to teach him the money. He happened to lean over and pull up his pant leg and, jeez, I saw a scar that went the whole length of his leg. I asked him, 'How did you get that?' Being stubborn, he was reluctant to tell me. So I said, 'I'm not going to teach you how to read and write if you aren't going to tell me how you got that!' Well, he was a striker on a whaler, up front with the ropes. After my grandfather struck a whale, the rope flew out and took a big turn on his leg and pulled him in. The whale, after he's hit, dives deep and this one took him deeper and deeper. My grandfather, like all the whalers, kept a knife sheathed to his belt and he took that out and cut himself free. When he did, he cut his leg open. He didn't feel it at the time, not underwater. He was in the water quite a time. There was blood, and there were sharks all around. After I heard that story, I knew what it meant to be a whaler."

His grandfather didn't tell him much more than that — he never told Flyer what it was like aboard the *Rose Dorothea* — but Flyer did a lot of reading. "When I was in school, I liked history, I liked geography very, very much. I always felt that I was going to sail around the world alone, like Joshua Slocum. The closest I got to doing that was reading the book three times."

In his reading in school, he found there were a lot of mistakes in the history books. "The Portuguese discovered everything, or just about everything, and when they got done discovering, they were nowhere big enough to own it, so the English came along and colonized whatever it was they'd discovered. Portugal was such a little country, you know, but they discovered the coast of Africa, where no one had ever been before; they discovered all of South America, and Magellan was the first man to sail around the world — you can go on and on forever."

Flyer has light green eyes and smooth tan skin. He believes that the Portuguese are a global race, a race that embraces the entire world. "A lot of people think that the Portuguese are black. My father-in-law, when I was going to marry my wife, he felt that the Portuguese were colored. And you can think that if you don't know any history, I suppose. The Portuguese could go anywhere. They could sail these big square-riggers, but they were at the mercy of the winds and the tides so they never could sail back. So they dropped everywhere — Africa, South America, all over — and they intermarried."

Flyer was leaning against his workbench. The window beside him was open and he looked out toward the harbor, which could be seen in a glimmer between the clusters of buildings. "You see, this is my heritage as well as that boat, and every time someone refers to me as black, they don't offend me. The Portuguese discovered ninety percent of the world.

"So, the history books know so little. Where I went to school, they taught that the first landing of the Pilgrims was in Plymouth. Well, the first landing of the Pilgrims was in Provincetown. They settled in Plymouth, but they landed here. They've got nothing to show for it — a little rock! We've got a monument two hundred and fifty feet high. Why did they let the schoolteachers put that in the history books?"

There's nothing much in the history books about the Lipton Cup race, which happened in Boston in August 1907. But Flyer can reel it off as if he'd been there. "The *Rose Dorothea* was a much larger schooner than the others, sailwise. She carried an awful lot of sail and there weren't many schooners that could even touch her. It was Sir Thomas Lipton, the greatest sportsman of all times, who offered the cup, the most expensive cup they make in England, plus six hundred dollars to the crew and captain. It was a forty-two-mile course off Eastern Point in Gloucester and near the finish the *Rose Dorothea* heeled over and her fore-topmast snapped. She kept right on going and won the race anyway. When you think of a town as small as this competing with Boston and Gloucester and you look at our town years ago, before anything was built on Cape Cod, at that massive and beautiful town hall, this will show you that we were second to none as far as the sea was concerned."

The Lipton Cup has been kept at the town hall all these years, and Flyer hoped that when he finished the boat, the cup could come over to the museum, alongside the *Rose*. "It's bigger and better looking than that New York mug, the America's Cup, I guess they call it," Flyer said.

Flyer didn't build the model alone, and he wants to be sure that everyone knows that. On the wall of his shop is a list of names of people who helped with the boat. He points to a name. "Now there's a girl who helped plane the mast." There are a couple of names that have been crossed off. "Whoever made this list tried to slip their friends' names in there. I blacked them right out to show no politics in this place." He points to David Ditacchio's name. "This is the guy that stuck with me the longest." Frank James, a Gay Head Indian, spent two years making the rigging.

There was one volunteer Flyer won't forget. Richard Meads, a house carpenter, would just show up on his way home from work and help Flyer with whatever needed doing. Richard Meads was Portuguese, and Flyer loved him like a son. Richard Meads died without seeing the project completed. "Thirty-nine years old and dead of cancer!" Flyer said, as if the injustice of it could be righted by pointing it out. "He loved to come down and work an hour or two. The last thing he did for me was cut out that ceiling." Flyer cannot speak of it without tears coming up in his eyes. "The first day I got down here to work on this boat after that — everything I touched, everything I looked at reminded me of him. I'd look at the ceiling. . . ." The death of Richard Meads slowed Flyer. It was the only time he lost enthusiasm for the *Rose Dorothea.*

Not only was Flyer's work on the boat volunteer, but everyone else's was also. "That's the only way we ever would have built this thing. We didn't take money. We had a lot of talk, a lot of plans, a lot of noise, a lot of volunteers, and no money."

Josephine Del Deo and the others at the museum organized auctions and concerts to raise money, and her husband Salvatore, an artist, made limited-edition silkscreen prints for $1,000 donations. "The reason it took Flyer all those years [to build the *Rose*] is because every time he did something, he'd have to stop and wait for us to raise some more money," Josephine explains. "This is without a penny toward his labor." The final tally was $75,000, including the sails that were stitched by an old master in New Bedford and cost $17,000. (The original *Rose Dorothea* cost $15,000 to build.) The Provincetown Heritage Museum is proud they had to borrow nothing to complete the *Rose*.

Flyer helped save money by using salvaged lumber. When they gutted the Provincetown Library during renovations, Flyer stood by and scarfed up the oak shelving, which he used to make hatches and grates on the deck of the model. "That wood is a hundred years old. It will never shrink. It acts the way wood ought to." And whenever he saw a builder on his way to the dump, his truck loaded with 2x4 scraps and pieces of plywood, he'd flag him down and rummage through to save what he could. The bowsprit of the *Rose* is made of four floor joists, glued and doweled together, joists he removed from the church ceiling to make way for the mast. "I had to take nails out of it and all that, but you can't see a joint. That shows what you can do with old wood." Flyer made the blocks in the rigging and the deadeyes and the hatches from used lumber. It's a little fact that evokes a small sermon from him. "I would like to teach that to the younger people. Carpenters today, over half their lumber goes to the dump! Big pieces of plywood, 2x4s, that's why our dumps are full and we don't have a place to put things. I don't throw anything away, and I use every single piece. What I see going to the Provincetown dump drives me crazy. It's costing millions and millions of dollars. Society has got all this education, and they don't know what to do with their own rubbish. That's about the simplest problem in the world, what you do with rubbish. It's not one of the big technical problems like how do you get to the moon."

Boatbuilders — Flyer believes there are really very few left — need to think in these impecunious ways, anyway, Flyer says. "Most kids today, they go to college and learn how to make money. If you're that much interested in money, you're never going to be a boatbuilder because a boatbuilder is like a priest. They both work for nothing."

Before I left that day, I asked him if, after all this work, he wouldn't like to see the boat in the water. "Well, yes," he said, almost surprised by the question. "But that would be a dream and I am not a dreamer."

IT WAS ANOTHER year before Flyer finished the *Rose.* He got the sails up — a huge amount of canvas ("These are not make-believe. They could go to sea, oh, yes.") — and he and Frank James worked on the rigging, an enormous and complicated task that involved three hundred and seventy-five pounds of rope and a skill that only Frank had. It was so close to being finished that the museum set a date for a ceremony to dedicate the beautiful boat. It only made sense that it should be the same weekend as the blessing of Provincetown's fleet, a custom there since the late forties. The fishermen, being devout and somewhat superstitious, decorate their boats with colorful flags and hand-stitched banners bearing bits of nautical wisdom such as this one: "Give me a fish and I eat for a day. Teach me to fish and I eat for a lifetime." It is a weekend of parades and celebrations that culminate in the blessing: the decorated boats make a wide circle around the harbor before passing in front of the bishop who stands on the wharf and casts holy water toward each one as it glides past.

For Flyer, it was a final deadline. He worked and worked as the time came closer. Details — a block out of place, spar varnish for the hatch covers — loomed. The two weeks before the dedication, he was down at the church every night until ten. At four o'clock the day before the dedication he raised the ensign, the original flag from the *Rose Dorothea*, a fifteen-star American flag, and then he went home. Irene was in the kitchen making salads and a roast beef, and Flyer set two pots of beans to baking, for there would be a crowd coming back to the house after the ceremony.

The next day, at the dedication, the odor of the fresh white paint on the front of the museum hung a little in the air, and the seams of the newly laid sod on the front lawn had not yet meshed. It was a warm day, the sun bright. A great crowd gathered and spilled out into Commercial Street, where passersby stopped to watch. The schoolchildren had written a song. "The Good Old *Rose Dorothea*" which they sang, and they'd prepared a pageant, "The Race of a Lifetime," which they performed, and there was a poem recited, all in honor of the *Rose Dorothea.* Josephine

Del Deo presented Flyer with a gold watch, the face of which had been painted by a local artist — a miniature picture of the *Rose* under sail. The Lipton Cup, that huge and ornate trophy, was brought into the museum with great ceremony. Inside, where the decks of the *Rose* had been decorated with baskets of roses — big pink garden roses that Flyer's brother had grown behind his house — Irene was to do the christening. It took her three tries before she could break the bottle over the bowsprit, and then the Reverend Bento Fraga blessed the boat and "all of those who have given the gift of self so that we may be better aware of our heritage."

There was a party at Flyer's afterwards, and every room in the downstairs of the house that Captain Marion Perry built was filled with people talking about the *Rose*.

Early the next morning a dark storm rolled in. Lightning and thunder rattled the windows and shook the foundations of many of the houses along the narrow strip of sand that is Provincetown. The boats of the fleet, waiting to be blessed on that Sunday, rocked back and forth in the waves of the storm, their colorful flags snapping in the fierce wind. I walked through the rain to Flyer's where an assortment of sons and daughters and grandchildren lingered with him. The electricity had gone out so he could not make "flippers" (a kind of Portuguese fried dough), which he enjoys making on Sunday morning. Two blonde grandsons, their hair cut in modified Mohawks, whirled about from room to room.

"Everything goes on around me," Flyer said. "Half the time I don't know what's happening." He was in his socks and had put on a heavy flannel shirt against the cool of the stormy morning. Lightning flashed and thunder rumbled as we talked of the day before. Aside from the work he has done building the boat, Flyer had also spent a good deal of time trying to find out who all the crew members aboard the *Rose* had been. There had been twenty-six, and he had unearthed the names of seventeen and tried to contact them. During the ceremony, a woman had come up to Flyer, full of excitement. She carried with her a framed photograph of a man who had been a part of the crew. The man was Richard

Meads' grandfather. Richard Meads never knew his grandfather had had anything to do with the *Rose Dorothea.* It seemed the most exciting part of the whole day for Flyer. "He had an attachment to that boat that he never knew!" Flyer said. "There was a reason why he kept coming back to work on that boat."

It is these mystical attachments that Flyer believes have kept the boat alive, a spiritual member of the Provincetown fleet.

In spite of the gold watch and the songs and the burst bottle of champagne, Flyer doesn't seem to think that his work with the *Rose* is over, not just yet. So far, the scale model of the *Rose Dorothea* has been thirteen years in the making. "You know, there's still a bit more to be done."

January 1989 Yankee magazine

FLYER SANTOS *is now ninety-six years old and still lives at his home on Commercial Street. He is very happy to welcome anyone who is interested in his scale model of the* Rose Dorothea *which is on display on the second floor of the Provincetown Heritage Museum. His pride in the accomplishments of his Portuguese forebears remains undiminished and he hastens to add that the Lipton Cup is on display on the first floor of the museum.*

The Black and White of Berenice Abbott

The winter sun hunches low, lighting up the snow that has drifted across Lake Hebron and mounded up around the log house. The porch, which in summer provides a quiet place for a solitary soul and a rocking chair to sit in and observe the lake, is buried by the height of the snow. The lake does not look like a lake so much as a field or a desert, a wide expanse of white dunes rimmed in the black silhouettes of bare trees. Inside, Berenice Abbott throws the dice with a triumphant flourish of her strong-looking hand and advances the red token one, two, three, up the ladder to Home. "Gotcha!" she says. She has won the last round of Parcheesi, and I part with another dime, which Berenice promptly deposits in the small cloth purse beside her and draws the string closed with a sly smile. "Had enough?" she asks, her pale blue eyes challenging.

The day has been spent in conversation. Though over the years there have been long lists of books and articles written about her photographs, Berenice, who is nearly ninety, doesn't like interviews. "I don't know what there is to write about me," she says. "If you want to write about my work, that is one thing, but about me there isn't a lot to say." When she tired of the questions, she suggested Parcheesi, which she plays daily with her friend and companion, Susan Blatchford, until Susan runs out of dimes.

Recent notices of her work — several shows in Boston and New York and a book, Hank O'Neal's *Berenice Abbott, American Photographer* —

have brought forth such descriptions as "American's greatest living photographer" and "a neglected genius." Such kudos do not turn her head. "My work is done," she had said, right at the start of the day. "Photography is a work of drudgery. You're on your feet a lot. It's very tiring. It's a labor of love. I loved what I was doing. But there comes a time when you don't want to do it anymore."

Her house is as comfortable as any could be in the Maine woods, though it is not the big "white elephant" she bought in the 1960s. It is a compact log cabin she had built for herself as a getaway, four miles down the road from her big house and her darkroom. She moved into it permanently when she went into retirement three years ago. A stack of split maple is in the corner beside the gray enamel parlor stove that provides an extra boost of heat for the house, whose walls are cedar logs and whose floors are thickly carpeted. There are four rooms downstairs and a loft bedroom upstairs, reached by spiral staircase that corkscrews up from the living room floor. Steam rises from the pot of black coffee sitting on the warming shelf of the stove, which is almost within reach of Berenice's plush, black easy chair.

With slow grace she rises and reaches for the coffee pot, a constant habit of her days. Dressed in black wool pants, a brown chamois shirt, and moccasin slippers, Berenice is slender and only slightly bent at the neck from her years of leaning over to peer through the lens of her heavy 8"x10" view camera. In Paris, in the 1920s, she used it to do portraits of such luminaries as James Joyce, André Gide, Djuna Barnes and Edna St. Vincent Millay; in New York her camera recorded the city during the 1930s in all its splendor; the camera traveled with her down the eastern seaboard in the 1950s when she went by car, photographing life along U.S. Route 1 from Fort Kent, Maine to Florida. It is also the camera she brought to Maine when she came to settle in 1960, buying an old rundown inn in Blanchard, a tiny town no one she knew had ever heard of.

On the far wall, facing Berenice's chair, is a black and white photograph that fills the wall. It is a view of New York City at night and seems to have been taken from a great height. The lights from the rows and rows of windows are a terrestrial constellation and here and there the lights are so bright they almost explode, like little suns.

It is a photograph Berenice took in 1932, as a kind of preamble to her series called "Changing New York," a project that consumed her from 1935 to 1939. In the series are photographs of Rockefeller Center and George Washington Bridge under construction, pawn shops and butcher shops and burlesque show marquees, and George Washington's statue being hoisted onto its pedestal in Union Square. The project was partially funded by the Works Progress Administration. In a 1930 Ford roadster, she traveled the city from neighborhood to neighborhood, selecting potential subjects. From the tops of high buildings, from the ends of piers, from the middle of the street, she found vantage points and set up her tripod-supported camera to record the city. She left few corners unrecorded and in fact was once chastised for taking photographs in the Bowery, where nice girls should not go. "I'm not a nice girl; I'm a photographer," was her reply.

"Night View" was photographed from a window, not from the top of a building, but just the same it was hard to get permission. "They always thought you wanted to commit suicide," she remembers. This print on her wall is blown up bigger than any print she ever made. Berenice can no longer work in a darkroom, and she no longer owns her negatives, or her camera, or even very many of her prints. They are owned now by Ron Kurtz, who lives in New Jersey. He produces Berenice's photographs under the name of Commerce Graphics. "I wasn't printing anymore, and there was more demand," Berenice explains. "So I thought, I could be dead and what would happen to them? They'd just go down to the dump." This notion is not the whimsy of an old woman who has lived in the woods too long. It ties into an experience in her life that had a profound effect on her. When she was a young woman, living in Paris, she came across the photographs of Eugene Atget. She was immediately struck by them — in them she found the sense of unadorned reality that many now admire in her work. Even though she knew that he was reclusive and that few appreciated him at that time, she sought him out and visited him many times, asking him questions about his darkroom techniques. Eventually she invited him to her studio so she could take his portrait. With the results of his sitting, she returned to his apartment to show him the prints, only to be greeted by the news of his death. She was stunned and deeply concerned about the fate of his life's work.

"Atget's photographs, the few I knew, somehow spelled photography to me. The deep response they evoked in me drove me to track them down with an instinctive fear that they might be lost or even destroyed. Had I realized at that time the general disregard and carelessness that exist — even today — with most photographs, my alarm would have been tenfold," she later wrote in her introduction to *The World of Atget.*

It is widely believed that if Berenice had not made efforts to salvage his work — thousands of glass plates and prints — it would have been discarded. Eventually she acquired much of the collection — there was little competition — and from there on made it an additional passion to gain recognition for this sadly neglected artist. Her efforts proved successful. He died without ever seeing his work displayed in public. Now, there is little dispute that Eugene Atget's photographs, which are now owned by the Museum of Modern Art in New York City, rank among the great. When she brought the Atget estate with her back to New York, she made prints of some of the glass plate negatives. Soon after her return, she became friends with the young Walker Evans. She shared these with Walker Evans. He later wrote that he was "electrified" by these images and Atget is regarded as a major influence on Evans' work. And so the wings of art are spread.

The sale of her own negatives and prints began only within the past four years, and though she has moments of regret, she appears to find someone else's vision of her pictures interesting. "They've enlarged some that I thought weren't much good." She beckons me to follow her into her bedroom where one of them, another oversized print made by Kurtz's company, hangs beside her bed. She photographed it from J.P. Morgan's office at the corner of Broad and Wall streets. In it there is a flag that seems to move, in the grandest way, above the figures that hurry along the street below. "There was a big flag from his window, hanging out over that famous corner. I was aiming toward the Treasury Building, the flag right in front of me waving around, like that," she says, making her hand undulate. "There was a spotty sort of a light and anything moving near the lens takes a much quicker exposure to stop it. It was a tour de force, and of course the whole negative was thin, too underexposed, so I thought it wasn't worth printing. Well, they bring this out and print it, and to my amazement, I liked it! I was smitten with it."

Of the "Night View" she says, passing by it on the way back to her chair, "I never would have thought to make it that big." It is so big, there on her wall, it seems almost like a window. She stands, hands on her hips, leaning back to look at it. "I was terribly excited about New York then. I had been away from it for a number of years, so it was very fresh. There were skyscrapers going up everywhere. I wanted to photograph it! I lost three years, talking myself out, trying to get some backing for the project. Nobody would help me. Meanwhile New York was changing before my eyes, literally from week to week. I have a picture I took on West Street, where everything was growing. There's just one little skyscraper, amid all these little houses down by the waterfront. It was the Hearst Building, sticking up like a sore thumb."

She returns to her chair, folding her hands in her lap, her eyes bright as moons, studying the picture. "A photograph is a document. What else can it be? And why? There is nothing more exciting than reality — nothing more fantastic or fanciful. All we can do is the present. Only in a painting can you paint the past or the future or wherever your fancy takes you — not in a photograph."

Though change excited her back then, she feels now that change has come too fast in this country. She was devastated last year to return to Columbus, Ohio — near where she grew up — only to find the city unrecognizable. "Americans have left nothing of their heritage. It is as if it didn't exist. Photographers should be taking their cities and their towns because they are changing like crazy."

To Berenice, New England is the only part of the country that has retained some tradition, some sense of heritage. She discovered Maine when she did her Route 1 project. Again, she had no backing and had to be creative in finding a way to fund the project, which she believed in but which has never to this day been published. "I talked a young man into making the trip. He wanted to be a photographer. I said, 'Go with me on this trip — you pay for it — and you'll learn photography.' So we did it. I discovered Maine out of it, and I liked it better than any other state. Maine was the least spoiled at that time — 1954. It was down to earth and unpretentious. It probably corresponded to south Ohio where I grew up. Simple."

The area around her is still simple — in town is a chainsaw dealer, a small store, and a post office no bigger than a kiosk — and far from almost everything except Canada. She is 80 miles from Quebec but a twelve-hour drive from New York City and a five-hour drive from Boston. It has changed very little since 1954, which delights her. "They don't like progress here, and I like that. There's times when it's better to be backward. They voted down a big highway that was going to go through here to Canada. Voted it down!" Berenice laughs. "I was so pleased! I mean, who wants *that*?

"I was never sorry I moved here," she goes on. "Never. Maine is hard to define. The minute you get over the bridge at Kittery you want to say hallelujah! I like it at this time of my life because I like peace and serenity and quiet. It was a tremendous adjustment, but it depends on your time of life. If I'd come up here when I was young, I couldn't have adjusted — I had too many interests; I was too active. Years ago, you couldn't have torn me out of New York. But now I go down there for a few days and I get so wound up, I have to get out fast to keep my sanity."

She was sick with emphysema when she first came to Maine, sick from spending too many years in an unventilated darkroom, breathing chemicals and bad city air. Fixing up the old inn in Maine became her obsession, and she designed a darkroom on the third floor that was not only well ventilated but even air-conditioned. And there she worked hard and long hours. She set about to photograph her new state, a project that resulted in her book *Portrait of Maine,* which some say is the best picture book ever put out about the state. She loved Maine and said she would never leave it — and she hasn't.

In her time, Berenice has seen photography become more widely recognized. "During the 1920s," she says, "photography was thought of as a rather inferior craft, like sewing or something. It's a tremendous art, a fine art, but it's still very primitive, much more appropriate to the time than painting. Painting takes time and patience. We have no patience, we have no time. We are run by dollar bills."

Though she makes it sound like an art for the impatient, hers was the work of the careful and painstaking artist. In her photographs, Berenice held patience and accuracy above all else. She took time, carefully examining each negative and thinking out each shot. She is baffled by what she has observed of many of the modern professional photographers who expose roll after roll of film, hoping for one good shot. "They are depending on luck," she says.

Though she says that photography went through something of a revolution in the 1960s, with faster film and more sophisticated equipment, she doesn't feel that people really *understand* photography. "They don't understand the difference between a serious photograph and just a snapshot, not yet. Everybody takes photographs now. Everybody reads and writes, but they're not all writers, are they?"

Many of her pictures — the Aroostook County potato farmers, the West Virginia miner's wife, the old men on the steps of Milliken's Store in Bridgewater, Maine — look as if they might have been snapshots, but they were not. At Milliken's Store, for instance, she says it was fortunate that the men didn't just leave when she arrived with her very conspicuous camera equipment and began to set up. "I would never let people just stand there and look like a snapshot — you can't do that. You have to talk to them or just be patient and wait. Soon enough they'll relax. People are always good. You have to be able to talk to them."

Berenice taught photography, but she does not believe schooling in photography is an effective way to learn. She learned from doing. She was a sculptor in Paris, where she knew slightly the photographer Man Ray. One day she heard him grousing about his assistant who thought he knew everything. "What I need is someone who knows nothing about photography," he said. And Berenice spoke up. "What about me?" She knew nothing and needed a job. He took her on and taught her darkroom technique. When she showed promise, he urged her to take some portraits. Within three years she was operating her own studio. Over the years, especially during her time in Maine, young photographers have come knocking on her door, eager to learn, and she has helped.

There are few photographers working today who have earned Berenice's admiration. "They're trying to do something original, and there's nothing new under the sun. Why try to be original? Just do what excites you, what you respond to." She is impressed by one, though, a New York photographer named Morris Engel. "I was very impressed with what he was doing, so I called him up and told him so. He sent me these." Berenice unfolds a large wide-angled color print. The photo is of a street corner. The lens was broad enough to see down both streets. In the center of the photograph, a man wrapped in overcoats and layers of heavy clothes sits on the sidewalk, leaning against the building, his legs outstretched. Next to him is a worn shopping bag that proclaims "I ♥ New York," the red heart big and vivid. Coming around the corner, her step determined, a young mother, expensively dressed, pushes her baby in a stroller. The fashionable woman is on a collision course with the homeless man, whom she cannot see. Berenice sits back in her chair and studies the photograph, which is bright with the reds and yellows of the streetlights and taxis. "Isn't that something? Isn't that interesting? You get an idea of our civilization there, don't you? I mean, what if we had pictures like that of the fall of Rome?"

Three weeks pass, along with three more snowstorms, and on a Friday evening, while a fine, powdery snow drives drifts against the log house in Maine, a hard rain turns the sooty snowbanks on the curbs of Fifth Avenue into ponds of slush. In the vestibule of the New York Academy of Sciences, people are shaking off their umbrellas and hanging up their coats. They have come for the opening of an exhibit of Berenice Abbott's science photographs, which she considers the most neglected of her works.

Like the prints in her cabin, these have been blown up to poster size by Commerce Graphics and displayed in mahogany frames. They are hung on the white alabaster walls of the hallways of the Academy, accompanied by long captions that Berenice wrote only recently, her recollections of how she made the photos. Beside the first photograph in the exhibit is a placard bearing a brief biography of and salute to the artist.

A woman in a pinstriped suit turns to her companion: "Look!" she says in a hoarse whisper. Like a vision, Berenice strolls into the arched entrance to the hallway, her hands clasped behind her back, a curious, who's-come-to-my-party look on her face. She is dressed in black and white — silky black slacks, a long black jacket, and a silky white blouse. "She looks stunning!" the companion whispers back. At once, admirers and old friends begin to crowd around Berenice, shaking her hand and bending low to speak into her ear over the noise of the crowd.

While tuxedoed young men pass silver trays of fresh asparagus and white wine and goose liver paté, Berenice settles into a velveteen chair in the ballroom and continues to greet all comers. Photographers angle front and side. Flashbulbs pop. Berenice looks startled and makes a funny face. It is something she has said she would never do, just go up to a person, without permission or preparation, and start snapping. More flashes and she holds her napkin up to her face. They persist and she waves her hand in disgust. "Take away the cameras!" she cries out.

Ron Kurtz is here, a stocky man with a ring of white hair around a smooth, sun-tanned head. Kurtz is a collector who first encountered a photograph by Berenice Abbott in 1962 at an auction. It was a print of "Night View," and it got by him. "It went for ten or twenty dollars, something like that," he said. "Whatever it was, I couldn't afford it, but eventually I did get one some years later at a gallery for five hundred." He has owned her life's work for three years, and some people are disturbed that Berenice has no artistic control and sees no royalties from any of the prints, now so much more pricey than when she handled them. But others say he has helped her work regain a foothold in the art world. Berenice is enthusiastic about him. "He really likes the pictures," she has told me.

He has organized this show in coordination with the Academy, and he is speaking to a reporter when he says, with conviction, that he would like Berenice Abbott to be a household name. "But she isn't! It's hard to say why. She spent so much more of her career promoting Eugene Atget than she did promoting her own work. She is very modest. Today her work is valued much the same as Ansel Adams', and yet she has never had his kind of publicity. Publicity? Berenice never sought it and she never got it. She never thought she was very good, but she had vision that most photographers only dream of."

It is not, however, as if her work is worth nothing. A Berenice Abbott print was recently sold at auction in New York City for three thousand eight hundred dollars, and Commerce Graphics sells portfolios of five prints each for thirteen thousand.

After two hours, a physicist from the Academy calls for the attention of the gathering. From a lectern near Berenice's chair he introduces her and says ponderous and eloquent things about her work. In closing, he notes how long she believed that photography and science should be used together and says, "I wish we had listened to you long ago." Softly, matter-of-factly, Berenice responds: "So do I."

THE HOTEL where Berenice likes to stay is down a little from the towers and canyons of midtown Manhattan, in Gramercy Park. Her room has remnants of old New York — the sink in the bathroom is on a porcelain pedestal and the doorknobs are rose-tinted glass. From her sixth-floor window she can look down on a little park that is bounded with a wrought-iron fence. You have to have a key to get in to the park, she tells me. The other buildings around the park are low, no more than four or five stories, and they seem European. They have arched windows with narrow balconies and French doors with black shutters. But the noises of the city cannot be fenced out. Horns bleat and toot; sirens wail and warble and whoop. Brakes screech. So many different sounds, they are like voices, speaking, repeating, quarreling. The night sky is as yellow as the streetlights. Lights burn in the windows of all the buildings outside the hotel. It would be a perfect night to find a high place and take a picture of the city lights. But Berenice has gone to bed. She will stay another few days so that she can visit with old friends. She would rather be in Maine, where the only sound is the wind moving snow in off the lake and where the night sky is always black and the moon and the stars are white.

December 1988 Yankee magazine

BERENICE ABBOTT *died in December of 1991 at her home in Maine. She was ninety-three. Her photographs can be found on postcards and posters and original prints frequently come up for sale.*

One Last Mountain

THE FIRST TIME I MET Bill House, he and his wife, Laney, had hiked through the woods to our house. This was some fifteen years ago, when we first moved to Chesham, New Hampshire. It was winter and they wore well-worn down jackets and hiking boots and they introduced themselves as my neighbors to the north. They were a handsome couple, he tall and noble, with a full head of snow-white hair, and she willowy and blue-eyed. They sat in our living room and we talked of neighborly things. Later, I found my way to their house, which is hidden from the road, on a rise with a fine view of Mount Monadnock. The walls of their kitchen were hung with framed photographs of a young man dangling from ropes draped over steep rock walls. "Is this you?" I asked him then. "Yes," he said, without elaboration.

In the years since, we have remained good neighbors, helping each other when the need is there, occasionally sharing a meal or an outing. Bill and I have served together on committees at the local church. Whenever our family has been in need, Bill is always the first to offer help. Bill is quiet and thoughtful, a man who rarely talks about himself but one who is always an interested listener.

Bill is well known in town, but few really know him. A measure of that is that few people in town — I among them — knew that he was, at one time, a "brilliant" rock climber, perhaps the world's best. In the early 1930s, he was among the elite few who climbed mountains and he was the first to climb Mt. Waddington in British Columbia (seventeen previous attempts had failed) and the first to scale the treacherous Devil's Tower, a sheer-sided mesa that rises straight up out of the desert in Wyoming. Perhaps his greatest achievement is that, halfway around the world, four miles up, on a wild and savage mountain called K2, the second highest mountain in the world, there is a gash that bears his name — House's Chimney. Recently, the one hundred and fifty-foot vertical ascent of House's Chimney was assessed as the hardest pitch in the Himalayas, harder than anything climbed on Everest. Among mountain climbers, that chimney is thought of with awe and a certain amount of desire, as is K2, the most perilous mountain in the world.

Until recently, I knew none of this. But two winters ago, Bill took a fall one night and at the same time, Laney threw her back out. I went up to visit more frequently. One afternoon, while Laney rested upstairs, Bill and I sat in his living room, in chairs side by side set to view the mountain outside his window. Our conversation turned to his years of climbing. He mentioned a book he had once written along with his friends Bob Bates and Charlie Houston. The book was called *Five Miles High*, and he pulled it from the shelf in his living room. Its red binding had faded pink with age. I turned its soft pages carefully and thought I'd like to find a copy, perhaps at a used book store.

The next day, I called a local bookseller and asked about this book. "Oh," he said, "I don't think you'd be able to find that. That book is so desirable among mountain climbers, if there ever were a copy available, it would go for four hundred dollars."

The next time I went to visit Bill, I reported this to him and he smiled. "Yes," he said, "I had heard that it was hard to find." Bill went right to the bookshelf and took down his only copy and handed it to me with a smile. "Keep it as long as you need to," he said.

And so, on a December night, I sat down beside my stove and read about this journey, which took place in the summer of 1938, ten years before I was born.

THOUGH IT IS a great adventure story, perhaps more than anything *Five Miles High* is the story of a friendship spawned in a desperate place where each person's life depended on the other's help and cooperation. In the beginning of the book, there were photographs of the young adventurers. The expedition's leader was twenty-five-year-old Charles Houston (pronounced *House*-ton), a medical student from New York and Bob Bates, then twenty-seven and a native of Exeter, New Hampshire; Richard Burdsall, from New York and Paul Petzoldt of Wyoming. Of the five, Houston was the most rugged looking, Bates, the most boyish and House, the most handsome. I looked into their young and eager faces for some time before I began to read.

K2 was among the last of the great peaks to be discovered. At 28,250 feet it is just shy of Everest's 29,000. Its name comes from a simple surveying identification, the K standing for the Karakoram, a ridge at the far eastern edge of the Himalayas, that remarkable chain of mountains that spans Nepal, Tibet, China, and Pakistan.

Bates, Houston, and House made their way to K2 by foot. They reasoned that by walking, they would acclimate themselves gradually to the higher elevation. Besides, it was also the only way for them to get there in those early days. The journey to the base of K2 was three hundred thirty miles, across desert, high hills, tumbling rivers, and glacial moraines. They crossed rivers by rope bridges of unknown condition and hoisted themselves over waterfalls by gliding on rope and pulley. They walked at night, by the light of the full moon, to avoid the daytime dangers of avalanche. They carried with them four thousand pounds of food and equipment, which required weeks of packing in wooden crates and some seventy-five porters and twenty-five horses to help transport the long journey to base camp. They suffered blisters, mountain sickness, dengue fever and other mysterious ailments. It took them a month to reach the mountain, which they had only heard of but never seen. Bob Bates recalled that moment in *Five Miles High*:

"Before us the valley was dark with sullen clouds, but directly ahead of us a rift in the vapor suddenly disclosed . . . the glittering apex of a ghostly summit. It was like something from another world, something ethereal seen in a dream. For a few stunned moments, we stared at the peak we had come so far to see; then it was gone. The glacier stretched ahead for miles into a void of blank, swirling mist."

After establishing a base camp, they began to survey the mountain, attempting various routes. Their task was to find a route to the summit, not necessarily to make it to the top. Prior to their expedition, only three attempts had ever been made to climb K2. Their climb was hampered not only by weather but by the steepness of its slopes. The higher they got, the more difficult it became to find a flat place to pitch their tents. One night, there was such a shortage of flat places in their path, they spent the night sleeping practically piled on top of each other.

They endured rock falls (one of which pierced their tent) and lay awake at night, listening to the ominous thunder of avalanches roaring down from the upper slopes. In *Five Miles High*, Bill House wrote of camping on the Savoia Glacier, just beneath the summit:

Long before dark we were in a twilight all our own. . . . Perhaps it was the darkening cirque that rose behind our tent to the unknown above the pass. Perhaps it was that we were actually in the shadow of K2 for the first time — not where it could be viewed from a distance, from the strength-giving companionship of our party, but with a single companion, temporarily cut off from all support, dependent on ourselves and ourselves alone. We were no longer the proud American Karakoram Expedition but two men slightly appalled at what they had challenged.

A few days after I had read this section, I stopped in for a visit with Bill and I asked him what had happened to the other members of his expedition. He told me that Dick Burdsall was killed in a climbing accident in 1953. Paul Petzoldt was now living in Maine. After their 1938 climb, he became estranged from the others. But with Bob Bates and Charlie Houston, Bill had enjoyed a close friendship of nearly sixty years, a friendship forged on that faraway mountain in that faraway time.

ON A COLD but brightening day last spring, the three of them came together once again. They met at Bill's house, in Chesham, where there was still a foot of snow on the ground. Charlie Houston drove down from his home in Burlington, Vermont. Bob Bates came from his home in Exeter, New Hampshire. The three men greeted each other warmly, not with hugs, for they are men of dignity, but with firm handshakes and sparkly eyes that recalled their youth. Though all are well into their eighties, each remain trim and compact and they moved in similar ways, their sneakered feet slow but agile, like the feet of aging dancers.

To appease my curiosity, they had brought with them tools from their expedition: from the trunk of his car, Bob Bates took his heavy leather climbing boots, the soles pierced with rugged metal spikes. From the space over his garage, Bill had brought down the lethal-looking eight-inch crampons he used to walk up ice walls, and Charlie carried with him, among other things, his climbing ax with a handle of smooth cherry wood and a head of bright steel. Also, he brought a buff-colored, moth-eaten wool sweater. "Let's see," he said, and he pulled the thinning garment over his head. Proudly, he smoothed the hem to his hips and his friends cheered to see that it still fit him, rather perfectly.

I watched as they passed the tools among themselves, turning them in their hands and staring into them as if they were crystal balls where they could look and see backwards, all the way to their youth.

Charlie also brought pages from his 1938 journal and he sat down on the couch and began to read at random.

"On July 8, a furious wind that shook the tent canvas with the sound of gunfire kept us from getting higher. . . . In the afternoon we mended clothes, read the *Oxford Book of English Verse* and planned what food we should have when we met at our reunion next winter."

The men burst into laughter. Nearly sixty years since, and here they were, about to join in yet another reunion, yet another meal together.

Charlie had also brought a video of their climb, created from the 16 mm. movie he filmed during their ascent. The four of us gathered around a small TV and watched the faded images of this early mountaineering effort. "It was just like the most wonderful dream," Bob Bates mused as he watched his young self on the screen. "Walking in, not knowing what you were going to see the next day. Everything was so different."

"And so exciting!" Charlie said. "Only a few Westerners had ever walked this route."

The men pass, single file, through the snow. They are dressed in heavy coats. "Those were those dreadful cloth parkas," Charlie pointed out. "They had a double layer, tightly woven. They were quite good but terribly heavy. But we never took our coats off."

"Did you sleep in your clothes?" I asked.

"Well, mostly. I don't remember that we ever took anything off."

In one segment, Charlie filmed Bill as he emerged from his chimney, a happy Santa, his strong, handsome young face swaddled in wool and goggles. Charlie had filmed this scene the second time Bill went up through, in an attempt to record it for history. As Bill appeared through the gash, he raised his heavily gloved hand in mock triumph.

"Boy, it was cold that day," Bob recalled. "Just a bitter cold day."

"That's still the only way up," Charlie mused as he watched the fuzzy scene. "No one climbs K2 without going through House's Chimney."

It would be fifteen years and a world war before Everest was conquered. In the calendar of mountain climbing, it was the age of innocence, a veritable high peaks Garden of Eden into which House and Bates and Houston stepped. They had no way of knowing it would bloom into an industry built on adrenaline and an appetite for danger where inexperienced climbers pay upwards of $60,000 for someone of skill to get them up and down a mountain like Everest, an industry rife with summit lust and regular reports of disaster.

"It's a lot different now," Bob observed. "Now, so many people want to be first. For us, the idea was to climb the mountain. If the mountain was climbed by your expedition, you all had a part in it, it was your mountain, your climb, your success. It didn't really matter so much who was actually the one to get to the top."

"In those days, the summit was important but it was not the most important," Charlie agreed.

"Yes, getting back was the most important," Bob said.

"We succeeded in finding a route. That was what we went there to do," Bill said.

Although they have lost many friends to the mountains, remarkably, none of the three of them ever had a serious climbing accident. Bill explained: "Well, we were all very cautious, very conservative. We were good climbers, we had good balance and good ability but we didn't take risks, although I suppose that you could say that just being on K2 was a risk."

"And we always climbed with men we trusted," Bob said.

"You're all roped together?" I asked.

"Oh, yes, I never climbed with someone I didn't trust," Bill said. "That must be an awful feeling."

I asked them what the most memorable moment on the mountain was for them and Bill said, "The decision to turn back. That was a very very difficult decision to make."

With dwindling food supplies and worsening weather, the decision had to be made, whether to try for the summit or not. Worse perhaps than food and weather, they were down to six matches. In a one-day assault, two in the party reached 26,000 feet and then, without much discussion, they turned back for good. Charlie Houston wrote this about that moment, when they reached five miles high, higher than any American had ever been, but still two thousand feet shy of the summit.

> *There was no question but what our work was done, and we turned to descend at 4 o'clock with mingled emotions. The whole world was deathly still; not even the clatter of rock-falls broke the calm. All the peaks about us seemed breathlessly awaiting our descent. We trudged down to Camp VII in a deepening twilight. About us the mountains turned first pink, then lavender, then purple. We reached camp safely, exhausted and cold but curiously content.*

Since 1938, over a hundred climbers have ascended K2 and several dozen have died in the process. There isn't another mountain on earth with such a gruesome reputation.

"Mountain climbing demands a certain amount of harmony for people to survive. A climb is only successful if you come down from the summit alive. It's different today," Charlie Houston said. "Many of the big expeditions today are chosen of climbers who have outstanding climbing records even if they are difficult personalities. Many of these parties end up in some kind of disenchantment or fights. One of the things that made (our trip) so great was that we ended up very very close friends. Forever."

During World War II, Bill and Bob served together in the Army's Quartermaster Corps, testing cold weather clothing and equipment (Bob is responsible for the design of that perennial favorite, the fatigue sweater.) In 1953, Charlie and Bob returned to K2 to try once more. (They invited their friend Bill to join them but, having been recently married, he declined, saying that "marriage and mountains do not mix," which would be the reason why all of them would eventually give up dangerous climbs in favor of more recreational climbing.) It was on this journey that Charlie Houston began to call K2 the "savage mountain," a term that is used to this day. Their efforts proved even more disheartening than their 1938 trip. One member of their party, Art Gilkey, fell seriously ill. As they tried to carry him down through a raging storm, one member of the party slipped and they all went like puppets on a string, down, down the terrible precipice. In one last desperate effort, the lead climber threw his ax into the wall of ice and, unbelievably, it held. They all came to a stop, together, the last man dangling in midair. This has become perhaps the most famous fall in mountain climbing history. When they recovered themselves, they decided to leave Art, secured with ice axes, and go for help. When they returned, he was gone. Some think that Art Gilkey pushed himself over the edge to prevent his friends from risking their lives to try to save his, which was seriously in question. A mountain mystery. His body was not found until six years ago when his bones came down in a spring thaw. Even now, the mere mention of Art Gilkey's name brings pain to their faces.

Though each of them has climbed many other mountains, the 1938 expedition remains, in their minds, the best of what they have done. "I can't imagine having a better trip than that," Charlie said. "We did what we set out to do, we came back well and we are still friends. I don't see how a trip could go any better than that — all for nine thousand five hundred dollars for five months, that's for *all* of us, for *everything*!"

Misfortune and death seem to make the story of the climb even more tantalizing than a safe ascent and clear roads back down. This may be one reason why the names of these three men are not better known. They blazed a trail so that others could accomplish what they did not. They went five miles high, higher than any American had ever been. In 1938, these mountains were our outer space, these men our astronauts.

THE SUN ANGLE is low and it is time to leave. They each rise from their chairs slowly and with caution. "Well, you characters!" Charlie says, chucking Bob on the shoulder. And then he turns to Bill and lightly touches his forehead, which is bruised. "William," he says, "when did you do this?"

It has been a rough winter. Within the last six months, each of them have had brushes with disaster. Bill had his fall in the night, which bloodied his forehead, and soon after, on an icy night, Bill's car landed in a ditch and rescue workers had to be called. Charlie confesses that he slipped on the ice and fell flat, blacking his eyes and leaving his face swollen and badly bruised. Bob also ran his car off the road, having fallen asleep at the wheel. He broke two ribs and bruised his heart. Ironically, he was on his way to visit his old friend, Bill, who he'd heard was ailing. They speak now of their accidents and they commiserate and they laugh at themselves and the unlikely occurrence that they should all endure these mishaps, roughly at the same time.

Each of them has recovered from their midwinter upsets. Still, it is hard. "Don't ever get old!" Bill sometimes says to me as we part.

That's their mountain now. They know the steps, one at a time, cautious but unafraid. I am standing among the quietest of legends, and it startles me to realize that, had Bill not fallen in the night, I might never have discovered all of this about him. I've never climbed a mountain and likely never will but these men have much to teach me: Take risks but never be foolhardy. Do your best but know that sometimes you will have to turn back. Keep an eye on the sky. Watch out for your friends and do what you can to bring them to safety. At all times, remain humble. Never climb alone. I hope that when I arrive at the base of this particular mountain, I can remember Bill and his friends, and the way that their feet touch the ground, ever so lightly.

May 1997 Yankee magazine

BILL HOUSE *died in 1997 at the age of eighty-two. Bob Bates died on September 13, 2007 at the age of ninety-six. Charlie Houston died on September 27, 2009 at the age of ninety-six. Their collected longevity seems to negate the oft-quoted saying that there are old mountain climbers and there are bold mountain climbers but there are no old bold mountain climbers.*

Edie Clark has been a writer and editor of books and magazines for the past 40 years. She has written extensively about New England in award-winning feature stories for *Yankee* magazine, where she served as Senior Editor, Fiction Editor and Senior Writer for twenty-four years. She is now Contributing Editor to that magazine. In her hundreds of published articles, she has written about food, travel, and personalities as well as controversial topics such as our northern borders, Lyme disease, land development, the Christian Science church and water pollution. Her memoir, *The Place He Made*, about her husband's death from cancer, was described by the *New York Times Book Review* as "a triumph of the human spirit [which] may take its quiet place among the best of the literature." She has been a fellow at the MacDowell Colony and at Hedgebrook Writers Colony, as well as a visiting writer at the University of Northern Michigan. She has taught in the MFA program at Emerson College and frequently conducts workshops. She currently teaches at Franklin Pierce University where she is managing editor of the *Northern New England Review*. Her earlier books, *The View from Mary's Farm* and *Saturday Beans and Sunday Suppers* have received generous acclaim. To learn more about her work, visit www.edieclark.com.